DECISIONS
a comparative critique

MICHAEL MURRAY
DePaul University

Pitman Publishing Inc. A Longman Inc. Company

Pitman Publishing Inc.
1020 Plain Street
Marshfield, Massachusetts 02050

A Longman Inc. Company
95 Church St.
White Plains, N. Y. 10601

Associated Companies
Longman Group Ltd. London
Copp Clark Pitman, Toronto
Longman Cheshire Pty., Melbourne
Longman Paul Pty., Auckland

© 1986 Michael Murray

Library of Congress Cataloging-in-Publication Data

Murray, Michael
  Decisions: a comparative critique.

  (Pitman series in business and public policy)
  Bibliography: p.
  Includes index.
  1. Decision-making.   2. Decision-making—
Case studies. I. Title.   II. Series.
HD30.23.M87   1986   658.4'03   85-16922
ISBN 0-582-98832-2

All rights reserved. No part of this publication may be reproduced, stored in a retrieval system, or transmitted in any form or by any means, electronics, mechanical, photocopying, recording and/or otherwise without the prior written permission of the publishers.

Manufactured in the United States of America
10 9 8 7 6 5 4 3 2 1

PITMAN SERIES IN
BUSINESS AND PUBLIC POLICY

CONSULTING EDITOR
EDWIN M. EPSTEIN
University of California, Berkeley

CURRENT BOOKS IN THE SERIES:

John D. Aram, *Managing Business and Public Policy: Concepts, Issues and Cases*, 2nd. Ed.

R. Edward Freeman, *Strategic Management: A Stakeholder Approach*

S. Prakash Sethi, Nobuaki Namiki and Carl L. Swanson, *The False Promise of the Japanese Miracle: Illusions and Realities of the Japanese Management System*

Charles S. McCoy, *Management of Values: The Ethical Difference in Corporate Policy and Performance*

Stefanie Ann Lenway, *The Politics of U.S. International Trade: Protection, Expansion and Escape*

Donna J. Wood, *Strategic Uses of Public Policy: Business and Government in the Progressive Era*

Michael Murray, *Decisions: A Comparative Critique*

To the memory of
Joseph A. Altsheler,
American Author

CONTENTS

PREFACE	xi
ACKNOWLEDGMENTS	xii
INTRODUCTION	1

One
DISINTEGRATED APPROACHES — 6
Definitions and Assumptions — 7
Rational Models — 13
Political Models — 29
Legal Models — 35
Conclusion — 41
Notes — 43

Two
RATIONAL MODELS — 48
Definitions and Concepts — 49
Case in Point: Modern Management Applied to Academic
   Decisions — 58
Case Review — 70
Conclusion — 75
Notes — 77

Three
IRRATIONAL MODELS 80
Definitions and Concepts 81
Case in Point: The Lordstown Fiasco 87
Case Review 93
Conclusion 99
Notes 100

Four
POLITICAL MODELS 102
Definitons and Concepts 103
Case in Point: Budgeting as a Political Process 107
Case Review 115
Conclusion 124
Notes 124

Five
ADMINISTRATIVE MODELS 128
Definitions and Concepts 129
Case in Point: The Blast in Centralia No. 5:
   A Mine Disaster No One Stopped 133
Case Review 151
Conclusion 158
Notes 159

Six
LEGAL MODELS 162
Definitions and Concepts 165
Case In Point: *American Textile Manufacturers Institute, Inc., et al.*
   v. *Donovan, Secretary of Labor, et al.* 169
Case Review 175
Conclusion 185
Notes 186

Seven
DISCRETIONARY MODELS 192
Definitions and Concepts 193
Case in Point: *Federal Crop Insurance Corp.* v. *Merrill et al.,*
   Doing Business as Merrill Bros. 199
Case Review 204
Conclusion 211
Notes 212

Eight
INTEGRATED APPROACHES 216
Common Qualities 217
Progress, Integration, and the Future 224
Notes 228

CONCLUSION 230

Standing Properly and First Steps 231
Notes 236

GLOSSARY: SOME IMPORTANT DEFINITIONS 237

ANNOTATED RECOMMENDED READINGS 242

AUTHOR INDEX 249

SUBJECT INDEX 253

QUOTE SOURCES 261

Strange is our situation here upon earth. Each of us comes for a short visit, not knowing why. . . . From the standpoint of daily life, however, there is one thing we do know: that man is here for the sake of other men. . .

Albert Einstein
Living Philosophies

PREFACE

Much of the suffering in the world is man-made. It is therefore unnecessary and wanton. Suffering can be ended only by man and only when man sees himself at one with his universe and with his fellow-man. The first step is to recognize the reality of oneness, the second step is to "unlearn" some bad habits; not ancient habits; just foolish habits. For example we must "unlearn" the habit of thinking that problems are discrete; that solutions are specialized; and that man somehow is separated from other men and from other living beings.

The purpose of this book is to expose useless habits and to encourage new ways of thinking. Its major goal is to teach; to inform business people about government and law; to introduce lawyers and law students to politics and business; and to instruct government students about business and law. As a present or former professor, lawyer, administrator and government employee who has wandered about these various institutional worlds for the past twenty years I am struck—indeed dumbfounded—that people in these different institutions know almost nothing about life in "other sectors".

This book is merely an introduction for those who might appreciate a basic and cursory look at these other zones. Critics will say the book is elementary; perhaps it is. They will say it is dated; some of it is. But the purpose is very limited. In plain, simple, straightforward English I wanted to offer the uninformed a closer view of distant parts of their universe. This book is only a superficial and preliminary first step. But the journey must begin somewhere.

Let's be off.

ACKNOWLEDGEMENTS

Twenty-five years ago at Kibbutz Gadot, Israel, Mr. Shlomo Sokol, a very wise and very kind teacher, pointed me in the direction of this book. My gratitude is boundless.

Dr. David Weinstein (Director of the Campaign for the U.S. Holocaust Memorial Museum), Ms. Judith Sharlin, R.D., M.S., (Ph.D. candidate, Tufts), and Mr. James E. Downey (President, C & D Plastics, Inc., Huntington Beach, California) nourished body, mind and soul during difficult days. Words cannot express my thanks.

Professors Edwin M. Epstein (Berkeley), R. Edward Freeman (Minnesota), and Victor G. Rosenblum (Northwestern) read and critiqued early drafts of the manuscript. Their support and comments were always helpful and deeply appreciated.

Brother Leo V. Ryan, C.S.V. (Dean, College of Commerce) and Dr. F. James Staszak (Chairman, Management) of DePaul University provided much appreciated supports. Miss Casan Grillo and Mrs. Dianne C. Chanski (Management Department, Secretarial Staff), were always helpful. Mrs. Pamela Schnitz (Graduate Assistant) was of great assistance during several revision stages.

Acknowledgements

The University of Arizona through its Management Department, particularly Dr. Gerritt Wolfe and Eva Ehrsam, provided gracious and timely support and a "home" away from home. The Library staff at the University of Arizona extended extremely competent assistance.

The staff at Pitman Publishing, Inc.—President William Roberts, Executive Assistant Jean Grissom, Production Manager Michael Weinstein, and copyeditor Susan Badger—was a joy to work with. Intelligence, competence, guidance, support, and encouragement all under one roof!

Miss Audrey Ivory, graduate assistant, did yeoman duty copying and assembling various parts of the manuscript.

During several summers of writing, the good folks of Washington Island, Wisconsin, provided an always friendly and peaceful environment for work and reflection.

When it came to the "critical crunch," my competent and dedicated assistant Ms. Joann Spires was there to pick up my spirits and pick up the pieces. The word appreciation or gratitude is insufficient. It was a tough, demanding job.

All of my students, my teachers (and coaches), and my clients over the past many years have added in countless ways to this study.

My family and especially my son John have always been a loving part of my professional life.

My gratitude to each and all is immeasureable.

When we speak of the world *of unreal objects, we use an inexact expression for the sake of greater convenience. A world is a unit in which each object has its fixed place and bears certain relationships to other objects. The very idea of a world implies the following twofold condition for its objects: they must be rigorously individualized, and they must be in equilibrium with a milieu. It is for this reason that there is no unreal world since no unreal object can meet this twofold condition.*

Jean-Paul Sartre
"The Imaginary Life"

Introduction

RATIONAL MODELS;
POLITICAL MODELS;
LEGAL MODELS:
AN INTEGRATED APPROACH
TO DECISION MAKING

The world of complex organizations, intellectually, is divided into sectors or pieces or categories. That these categories are abstract in origin, and that they ignore the basic law of life (and of systems analysis) that everything is connected to everything else, does little to reduce their potency. For example, we think automatically of the "public sector" and the "private sector" (or if we are truly open-minded and innovative, of the "third sector"). We think, almost without thinking, that there actually exists a "sector" that is private, or public, and that in some purified atmospheric sense operates as a separate, discrete unit. This segregated unit, if not wholly uncontaminated by other sectors, is nonetheless viewed intellectually as a discrete, isolated entity.

To be sure, no serious philosopher holds the view that everything is disconnected. Nor do academic disciplines assume, as an operational reality, that interconnections do not exist. But since Sartre's departure, where is a serious philosopher? To whom does the world turn for answers to

1

simple but profoundly disturbing human questions? Is there a serious philosopher who can overcome the entrenchment of established academic disciplines, someone who with a sure sense of authority can say, "You guys, with your narrow categories, you have it upside-down; you are doing it backwards" Isn't this precisely why Elie Wiesel must scream quietly over and over and over again that the horror affects every human and every aspect of human life?* We do not see the interconnectedness. We are conditioned, trained, expected, and rewarded to see "special" (specialized) parts. This is the problem.

Today, for example, it is as if our intellectual abstractions envision a jumble of rocks, and each rock is neatly labeled public or private, capitalist or socialist, or business or government. Consequently, each rock can be plucked out of the pile and examined as though it is a completely segregated unit. This is the consequence of our "unreal" intellectual abstractions. Analytically they are very powerful. Practically they are deadly. The potency of such abstract categories causes entire disciplines, faculties, colleges, and societies to begin to mimic and mumble the abstract categories as if they *actually* existed. And of course this is the difficulty—because after a while, they do begin to exist. These categories and abstract distinctions take hold, grow roots, spread out, and eventually take on a life and force of their own.

And so today, we have a public sector and a private sector (and other sectors), and very little is done to examine the interaction or the wholeness of the "system."

So, too, with decision making. Intellectual models—abstract intellectual categories—dominate and influence reality. Likewise, these models dominate and influence decision making. And because these intellectual models are based on distinct and discrete approaches or categories, they force decision makers to take narrow and discrete approaches. This means that decision making operates with blinders on.

Consider the following illustration. Any observer of decision making in the business world, in the government world, or in the legal world would agree that most practitioners in these three fields are trained professionally and intellectually to think in quite discrete and categorical ways. For example, businessmen, or at least products of traditional business schools, are trained and steeped in the so-called rational approach. This approach is premised upon a value-free method of *rational* decision making, expressed by the illusory but popular phrase the "bottom line."

---

*To the point where the repetition becomes frighteningly trivializing.

Introduction

The rational model is based primarily upon quantitative methods and mathematical skills that assume a nonideological, nonintuitive approach to decision making. While very few academics (or practitioners) actually believe that their choices are as value free as the Decision Tree of means-ends analysis would suggest, the prevailing decisional norm in the private business sector is governed by the rational approach. This model itself has given birth to a whole generation of analytical models such as managment by objectives, cost-benefit analysis, and zero-based budgeting.

In the public sector, while some deference is paid to quantitative technique, the prevailing mode is still *political*. The term refers not to electoral politics or to overt lobbying methods but rather to the covert process of decision making based on self-interest, careerism, personal preference, or ideology. Students and practitioners of political science and public policy assert not only that the political mode is the dominant mode but that it is the preferred mode. The argument is that an intricate system of institutional checks and balances and governmental interplay ensures that ultimately a political decision, which is by process definition the right decision, will wash up.

In the legal sector, primarily in the developing field of administrative law, the truth-seeking or intellectual approach to decisions follows a pattern quite different from the rational and the political models. The *legal* model is based upon, and derives from, a set of fixed principles and precedents. These governing principles and case precedents are expressed in the form of positivistic statutes, codes, and regulations, which theoretically form the basis for legal decision making.

The problem with pursuing such discrete or distinct modes of thinking is that in reality they are not discrete. And it is intellectually absurd (or worse) to continue to promulgate the fictions that businessmen make decisions devoid of societal values or personal preference, that public officials and bureaucrats pursue only narrow ideologies and self-interest, and that lawyers or judges adhere inflexibly to "the law" as expressed in concrete rules and regulations. The reality is that there is a great deal of interplay between the three selected models.

The purpose of this book is therefore twofold:

1. To discuss and discredit the illusions that the business sector follows only a quantitative approach, that public administrators are purely political, and that legalists do not exercise discretion; and
2. To attempt to build an intellectual framework that outlines an integrated approach to decision making based on the tools or methods of these three approaches.

The gap between the intellectual approach and the reality only recently has become the subject of some fresh thinking in business schools, in public administration programs, and in law courses. The ultimate purpose of this book is to fill the gap and to provide an integrated framework for teaching new courses and for making sound decisions. In short, the purpose is to dispel some unhealthy mythology and to construct more useful alternative approaches.

(The Hypothesis of One)

"Let us . . . consider whether this hypothesis must not necessarily show that one is of such a nature as to have parts."

"How does that come about?"

"In this way: If being is predicated of the one which exists and unity is predicated of being which is one, and being and the one are not the same, but belong to the existent one of our hypothesis, must not the existent one be a whole of which the one and being are parts?"

"Inevitably."

"And shall we call each of these parts merely a part, or must it, in so far as it is a part, be called a part of the whole?"

"A part of the whole."

"Whatever one, then, exists, is a whole and has a part."

"Certainly."

"Well then, can either of these two parts of existent one—unity and being—abandon the other? Can unity cease to be a part of being or being to be a part of unity?"

"No."

Parmenides
Plato on the One

CHAPTER ONE

DISINTEGRATED APPROACHES

The purpose of this book is to help the reader understand organizational decision-making processes and to build a framework for developing more intelligent and realistic decision-making methods.

The study focuses on three primary intellectual approaches to decision making: the rational approach, the political approach, and the legal approach. Each of these approaches—or "truth-seeking" methods—operates as a separate and discrete intellectual model. Each is based on separate and distinct assumptions. Each triggers its own counter-model. And each carries grossly divergent consequences and implications.

The purpose of this chapter is to review and to analyze some of the methodological and practical limitations of these separate and discrete truth-seeking approaches. But first certain definitions and clarifications are in order.

DEFINITIONS AND ASSUMPTIONS

Systems and Organizations

What is *decision making* in the context of an organization? To focus on decisions within organizations we must first define what is meant by an *organization*. This necessarily involves a discussion of the related concepts of a "system" and of "systems analysis."

Within an institutional context, an *organization* will be defined in the behavioral sense as a structure consisting of two or more persons who accept coordinated direction to achieve certain goals; this structure has certain functions (or consequences). As conceptually derived from structural-functional analysis, an organization, whether a business firm, a government agency, or a judicial body, operates within a social system.[1]

As used in systems analysis,[2] the word *system* refers to a bounded region in space and time, with component parts that interact with each other, causing stresses and strains, inputs and outputs, and feedback over time. Systems are involved in a functional relationship with their environment. Systems analysis allows us to segregate out of a bewildering and complex universe of infinite data certain finite phenomena and discrete data.

In use for several decades, systems analysis has provided a marvelous heuristic and intellectual framework for isolating and selecting out of a "total" universe those parts or entities (for example, the "political" system or the "economic" system) that researchers choose to examine and analyze. As an abstraction, systems theory has done much to allow analysts to manage their data. In its practical effect, however, systems theory also has done much to allow analysts (and decision makers) to segregate the universe, to oversimplify a world of complex interrelationships, and to reduce whole cloth to strips and pieces. What began as "a search for unity" out of a variegated manifold bias had the unfortunate side effects of reducing analysis to egg-crate reasoning and of setting up categories and abstract subsystems that assume a life of their own.

The premise of this study—that whole cloth has been reduced to rag strips—is hardly startling; nor is it necessarily undesirable. Rag strips may be more functional in some environments than seamless artwork. Moreover, the implicit meaning of words, with the complexities of synonymy, further complicates any evaluation. That is, this study presupposes a "beauty" or eufunction in interrelated methodologies or in truth-seeking devices that have common integrators. However, such a view of the world does not necessarily square with reality. More significantly, such a view (or hope) does not jibe with common processes of reasoning that rest primarily on the meaning of words.

For example, William Alston demonstrates that it is impossible to find even a pair of words that are exact synonyms, much less a pair of methodologies that are perfectly synonymous or integrated.[3] The main reason, Alston argues, is that

> practically all words have more than one meaning. The more meanings a given word has, the more unlikely it is

Definitions and Assumptions 9

that another word will have exactly the same range of meanings over the same range of contexts.[4]

Thus although the words *rational* and *political* and *legal* may share the common meaning "efficacious," in their individual contexts each word has other meanings ("efficient," "purposive," "legitimate") that are not shared by the others. Consequently, it may amount to nothing more than constructing a "straw horse" to assume that language and decisional methodologies allow for integration or can lead to synonymous, consistent processes and results. It may indeed be dysfunctional or undesirable to wish such a result, however improbable.

At the same time, although perfect synonymy and interrelatedness may be elusive goals, more realistically there is a range of interrelatedness that is possible, a degree of synonymy that is helpful. This text argues only that it is important to attempt this median range of interrelatedness—or at the very least, to minimize the dysfunctional segmentation that currently besets many academic and practical disciplines.

To illustrate, it is one matter to utilize systems theory to analyze behavioral factors within an organization. According to this approach, one might establish the parameters (bounded region in space and time) of the social system within the organization, focusing on group entities and on individual units as subsystems. Figure 1.1 illustrates this principle.

Figure 1.1

"The Black Box"
A Systems View
of the Organization

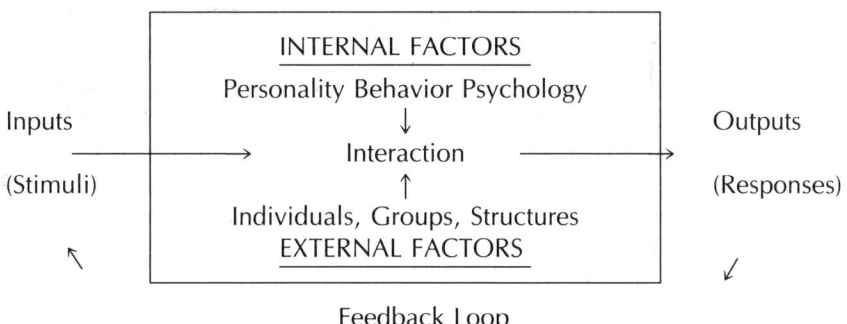

In its simplified version, systems theory is nothing more than the "black box" approach, which sees inputs first filtered through an abstract system of interacting parts and then ultimately converted into outputs, which in turn are transformed via a feedback loop into other inputs.

It is an entirely different matter to carry systems theory to the extreme of actually building decisional approaches that presume separate and isolated realities. For example, it may be useful as a heuristic device to imagine a business world, a government sector, or a legal entity. Thereby one might examine as analytic entities the structures and functions of the organizations involved in these sectors. It is a radically different matter to build and to operationalize intellectual disciplines that *establish* separate methods of reasoning built upon a rational approach, a political approach, or a business approach. This is systems theory run amuck. And yet this is precisely what has happened in business schools, in schools of public administration, and in law schools. Students and practitioners are trained to think and to act (to make decisions) based upon separate tracks of reasoning and according to models of decision making that exist only in the most abstract of worlds.

Consider as a logical extension of this egg-crate reasoning the phenomenon of current decision making within organizations.

What is Decision Making?

Within the context of organizational activity, decision making is the process by which courses of action are chosen (from among alternatives) in pursuit of organzational goals. To be acceptable a course of action must satisfy a whole set of requirements or constraints.

The choice of one constraint over another generates an elaborate goal-action interplay, and in this context, the decision-making process itself is thought to involve at least three major phases. These include:

1. *Analytic Phase*. In this phase, situations that affect goals (problems and opportunities) are perceived and information about them is gathered.
2. *Design Phase*. In this phase, courses of action (options) are crystallized to deal with the problem situation.
3. *Choice Phase*. In this phase, the alternatives proposed in the design phase are evaluated, and some are selected for implementation.

In addition, several analysts include the threshold phase (pre-analysis) of self-evaluation[5] as important, and most writers at least touch upon implementation as a separate, last phase.[6]

Although decision making can be viewed as a process divided into three (or four or five) distinct phases, the process is not goal free. That is, the circumstances in which decisions are made complicate the process. John Steinbruner refers to these circumstances as "complex situations" with the following characteristics:[7]

1. (a) Two or/more values are affected by the decision.
   (b) There is a trade-off relationship between the value such that a greater return to one can be obtained only at a loss to the other.
2. There is uncertainty (i.e., imperfect correspondence between information and the environment).
3. The power to make the decision is dispersed over a multitude of individual actors and/or organizational units.

It would be difficult, especially in this initial chapter, to overemphasize this central point: that decision making is not a value-free process resulting in value-free choices. For example, in the business world it may be entirely "rational" to choose to locate the headquarters of a corporation such as Union Carbide in a nonurban, campuslike setting. The cost projections, technical problems, logistical issues, and architectural plans all may be entirely rational in that they are consistent with the chosen goals of the organization. Nonetheless, the ultimate choices of site, style, image, size, and the like, reflect values. Usually the choices reflect one party's values over another's. Thus the process of choice is hardly value free. People in organizations argue even (or particularly) over the color scheme in their offices. The price of paint may be based on rational cost-benefit analysis, but the choice of color is not.

Likewise, this is so in the government world of sanctioned "officialdom." Majority rule in legislative bodies does not equate with complete consensus. Policy decisions and resultant programs in administrative agencies like the Occupational Safety and Health Administration (OSHA) or the Environmental Protection Agency (EPA) are the product of intense staff infighting, conflict, and sometimes partisan sabotage. Very little in government is value free. Even, or especially, "pointy-headed" bureaucrats hold deeply valued convictions and passionate preferences.[8] This may explain, more than anything else, why these much maligned bureaucrats last so long. They have a mission.

It is the same in the world of law and with regard to the legal process. Any seasoned trial lawyer knows and understands that judges and juries are human. In fact, it is this very humanness, common sense, or sound judgment that lawyers rely on in arguing cases. The legal process itself has never pretended to be value free. On the contrary, the beginning and the end of the Anglo-American tradition of law reflects a moral position or a moral theory. In the infamous shipwreck/cannibalism case of the *Queen* v. *Dudley and Stephens* (14 Q.B.D.273 [1884]), an English court found crewmen Dudley and Stephens guilty of the willful murder and consummation of the body of cabin boy Brooks. The court, recognizing the extreme conditions of starvation and thirst nonetheless held that

> though law and morality are not the same, and many things may be immoral which are not necessarily illegal, yet the absolute divorce of law from morality would be of fatal consequence.

In finding the sailors guilty of murder (and passing a sentence of death, later commuted by the Queen to six months in prison) the court went on to recognize, "We are often compelled to set up standards we cannot reach ourselves, and to lay down rules which we could not ourselves satisfy."

In each case and in all decisional processes, it is clear that values are a critical element and that no process is value free or neutral.[9] Decision making, in short, is more than neutral means-ends analysis. In the context of organizational settings, it is the behavioral process by which actors choose among ends and means. This process is not value free; it involves preference. Consider three major types of institution-based decisional processes: the rational model of the business firm, the political model of the government agency, and the legal model of the judicial process.

Models, Models, Everywhere: What Are They?

Models have been defined as "abstractions of reality" or as "simplified representations of some real-world phenomema." Models, and modeling, are useful to analysts of decision making and organizational behavior. They help to simplify otherwise complex fields and to build integrative wholes.

Decisional models do not fall neatly into any one typology. They are based on subjective approaches and often include objective content. They derive from abstract concepts but often have concrete expression. Although descriptive, they carry value-based assumptions.

This book focuses only on three major decisional-making models or methodologies. The choice of these models is linked to the present realities of institutional life and to the need to understand decision making within the context of our most potent organizational settings.[10]

RATIONAL MODELS

In the rational model each of the three phases of decision making is performed deliberately and consciously. Problems and opportunities are actively sought. As problems are discovered, the decision maker gathers information relevant to them. He analyzes their impact on organizational goals. Next, he determines possible courses of action.

In complex situations the decision maker weighs competing organizational values and possible trade-offs among them; and he explicitly evaluates which among his competing values are most important. He then calculates which of his options most assures his goal, which maximizes his important values, or which at least addresses the problem situation at the least expense. Steinbruner states the minimum conditions of rationality:

> A given process of decision is analytic (i.e., rational) if upon examination one can find evidence that there was at least limited value integration, that alternative outcomes were analyzed and evaluated, and the new information regarding variables of the problem did produce plausible appropriate subjective adjustments.[11]

Within an organizational context, the rational model assumes that organizational goals are implicitly known and explicitly articulated by the decision maker prior to the design phase of the decision process. Hence it is possible intellectually to assert that the traditional, rational model of business firm behavior is based on the premise that profit maximization is the organization's primary, if not its single, goal. Lawrence Gordon, Danny Miller, and Henry Mintzberg corroborate bottom-line goal orientation with regard to most current prescriptive models of managerial decision making.[12]

By definition, however, the goals of most organizations are numerous: organizations are complex structures with multiple units. In addition to financial goals, an organization might have legal, political, or more broadly, social goals. Obviously, these goals may be perceived as being in conflict. Equally likely, different units (for example, sales versus research and development) within the same organization may pursue conflicting goals. There is, however, no inherent reason why a rational model of decision making must exclude policies involving more than one goal. The rational model only requires that goals be known before courses of action are proposed, and that the decision maker explicitly make choices among his goals when they are in conflict. In this sense the very nature of the rational model is deliberate, comprehensive, and goal exclusive; that is, certain goals (A,B,C) are selected over other, less-preferred goals (X,Y,Z).

In a classic essay the rational decision-making process has been described in step-by-step fashion by Charles Lindblom. The decision maker starts

> by trying to list all related *values* in order of importance, e.g., full employment, reasonable business profit, protection of small savings, prevention of stock market crash. Then all possible *policy* outcomes could be rated as more or less efficient in attaining a maximum of these values. This would of course require a prodigious inquiry into values held by members of society and an equally prodigious set of calculations on how much of each value is equal to how much of each other value. He could then proceed to outline all possible policy alternatives. In a third step, he would undertake systematic *comparison* of his multitude of alternatives to determine which attains the greatest amount of values.
>
> Finally, he would try to make the choice that would in fact maximize his values.[13] [emphasis added]

It is this clear reliance on systematic means-ends analysis that characterizes the rational approach. Proceeding from analysis of a problem condition, the decision maker seeks to deal with the problem by a systematic and comprehensive matching of means with ends. Almost all accounting methods derive from this procedure, whereby the decision maker lines up on one side of the ledger (and rank orders) all of his goals (A,B,C, . . . , n). On the other side are listed the means or resources available (1,2,3, . . . n). The decisional task is to match the preferred goal with the efficient means. (See Figure 1.2.)

Another way of looking graphically at the same decisional procedure would be to imagine a decision-making tree with many branches; the decision maker simply follows the path of predetermined choice.

Within the context of path-goal decisional models, a recent addition to rational approaches has been the contingency[14] theory of Fred Fiedler, Robert House, and others.[15] And a recent addition to the contingency approach is the leadership-participation model of V. H. Vroom and P. W. Yetton, which relates leadership behavior to decision making. Some approaches view the rational model as a "decision tree" with limbs encompassing a set of rational, sequential, normative rules branching off (depending on contingencies) into alternative leadership styles. While the

Means-Ends Analysis

GOALS	RESOURCES
A	1
B	2
C	3
n	n
Rationality: Match Up Means and Ends	

Figure 1.2

model confirms that decisional research should be contingent or situation based rather than value directed, the model has the larger effect of saying that leadership (the penultimate management goal) is nothing more than a clearly defined set of rational choices or means-ends matchups.[16] Or, at any rate, this is the "purist" position.

More modern and sophisticated rational choice models introduce the element of self-interest, which seeks to explain the "flagrant" inconsistency between, say, the rational goals of the organization (O) and the individual interests of the actor (A).[17] The notion of self-interest, stripped of all its academic jargon, is nothing more than a common-sense explanation for irrationality. That is, we can understand irrationality not as a "logical inconsistency" but as a combination of conflicting objectives, between O and A. In this sense the concept of self interest points irrationality as the related counterpart of rationality.

Moreover, the concept of self-interest enriches the concept of rationality per se. At its core the concept of self-interest compels a discussion of relativism. That is to say, rationality is a relative concept based partly upon self interest. For example, separate cultures, biologically and socially discrete, possess their own system of values. Values in this context are relative. Moreover, rationalism and the sociology of knowledge not only tolerate relativism but actually require it.[18] Thus the quest for scientific truth, and the rational process of investigation, require a step-by-step programming or relative comparison. But relativism means more than relationship. Philosophically, the value of rationality does not float "free of the educational and institutional patterns of the day."[19] Relativism is the explanation of this seemingly lesser standard.

Thus no serious philosopher would argue that rationality, or the rational model, actually produces the value-free, absolutely objective results claimed by proponents of management by objectives (MBO), program planning and budgeting system (PPBS), or cost-benefit analysis. This is not the argument here.

The issue here has to do with the complex matter of definition and criticism: definition of the word *rational* and a critique of its operable elements. The notion of self-interest does much to temper our naive thoughts of rationality and to explain how economic man and rational man can be one and the same.

Whether viewed as double-columned goal-resource matching or means-ends decisional sequences or as self-interest—collective choice mechanisms, rational models posit the absurd assumption that the end or the goal (a value-laden concept) can be achieved by a series of neutral (value-free) choices or steps. It is this logically unsound relationship between means and ends that ultimately disturbs critics of the rational method.

In addition to self-interest and the corollary concept of relativism, the notion of conflict does much to explain a central paradox of the rational model, namely how differences among individuals and between individuals and organizations are reconciled through collective choice mechanisms. Conflict and conflict resolution models are traditionally discussed as political processes (Chapters Four and Five herein), but for conceptual purposes, conflict must also be addressed in the context of the rational approach.[20] In fact, introducing the problem of conflict resolution at this point (as a rational process) only illustrates the central point of this text: that rationality and politics and legalisms are one and the same.

At any rate, rational choice models do not preclude conflict resolution and resultant collective choice objectives. Nor do rational model theories ignore the prerequisite realities of value conflict, irreconcilable differences, and intraorganizational disputes. The popular misconception, and the academic absurdity, is the misguided presumption that rationality precludes conflict. It does not. As Russell Hardin so adequately illustrates, "narrow rationality" or self-interest is often perfectly consistent with "collective" rationality.[21] In short, rationality also means "broad" rationality. Accordingly, rationality means being "efficient in securing one's self-interest"; and of course this may be done through economically based collective choice processes. George Stigler and others show how perfect competition reconciles the paradox of irrationality.[22] In this book, the political model is used to illustrate the same phenomenon.

There are other less philosophical, but nonetheless relevant, concerns and criticisms.

The Rational Model Critiqued

Criticisms of the rational model focus on three of its aspects: assumptions regarding the societal nature of goals, assumptions regarding internal subunit conflict, and assumptions regarding human perceptual and cognitive abilities. Critics claim that the model's assumptions are simplistic in the first instance and unrealistic in the second and third.

The Societal Context

The idea that values should be clarified rationally even in advance of examination of alternative policies is appealing. But ask, What happens when we seek rationality for complex social problems? The first difficulty is that on many critical values or objectives (the end state) businessmen disagree, legislators disagree, judges disagree, society disagrees. This leads to a second problem of ranking or, as managers say, "prioritizing."

> Even when the administrator resolves to follow his own values as a criterion for a decision, he often will not know how to rank them when they conflict with one another as they usually do. . . . Somewhat paradoxically, the only practical way to disclose one's relevant marginal values even to oneself is to describe the policy one chooses to achieve them.[23]

There is a subtle, but powerful, third point underlying these first two realities. It is the obvious fact (discussed above) that social objectives do not always have the same relative values. Clearly, means and ends (the bedrock of rationality) are inextricably intertwined. Both rank ordering and decision trees are mere abstractions. One chooses among values and policies (ends and means) *simultaneously* if at all.

What does all of this mean in the real world of day-to-day decisions? A brief example might illustrate the fundamental absence of rational goals in the larger societal context.

In his classic study Amitai Etzioni wrote that goals (or values) have two aspects within organizational life:

1. Goals constitute a source of legitimacy which justifies the activities of an organization and, indeed, its very existence.
2. Goals serve as standards by which members of an organization and outsiders can assess the success of the organization.[24]

In terms of organizations, societal goals may be considered from three perspectives:

1. Social goals (imposed on the organization),
2. System goals (operational goals), and
3. Participant (intrapsychic) goals.[25]

Social goals are encountered at the environmental level. System goals apply to the organizational level and are similar to the operative goals—as opposed to the official goals—of the organization.[26] Participant goals are those of the individuals constituting the membership of the organization. What happens to the rational decision-making process when an external social goal is imposed on the organization? Consider the following case of goal incongruence involving the Foreign Corrupt Practices Act and its impact on a large organization.

THE SOCIETAL CONTEXT: A CASE IN POINT

ABC, Inc. is one of the world's leading manufacturers of electronic equipment and components. The 1982 Annual Report describes the company as being engaged in the design, manufacture, and sale of two-way radios and other forms of electronic communications systems; semi-conductors, including integrated circuits, discrete semi-conductors, and microprocessor units; electronic equipment for military and aerospace use; electronic engine controls; digital appliance controls; data communications products such as high-speed modems, multiplexers, and network processors. These products are manufactured for both U.S. and international markets.

Over the last three years, the company has reported an average annual growth rate in sales of 17 percent and in earnings of 13 percent. Sales for 1981 were more than $3.3 billion. Over 30 percent of the company's business is in international markets, where the company has 27 major facilities and approximately 85 non-U.S. sales offices.

A significant aspect in the development of the company and its current competitive position is the synergistic relationship between the technology of the company's semiconductor operations and the company's other products, which utilize microelectronic components. The rapid growth of semiconductor science has pro-

---

This case is based on a study by Gene O'Rourke submitted for a course in macro-organizational behavior, DePaul University, 1982. Michael Murray, editor.

vided other operations of the company with a technological base to further expand and develop product offerings.

The overall structural form of the company is the conglomerate. The company has five major businesses that are structurally designated, in order of decreasing size, as either sectors or groups. The specific structural divisions include: the Communications Sector; the Semiconductor Products Sector; the Information Systems Group; the Automotive and Industrial Electronics Group; and the Government Electronics Group.

The sector-group-division form of structure is also used to subdivide the businesses. For example, the International Group is a subunit of the Communications Sector. Groups and divisions have a mixture of departmentation schemes with functional and divisional structures predominating. The International Group uses a modified functional departmentation scheme that divides work into subunits by function and geographical location.

Two important subunits are the Distribution Operations Subunit (distribution) and the International Finance Subunit (finance). These are interdependent subunits with a line-staff relationship, but both report to the group vice-president. There is also a parallel reporting path for the International Finance Subunit, which ultimately leads to the corporate controller. This parallel path was set up by corporate management to ensure that financial standards would be maintained regardless of pressures brought by sector or group managers.

The Foreign Corrupt Practices Act passed by Congress in 1977 in response to controversy regarding commission payments to foreign agents by U.S. companies has had a major impact on the company and especially on the International Group. Since the act contained ill-defined but broad provisions that could be selectively enforced by the government, the company formed a Business Ethics Compliance Committee, responsible to the board of directors, to monitor compliance with existing ethics policies and to further define and modify those policies where needed. Managers in a position to have knowledge of dealings with distributors, agents, customers, suppliers, or political entities were required to sign an affidavit affirming that their actions were in accordance with the company's Code of Conduct.

Standard operating procedures (SOP) were revised and tightened up to meet the strict guidelines set by the Compliance Committee. These guidelines defined who could be paid sales commissions and how the commissions had to be paid. To enforce these guidelines, the corporate controller directed finance to monitor closely the details of sales transactions. These actions did not change the substance of previous operations; strong guidelines had been used for years, and finance had always had approval authority over commission payments. However, this increased emphasis did change who was empowered to interpret the circumstances connected to a sales transaction. Before, distribution was the dominant factor in deciding how circumstances fit the guidelines. it alone had knowledge of the political, cultural, legal, and business complexities of a marketplace that consisted of almost 100 countries. Now, finance was a more equal party to such decisions, and it brought with it a mandated attitude that circumstances should clearly fit the guidelines with little, if any, interpretation. Although finance did not have a clear veto power, a challenge to a distribution decision was sufficient to cause a series of reviews that took several weeks. Since then, these two subunits have interacted with an increasing amount of friction, quite often requiring the corporate legal department to resolve their disputes.

In short the imposition of the Foreign Corrupt Practices Act has generated a great deal of internal conflict. In part, the conflict results from organizational conditions such as task interdependence, (the requirement of coordinated action); status inconsistencies (unbalanced relations between subunits); and jurisdictional ambiguities (lack of clear lines of decision-making authority). In addition, however, there are deeper value-based obstacles. One obstacle has to do with communications that impact finance and distribution. For example, distribution personnel must focus their attention on the marketplace outside the organization, whereas finance personnel focus their attention on elements inside the organization. Dealing with the marketplace gives distribution specialized knowledge. Dealing with internal financial statements gives finance specialized knowledge. The two subunits must coordinate their respective specialties to produce a forecast, but the exchange is not equal. Distribution has to give up its knowledge to provide the substance of the report and bears the risk for accuracy, whereas finance bears no risk and does not have to divulge current financial information to distribution.

Another factor, equally divisive, concerns goal incongruity. Theoretically, distribution and finance should have the same goal: meeting forecasted sales and profit targets. However, each subunit tends to suboptimize the element over which it has more control and for which it is

The Societal Context: A Case in Point

rewarded. Distribution concentrates on sales volume. Finance concentrates on bottom-line profit, which it can influence by controlling distribution cost. Simply put, distribution wants more resources to develop the marketplace, whereas finance wants to reduce the amount of resources used. Clearly, compliance with the Corrupt Practices Act means many things to many people.

Without considering whether the members of the units have internalized the internationally shared values of the Corrupt Practices Act, it is obvious that imposition of a broad societal goal triggers internal goal incongruence. Query the results when external agencies set pollution standards or racial regulations or ethnic standards. Preferred choices within an organization are hardly rational (value-free) choices.

The Subunit Context

That various parts of an organization have different and conflicting values need not necessarily be a problem for a rational model. The model does not claim that disagreements evaporate. It maintains only that disagreements can be resolved through evaluation and choice. Furthermore, as Herbert Simon contended in his dated but classic study, the decisions (ends) reached in any one part of the organization frequently enter as constraints (or means) into the decisions being made in other parts of the organization. To the extent that this happens, elements of an organization naturally (although not necessarily easily) accommodate. It is important to note, however, that once again means and ends are inextricably intertwined. According to Simon, "[B]ehavior . . . is rational insofar as it selects alternatives which are conducive to the achievement of the previously related goals."[27] A hierarchy of means and ends emerges, based upon conflict and choices. In the context of multilayered, multidivisional institutions, organizational conflict may be viewed as a condition that exists when the goal-oriented behavior of one unit results in the blocked goal-directed behavior of another unit. The inevitability and pervasiveness of conflict have led to a contemporary view of conflict as "not inherently good or bad." Rather, conflict is viewed as an integral part of an organization and needs only to be managed effectively in order to contribute to organizational effectiveness.[28]

The contemporary view that conflict inherently exists and needs only be managed is a far cry from the traditional view that the decision-making process is entirely rational and free of inherent disagreement and divisiveness.[29] To be sure, neither Simon nor modern analysts argue that rationality cannot be "practiced." Again it is a matter of definition, but Oliver Williamson offers the notion of "bounded rationality" (that is, Simon's idea of limited rationality) to explain the dynamics of subunit context.[30] For example, uncertainty and complexity are like self-interest—they define the limits and the direction of rationality. Thus a pricing system (or market) that only publicly omits power as a factor operates rationally to allocate resources in a generally useful and acceptable way, at least for market participants. In this sense rationality may be seen as a contingent phenomenon. Nonetheless, logically, rationality as a value-free choice or as a purely mechanistic means-ends process is no longer credible in the subunit context, where inherent conflict inevitably occurs. Consider the following case involving a large organization with inapposite subunit goals.

THE SUBUNIT CONTEXT: A CASE IN POINT

DEF Corporation is a major international producer of chemicals and machinery for agriculture, industry, and government. Headquartered in Chicago, the company has almost 40,000 employees located at 129 manufacturing facilities and mines in the Untied States and abroad. Following a period of acquisitions in the 1960's and early 1970's, the company eventually grew large enough to require additional manufacturing space, and by 1976, plants were set up in Lexington and Bowling Green, Kentucky. Lexington was set up as the Hydraulic Crane Division with its own departments for engineering, purchasing, service, marketing, and so on. Bowling Green remained part of the Cable Crane and Excavator Division along with the Cedar Rapids plant. In spite of this, Bowling Green has a retinue of departments that is nearly as comprehensive as that of Lexington.

In 1978, upper mangement decided to establish a group headquarters and service parts operation in Bannockburn, Illinois. In addition to headquarters and the parts operation, the machine sales and distribution operation (CEDO) was established at Bannockburn. Most of the functions located here were moved from the Cedar Rapids plant where they had existed in roughly the same form, and with many of the same people as they do today.

The notable exception to this is the parts operation (CEPO), which was a new concept to DEF and the crane industry in general. Over three years since its inception, CEPO is still the only separate

---

This case is based on a study by Ruth Balfe submitted for a course in macro-organizational behavior, DePaul University, 1982. Michael Murray, editor.

parts facility in the industry. CEPO consists of the central parts warehouse in Bannockburn and departments ancillary to parts distribution, including parts sales and parts marketing. Since CEPO is an operation rather than a division, it does not have a separate purchasing department, and profits on parts sales are not retained but rather are allocated back to the source plants within one of the divisions.

While many analysts see communication breakdown as a factor in subunit conflict, a more realistic view is that poor communication is merely a symptom of a more fundamental disparity in value orientation or "frame of reference." The DEF case is a classic illustration. Since the parts operations is more functional than divisional in design, CEPO employees view the functional organization as the more desirable structure of the two; and conversely, the divisions see the parts operation as a departure from the divisional structure ideal.

For example, the divisions have a different *priority orientation* than the parts operation. CEPO employees lean toward product support and cling to the philosophy of "You can't sell more machines if you don't support the one already in the field." Divisional employees look at parts as a necessary evil and express the diametrically opposed belief that "You can't sell parts if you don't have machines out there to put them on." Since this is a "Which came first: the chicken or the egg?" type of dilemma, it sets the stage for communication problems and subunit conflict.

The source of conflict is not mere breakdown of communication but deeper underlying conditions such as *competition for scarce resources.* As analysts note: "A . . . major source of conflict involves competition between two or more groups for what their members identify as a finite set of scarce resources."* The two resources for which the plants and Bannockburn compete most directly are operating budgets and human resources (headcount). With the growing realization at the plants that overlapping functions are being centralized at Bannockburn, there comes an intensification of this competition. The struggle for people and budgets seems to be viewed as a "zero-sum" game in which, if Bannockburn wins, the plants lose, and vice versa.

---

*Paul R. Lawrence, Louis B. Barnes, and Jay W. Lorsch, *Organizational Behavior and Administration* (Homewood, Ill.: Richard D. Irwin, 1976), p.295.

In short, the goal orientation of the divisions versus the parts operation are quite different. Divisions are set up as profit centers with formal goals beings primarily profit oriented but with informal goals that emphasize the number of machines sold rather than the degree of profitability. CEPO is set up as a cost center with formal goals that revolve around product support and customer service, yet the general manager's performance is measured largely on profitability.

But profit orientation is not the only disparity. Other value (or resource) disparities are evident. For example, differences in orientation toward time between plant people and CEPO employees may be necessary for efficient performance, but it is nevertheless a potential area of conflict. Plant production and purchasing people are geared toward building schedules that are planned 3 to 12 months in advance. CEPO parts expediters, in most cases, are at the opposite end of the continuum and relate to a time frame of two days to two weeks, since a customer's machine may be sitting idle for lack of a part.

Divisional machine marketing people think in terms of two to five years into the future. The length of time it takes to move an idea from prototype to production dictates this type of long-range planning. CEPO parts marketing people, on the other hand, operate in time frames of 3 to 12 months, since parts markets are far more volatile than machine markets.

A note on differences in unit orientation and the temptation to reduce those differences is provided by Edgar Huse. "Increasing shared perceptions is usually good for the organization . . . [however,] differences in perceptions in such areas as time, goal, and interpersonal areas may be needed"* to enable an organization to function in an unstable, uncertain environment. This may be true, and in the end it may be rational (in the sense that it is desirable), but it is not an example of value-free, purely objective decisional frameworks. Values in conflict, of course, are values that must be "traded off" or otherwise negotiated.

The Individual Level

Although the rational approach is easily described, except as bounded rationality or as contingent rationality, or regarding relatively simple problems, it is not easily practiced. One reason, critics claim, is that the

---

*Edgar F. Huse, *Organization Development and Change*, (St. Paul, Minn.: West, 1975), p.243.

rational model attributes unrealistic perceptual and cognitive abilities to the decision maker. At the very least it ignores fundamental human limitations. Perhaps the problem is overstated by assertions that the rational decision maker bases his choices on an "omniscient analysis" of all the available alternatives. However, most analysts agree that the rational-comprehensive model in pure form assumes that every important relevant factor is taken into account in the decision process.

The problem is that because the environment contains an infinite amount of "data," that is, an infinite number of sensory clues that could be perceived, the decision maker cannot perceive all of the them.

Clearly, aspects of perception and cognition bear on the rational model—or for that matter, on any model of decision making. For example, it is well known that in the process of perception itself, data are organized or structured. Certain information may be suppressed, other data are given greater emphasis, and still others may be added by the observer himself to complete anticipated or preconceived patterns. Consequently, the very basis of decision making, the information gathered in the analytic phase, cannot be assumed to be wholly accurate, much less objective. This, say the critics, undermines an important assumption of the rational model.

Equally important, perception and beliefs are maintained in ways to ensure their consistency. Some writers argue that this phenomenon is demonstrated convincingly in certain optical illusions; and of course, this forms the basis of the theory of cognitive dissonance.[31] Beliefs and attitudes are pruned, modified, even discarded to eliminate disharmony. What makes this process inapposite to the rational model is that it often happens unconsciously. Hence it is doubtful that a decision maker can be fully objective, even assuming that all the facts are available to him. In short, beliefs, attitudes, and values are sustained, not reevaluated, as rational data enter the process of cognition.

Criticisms directed against the rational model focus on key assumptions regarding the nature of goals and the limits and the nature of human perception and cognition. First, organizational goals often are so complex that the rational model is operable only if it assumes a near omniscient decision maker. Second, the rational model does not take into account certain factors that shape and limit perceptual and cognitive processes.[32] To be sure, these critiques often overlook the compensating effect of numerous participants in the decision process and of group dynamics with its supplementing mechanisms. But do group settings actually induce greater rationality? An example or two should illustrate the fundamental limits of individual rationality, even when (or particularly when) working in group settings.

Nowhere are the difficulties of rational decision making more severe for the individual than in the complex and highly pressured world of the Internal Revenue Service (IRS) data manager. In an organization that bases its decisions on the most objective factors (quantifiable data), the limits of human perception and cognition are nonetheless dramatic. Consider the realities in the case of the IRS agent.

THE INDIVIDUAL CONTEXT: A CASE IN POINT

It is no secret that the Internal Revenue Service (IRS) uses various degrees of power in order to collect the federal taxes imposed by Congress.

But what about the internal structure of the IRS? Does the same organization that pumps fear into the American people use the same power techniques to manipulate and control its own employees as they go about their neutral, objective national activities? This case will examine the concept of power as it relates to the audit function, one of the many divisions within the IRS, and the activities of the Internal Revenue agent. The term *power* as it is used in this case shall mean: the capacity of one party (subunit or individual) to modify the conduct of other parties (subunit or individual) in the organization in a desired manner and to prevent having one's own conduct modified in undesired ways.

The IRS is an administrative agency of the Treasury Department. The service is headed by the commissioner of Internal Revenue, who serves under the Secretary of the Treasury. The organizational structure of the IRS is divided into three basic levels: (1) the national office, (2) the 7 regional offices, and (3) the 58 district offices.

The national office has the mission of developing broad policies and programs for the administration of the revenue laws. This office is located in Washington, D.C., and is headed by the commissioner of Internal Revenue, who is appointed by the president and approved by the Congress.

The seven regional offices act as intermediaries between the national offices and the various district offices. They are responsible for coordinating the broad policies of the national office with the district offices within these regions. The regions are broken up geographically and are headed by seven regional commissioners.

This case is based on a study by Michael Curley submitted for a course in macro-organizational behavior, DePaul University, 1983. Michael Murray, editor.

The district offices administer the collection, audit, intelligence, and administration programs of the Internal Revenue Service. It is at this level where the day-by-day routines are carried out. The district offices are headed by the district director. Within each district there is an Audit Division (also referred to as the Examination Division). The Audit Division is headed by the chief of audit. This division is further broken down into various branches. These branches are dispersed in the district by geographical location and in some cases based on the type of taxpayers where the branch is assigned. Each branch is headed by a branch chief and has from four to eight audit groups under its control.

The Audit Group is the lowest organizational division in the IRS with respect to the auditing of federal income tax returns. The "group," as it is called, consists of from 10 to 20 revenue agents, 1 or 2 group clerks, and a group manager.

Although performing a theoretically objective activity, the Internal Revenue agent feels the impact of power from various sources, including: the group manager, the review staff, and the inspection service. Power or control is felt in the form of direct personal influence, compliance with laws and procedures, and latent criminal charges.

The group manager exerts personal pressures directly upon revenue agents. The IRS is a centralized bureaucracy; therefore, lines of command are rarely broken. The group manager has various objectives upon which he is evaluated, including: the number of cases closed out through the group, the number of cases closed with no audit change, the number of cases referred for criminal prosecution, and the number of prepared penalty cases. Obviously, the qualified evaluation mandates that the success of the group manager is contingent upon the quantifiable product of his subordinates. It is the revenue agent who investigates and turns in the finished product. This product is the audit report, referred to herein as the "case."

In order to meet the requirements of the IRS, the group manager must exert direct control over his agents. He must motivate them one way or another so that he may achieve his desired goals. The group manager, by the nature of his position, has a variety of resources. These resources are given to the manager in the Internal Revenue Manual (IRM), Chapter 1000, as well as in the Multi-District Agreement between the IRS and the National Treasury Employees Union. These documents give the manager the responsibility of occasionally reviewing cases in depth. Upon completion of this in-depth review, the manager prepares a written evaluation.

The written evaluation then becomes part of the employee's permanent personnel file. This file is later used as a basis for promotions and reassignments.

The IRS is a very mobile organization; that is, the employees are constantly being moved to different geographical locations within the organization. There is also a high level of external mobilization of employees to the private sector. Owing to these facts, chances are that an agent will have a new manager at least once every two years. Therefore, it is very often the case that the employment file is the only basis for evaluating the performance of the revenue agent. A smart agent who wishes to progress in the organization will pay keen attention to the manager and the manager's values and attitudes regarding group goals and deficiencies. In addition, an agent is constantly facing new and complex cases involving a myriad of data. Not knowing what will be the reaction to his analysis and decision, each agent is guided by the direction and input of his group manager.

The review staff (a group of experienced revenue agents who have the duty of reviewing the cases submitted by other agents) exercises a disturbing kind of influence based on a formal review system. Not all cases submitted are reviewed. Some cases are selected on a random basis, while others are a must-review based on the nature of the case. When a reviewer analyzes your case and sends it back to you for further development, it has been rejected and must be redone. On the other hand, he may accept your findings and send it through to the processing center. Finally, he may not only accept your case but also write a memo praising your work. Any of these three situations may occur when an agent presents his case for review. The review staff sends out memos explaining the format and requirements of the case. An agent will try to comply with their procedures and format, even in the face of seeming absurdity, in order to avoid a bad evaluation.

Inspection is a separate division of the Internal Revenue Service with the responsibility for auditing the IRS. Activities include developing background reviews on new employees, investigating corruption within the service, and making sure employees maintain good conduct outside of work. The IRS uses this form of latent power to attempt to maintain credibility with the public.

Whether or not this exertion of power works in controlling the behavior of off-duty agents is questionable. However, in terms of influencing on-duty activities, these techniques are very functional. For example, revenue agents are given access to highly confidential

> material. Care must be taken so that this information does not get disclosed to others. Disclosure is a criminal offense and thus can result in a prison sentence. It is not at all unusual to see an agent checking his cabinet two or three times at night to make sure it is locked. One fact not disputed among revenue agents is that the power exerted by the Inspection Division is most feared. As one agent said: "The fear of inspection goes home with an agent every night."

Clearly, this case reveals that even in the most neutral and objective of activities individual perceptual and cognitive abilities are influenced by a number of factors and forces. Concern with personal promotions, compliance with review standards and forms, and the ever-present fear of wrongdoing make the work of the IRS agent anything but rational.

Even if an action is viewed as rational to the extent that it maximizes *net* goal achievement, in this circumstance even this minimal view of rationality fails. Reconsider the case and the reality of the work a day world as revealed by an IRS agent:

> During a group meeting the manager stated that the no-change rate within the group was considerably greater than the district rate. The next day the agent was out on an audit and determined that there were no material discrepancies on the taxpayer's return. However, he saw that if he spent another day on the case he could find some error, however small. He knew his time would probably cost the government more than the additional revenue brought in and that this uncalled-for probe would actually reduce the taxpayer's future compliance. But since he wishes to meet the manager's criteria, he goes right ahead and tries to find something.[33]

POLITICAL MODELS

The word *politics* might be defined as any activity that influences the distribution of power among groups or within societies. In its broadest sense the notion of a "political system" involves the complex of processes and institutions that allocate the authoritative values for a social system.[34]

The notion of a *political system* is significant. It presumes that the study of political phenomena can reach the level of other social sciences—

that politics constitutes as separate and distinctive a theoretical field as economics or law.

The conceptual force of the notion of a political system allows the analyst to "abstract from the whole social system" those variables that seem to be distinctly political. What are these political variables? "Neither the concept of the state nor that of power offers a gross description" of the central concept of political life.[35] Hence we look elsewhere.

In the concept of authoritative policy for a society (the authoritative allocation of values), we find a set of orienting concepts for political analysis.[36] By this definition, political activity may occur in a variety of institutional settings, public and private, formal and informal. Politics (the authoritative allocation of values for a society) may be expressed in a legislative body or in a corporate boardroom. Politics may take a formal (legal, public) character as in desegregation laws; or it may take a nonformal (illegal, unofficial) form as in actual segregation practices. The notion of politics thus forces us to a focus on those policies (whether public or private, legal or extra-legal) and those activities that influence values for a society.

If the political system involves the *complex* of processes and institutions that allocate authoritative value for a society, then we can further analyze the political system by considering the notions of micropolitics and macropolitics. Micropolitics looks at the individual and his attempts to influence the operation of the system (an organization) or a subsystem such as a unit or group. Macropolitics views the operation of the entire political system as it interacts with individual groups and members within it.[37]

Importantly, the notion of a political process embraces a method as well as a phenomenon. The latter suggests that a distinct dynamic of life is interaction among social groups and individuals and that one aspect of this interrelationship involves specifically political matters (value allocation for that society). The notion of process suggests a distinctly political *way* of making decisions regarding politics (values to be allocated).[38]

Charles Lindblom has referred to this process of making decisions (the policy-making process) as the "Science of Muddling Through." Although sharply different from the linear, orderly, rational process, the political process has distinct and unique qualities. Lindblom contrasts the political decision maker with the rational decision maker. Remembering that the rational approach would proceed by "scientific" or sequential means-ends analysis, Lindblom outlines a "process" whereby vaguely formulated and simple goals are matched in a fragmented fashion with relatively few policy alternatives, which results in unclarified and only partially satisfying decisions and which of course compels a repetition of the same unpredictable process.[39] Writing twenty years later and still arguing that "muddling through" (or incrementalism) "is and ought to be the usual method of policy making" Lindblom elaborated on the meaning(s) of incremental analysis as a "political pattern", and found three distinct forms of incrementalism.

1. Analysis that is limited to consideration of alternative policies all of which are only incrementally different from the status quo.
2. Analysis marked by a naturally supporting set of simplifying and focusing stratagems of which simple incremental analysis is only one.
3. Analysis limited to any calculated or thoughtfully chosen set of stratagems to simply complex policy problems, that is, to short-cut the conventionally comprehensive "scientific" analysis.[40]

Several years ago James March and others developed what is termed a "garbage can model" of decision making. This "model" is essentially a set of ideas about decision making under conditions of ambiguity. The model initially was used to describe academic decision making and later was extended to other organizations including large public bureaucracies (the military).[41] The garbage can model (or set of ideas) provides an important theoretical transition from strict rational models (clear objectives—clear choice) to muddled political models (conflicting objectives— compromised choice).

It is important to understand the March model as a transition point in the development of intellectual approaches, which is what the garbage can theory represents. Recent work by James March offers the important recognition that the fact that things are not exactly what they appear to be does not imply that they are necessarily the opposite.[42] For example: the fact that a decisional approach is not orderly does not necessarily mean it is chaotic. The garbage can model makes this point by illustrating that the range of conditions and characteristics of decision making embrace more than the extreme opposites of clarity-confusion/predictable process— chaotic process. Somewhere between pure rational models and pure intuitive models lies something termed *ambiguity*, which stresses the "unfolding" nature of activity in organizations. The term means that because decisions are segmented and discontinuous, and because objectives develop and change over time, behavior and decisions must be viewed in the context in which people, problems, and solutions come together. Thus solutions (decisions) are not determined a priori but are the products of solutions and problems joined together by "simultaneous availability" and by coincident but simultaneous demands on decision makers' time. Pure accident? No. Pure chaos? No. Pure rationality? No. March and others see the process as *ambiguity*, which refers to decision making in situations where objectives, procedures, technology, and experience are unclear but where simultaneous availability (the garbage can) compels a choice, often the right one (politically, legally, or rationally).[43] It is against this transition theory that one can best understand the political model.

Whether viewed as a procedural alternative to rational processes or as a substantively preferred series of choices on an incremental continuum, the political model, theoretically, is of a type different from the rational model.

At the core of the political model lies a preference—a preference for this value of the model itself. Roughly summarized, this preference is grounded on the thought that since the ideal (rational) model is elusive, the feasible (political) model is best. It is best not because it works ideally but simply because it works. And in working, the model precludes a basic assault on a consensus-compliance system of democratic government.

The Political Model Critiqued

Whether called "incremental analysis" or "strategy of decision" or "political approach" the political process model has gone through several stages. As evolved, the political model is not without criticism. The most frequent and fundamental objection is not to the procedural analysis of incremental alternatives; it is instead to the political practice of change only by increment. As Lindblom argues, "[T]he objection is not to incremental analysis but to the incremental politics" to which incremental analysis is nicely suited.

In short, to get rid of incrementalism, the decision maker would have to be rid of an elaborate constitutional system of checks and balances, divisions of power, and consensus-binding structures that contain almost ethical precepts.

Should we throw this baby (the laissez-faire system of incremental, fragmented decisions) out with the bathwater (the frustrating process of starts and stops)? Most analysts say no:

> [P]oor as it is, incremental politics ordinarily offers the best chance of introducing into the political system those changes and the change-producing intermediate changes that a discontented citizen might desire. That holds out no great hope, only as much hope as can be found in any style of American politics. If we live in a system designed

by the constitutional fathers to frustrate in large part the popular will, their success in doing so reminds us that even if we attempted a new constitutional convention the same consequences might follow.[44]

But is the preference for incrementalism so obvious? Does the political model really work? Are the choices so clear and ready? Consider the problem in detail.

A perfect and contemporary illustration of the impact of politics on the decisional process may be found in a recent public sector budgeting case.

POLITICS AND DECISIONS: A CASE IN POINT

The Congressional budget process is dying. Should anyone care? Yes, I care.

The budget process was born in 1974, and at the time, it was hard to believe that it would not increase the rationality of Congressional decision making. Prior to the new process, spending and taxing committees did their work individually without paying much attention to their impact on total spending, receipts, and deficits. The new process forced the Congress to vote explicitly on the totals. How could that be bad?

It is not clear whether it was or was not bad on balance, but like all new processes, the new one had some unintended consequences. As Allen Schick, professor in the School of Public Affairs at the University of Maryland and a participant in the forming of the Congressional Budget Act of 1974, has pointed out many times, a new process cannot overcome the incentive structure facing politicians. In most cases, it is their goal to get reelected. If there is a collision between the process and the pursuit of that goal, the process almost always loses.

A new process will only be successful if it generates new information that makes it harder for the politician to pursue re-election successfully while voting against the national interest, or if

---

Rudolph G. Penner, "The Budget Process Is Tied in Knots," *New York Times*, February 28, 1982 p. F3. The article is only partially reprinted here.

it gives the politician better information as to where the national interest lies.

To some extent the process has provided useful information to voters and politicians. It has made it a bit harder for politicians to vote for numerous program increases while claiming to be against higher deficits or higher taxes.

But it is remarkable how many politicians still feel uninhibited about voting for large deficits within the budget process and then voting against increasing the debt limit. By and large, the press fails to report on such inconsistent actions by individual members and the voter remains uninformed.

By creating budget committees in the Senate and House, the budget process has also provided new sources of information about inefficiencies in program design. The substantive committees that rule over individual programs are likely to be more tolerant of inefficiency because they are more obeisant to the narrow constituencies who find inefficiency to be profitable.

The Congressional Budget Office was created to provide technical assistance to the new process and has aided the effort to root out inefficiency. Recent budget office compendiums showing options for cutting spending programs and eliminating tax preferences may be the most valuable budget documents produced in either the legislative or executive branch.

But unfortunately, in its early years, the budget office gave much advice about stabilizing the economy and that advice was based on a rather naive Keynesian view of the world. In the late 1970's, it may thus have done more harm than good. Now, budget office analysis has become much more sophisticated and useful, but the problems that all economists had in explaining the world of the late 1970's opened the door to new unsubstantiated theories.

The political system, which had earlier twisted Keynesianism into an unintended promise of a free lunch, quickly seized upon supply-side economics as providing a new free lunch to replace the discredited Keynesian variety. In 1981, the Congress felt unrestrained by the more sober (and more accurate) analysis coming from the budget office.

While, in the early days, the Congress may have been misled about the impact of the budget on the economy, it quickly acquired a very valuable education regarding the impact of the economy on the budget. Few had paid attention to this before, but with the new process, the Congress frequently saw its efforts to achieve certain outlay and receipts targets overwhelmed by unexpected changes in inflation and unemployment which had profound effects on tax receipts and outlays on indexed entitlement programs.

This has proved to be the Achilles heel of the process. The process forces the Congress to vote on very precise outlay and receipt targets that are based on a very imprecise economic forecast. No progress has been made in resolving this paradox. It may be fatal because it creates strong political incentives to adopt forecasts that are overly optimistic.

The incentives for optimism are particularly strong when making long-run budget projections. There, politicians feel unconstrained by the consensus forecast coming from economists because no one really knows what will happen in the long run. Although the fact that the new process required five-year projections of budget totals and should have enhanced the rationality of decision-making, it is clear that long-run planning based on bad assumptions may be worse than not having long-run planning at all.

That was certainly true last year. The Administration persuaded the Congress to adopt preposterous assumptions about the future that made it seem possible to have an enormous tax cut and a balanced budget in 1984. Now we are left with huge deficits. All the goodies have been given away and the cupboard is bare. There is no grease left in the system to smooth Congressional efforts to make difficult decisions. As a result, there may be no Congressional budget this year. Without a budget, Congress will most likely end up continuing last year's policies. Spending controls and tax increases will be much more difficult to enact and deficits will soar far beyond the high levels now appearing in the President's budget.

Lamenting the loss of rationality, the author fails to see the beauty, however abstract, of the constitutional system of checks and balances (Congress versus President), of fragmented decisional bases (committees in House and Senate), and of structured incentives (getting reelected) in single-member districts. The current debate over the national deficit is beset with these very concerns.

LEGAL MODELS

Although he would no doubt decry more centralized regulation, perhaps the rationalist writer above is at heart a closet legalist. Or, to reverse the situation, perhaps the apologist for the abstract beauty of the political process is at heart an antilegalist. Regardless, "in a country with a strong rule-of-law tradition," the legal process itself stands as a third and theoretically discrete and powerful means of decision making.[45] Hence legal decision making will be analyzed as a separate and significant truth-seeking model.

What are the elements of this legal decision-making process in organizational life? Is the legal model different from the rational model and from the political model?

Consider first that the rationalist business organization has little tolerance for the imposition of laws regulating product quality or protecting consumer rights. Note that the imposition of laws (the legalist approach) is to be distinguished from the role of government as guarantor of business.[46]

Consider next that "interest group liberalism" (based on notions of fragmented power and incremental decisions) has "little place for law because laws interfere with the political process."[47] Remember that the abstract apology for the political model is that it works; thus it is preferred. In short, it is not ideally perfect, but its intricate systems of checks and balances, multiple points of access, and fragmented review procedures ensure a kind of "hidden hand" corrective process. But the legal approach changes all of this.

> The political process is not perfectly self-correcting if it is not allowed to correct itself. Laws change the rules of the game. . . . Laws set priorities. Laws deliberately set some goals and values above others.[48]

It is in fact the authoritative impact of the "rule of law" that until the late 1880s had "deterred the growth of large and formalized" public bureaucracies[49] and that made the American minimalist administrative structure so different from the huge bureaucracies emerging in Europe. And it is this reverse trend, the authoritative impact of law in the regulatory area, that since the late 1880s has impacted the development of the contemporary private sector.[50]

Understanding its historical significance, what is the rule of law and what are the elements of this legal model—in theory and in reality?

In its most simple and direct form, law concerns the conduct of individual human beings with each other in the context of the social, political, and economic order. In its simplest framework, the legal model consists of the sum total of principles and procedures that a legal society has adopted and that it relies on and enforces in order to function properly.

The Legal Model Critiqued

As contrasted with the traditional jurists Oliver Wendell Holmes and Benjamin N. Cardozo) who defined *law* in a functional sense as court-based principles (akin to William Blackstone's view of the law as the rule of conduct or the supreme power of the state), many contemporary theorists view the law as a fluid, adaptive system of decisions and rules. Judge Jerome Frank observed that the fluidity of the law lies at the core of a meaningful definition:

> The law always has been, is now, and will ever continue to be, largely vague and variable. And how could this well be otherwise? The law deals with human relations in their most complicated aspects. The whole confused, shifting helterskelter of life parades before it—more confused than ever in our kaleidoscopic age. . . . Much of the uncertainty of law is not an unfortunate accident: it is of immense social value.[51]

The word *law* has many meanings. But whether we think of the law as the legal order (the entire apparatus of social control), as the aggregate of legal precepts (judical and administrative rules and regulations), or as the judicial process (the ritualized formal institutional system), it is the vagueness, the fluidity, indeed the *discretionary* aspect of law that distinguishes this truth-seeking methodology from the rational model and from the political model.[52]

Viewed as "efficacious social engineering," the legal approach as a discretionary method is grounded on distinct characteristics. First, law or legal reasoning is not scientific; it is not based on statistically valid cause-effect relationships. Nonetheless, the law relies on experience, history, tradition, and custom and in this sense uses the inductive method of science.[53]

Second, the law is not philosophically incrementalist; however, the logic of legal reasoning rests on the bedrock of stare decisis ("stand by the decision") and in this sense reflects previous decisions and facts.[54]

Third, although the hallmark of legal reasoning is its discretionary character, the law rests on, and is framed by, certain moral and ethical principles relating to fixed notions of justice, welfare, and public policy.

In sum, legal reasoning is inductive in procedure, rests on precedent for legitimacy, and derives from fixed moral precepts. How then can legal reasoning be characterized as discretionary in nature? Kenneth Culp

Davis explains this methodological phenomenon. Davis specifies the nature of discretionary decisions, isolating three factors.

> When we isolate what we regard as the exercise of discretion, we find three principal ingredients—facts, values, and influences. But an officer who is exercising discretion seldom separates these three elements; most discretionary decisions are intuitive, and responses to influences often tend to crowd out thinking about values.[55]

In short, the legal model as a discretionary process involves both the goal of optimization and the method of intuition. In this synthesis the legal process model is unlike either the rational or the political model.

The legal model as based on fact, value, and influence (or circumstances, precedents, and norms) maximizes discretion, at least at the theoretical level. In this the legal model stands in sharp contrast to the political and rational models. In addition, in actual operation the legal approach is very distinct from the rational and the political methods.

Consider the difference between the "administrative technique" (the nonlegalistic approach to the problem of controlling human behavior) and the "legal technique" (rules sanctioned by penalties). The distinction is between attempts, on the one hand, to effect maximum compliance (rational goal achievement) without generating political opposition (political preference) and attempts, on the other hand, to secure maximum compliance without regard to bottom lines and without regard to political factors. The difference between the nonlegal administrator and the legal enforcer is dramatic. The legalist, with law training, is concerned with enforcement per se; he takes the content of the laws very seriously. The rational planner or the agency official is exposed to different facts and goals; he seeks merely to maximize compliance and not necessarily to punish lawbreakers. In short, the administrative technique focuses on the vast majority who comply; the legal technique focuses on the small percentage who violate the law by noncompliance. The administrator is concerned with a statistically good record as opposed to total maximum compliance. The lawyer is concerned with catching and prosecuting the last lawbreaker.

In short, the legal technique frequently gets in the way of, or fails in, overall compliance and program success. For example, if the central purpose of the Office of Economic Opportunity was to remind people that poverty was a national problem rather than actually to redistribute wealth, then the strict enforcement/nuisance procedure of lawyers pressing for maximum feasible participation formulas was irrelevant, if not counterproductive, to the overall goal.

Critical analysts of the legal approach suggest that the theoretical notion of law as the discretionary application of a rule of conduct does not fully explain the more subtle nonlegal behavioral elements of social rules and regulations. Consider what happens when laws are applied in an administrative or organizational context. The inherent nature of law as discretionary when coupled with its legitimate solutions leads to very interesting behavioral patterns. Using a classic familiar example, Murray Edleman explains this element of discretion as game playing:

LAW AND LEGALISM: A CASE IN POINT

To control automobile speeding within a 65-mile-an-hour limit or to enforce a $1.15 minimum wage provision are concrete administrative objectives. In these and similar cases the administrator's problem is to maximize compliance and cooperation, for there will always be resistance, footdragging, and some overt defiance. If there were no resistance, there would be no need for the administrative program at all; and if it were impossible to increase the frequency of compliance through governmental action, there would equally obviously be no reason for administrative action.

Both the supporters and the defiers will, however, be clear as to what they are supporting or defying. They will talk and act with respect to the same concrete issue, and they can rationally choose behaviors which will further their objectives (though probably not in optimal fashion). In this kind of situation an administrator will try to achieve a satisfactory degree of compliance by increasing the material, moral, sunk or other costs of defiance or by rewarding compliance.

Concrete legal objectives are ordinarily pursued as though administrators and potential defiers were involved in a game with rather clear rules. The basic rule is that a fairly large proportion of the instances of noncompliance will not be detected or penalized. Automobile drivers and policemen are both aware that most speeders will not be caught or fined, and both adapt their behavior to this assumption: drivers speed when the chance of being caught is slight or considered worth taking. Policemen stop some but not all violators, and let some of these off with a warning. As long as the game is played in this way, both drivers and policemen accept the order of

---

Murray Edelman, *The Symbolic Uses of Politics* (Urbana: University of Illinois Press, 1964), pp. 44–47.

things fairly contentedly: drivers paying occasional fines complainingly but without massive political protest, policemen noticing a certain amount of modest surpassing of the posted limits without further action. Similarly, employers accept health, safety, child labor, and minimum wage laws on the assumption that inspectors will appear at the plant only once in a while, and that if they are caught in violations of these occasions, a fine may have to be paid. The game of taking calculated risks in filing income tax returns is so clearly understood and so universally played that it needs only to be mentioned here.

Fortunately for scholarship and for "constitutional" government, we get just enough administrators ignorant of this rule of the game to serve as an objective lesson in the disaster that its violation brings and in the wholly new symbolic relationship that then occurs. Officer Muller of the Chicago police force dismayed and pained his superiors some years ago by systematically ticketing every good citizen who took advantage of the long-standing practice of parking in a no-parking zone near City Hall. After high state and city officials had received this treatment, the conscientious Mr. Muller was assigned to a remote beat. It was never assumed by either the Police Department or the public that enjoyed the story in the newspaper that such substitution of ordinances for the game could be allowed to continue. Similarly, national and local automobile organizations protest and citizens grow righteously irate when a village creates a speed trap and really penalizes every violator.

Each legal offense or administrative enforcement program is a separate game with its own stakes, one such game to another. Not the size of the stakes or the penalties, but rather the meaning of the offense to enforcers and possible violators is what determines whether a game or a dogma is involved. Each murder falls into the game class in our society, though as a kind of limiting case. Here the stakes and the penalties are high; but the rules prescribe many avenues for avoiding detection and even more for avoiding conviction if detected. If we really regarded murder as an unacceptable and unforgivable act, as we pretend to do, we would certainly put more of our resources into its detection, and we would not write into the laws a long series of acceptable excuses, from insanity to self-defense (usefully ambiguous terms, serving in practice to allow juries, lawyers, and judges to play the game). Our equivocation in these matters no doubt reflects quite faithfully the ambivalence we feel about murder and our occasional temptations to indulge in it ourselves. Such widespread personal ambivalence or shared role-taking very likely underlies all substitution of game playing for unequivocal legal enforcement. The popular response to television programs that treat crime and law enforcement as a game of wits is another clue to our deep-seated feelings about the matter.

What distinguishes a game from other forms of competition? The essential agreement on rules which fix or shape obstacles, stakes, and penalties; agreement to accept the result for each round of play; and inability to play at all unless your opponent plays, too, either because there is then nothing to win or because the victory is empty and unrewarding if it is won without opposition. *The keynote in these rules of a game is mutual dependence, and in every one of these respects legal regulation meets the test of a game and not the test of an all-out, no-holds-barred strike for booty.* [emphasis added]

But the pervasive impact of discretion and its resultant behavior of game playing does not completely describe the inverted process of legal enforcement. As Edleman explains, mutual role playing is the key element. Because mutual role playing is fundamental to an analysis of the legal method and the discretionary enforcement of rules, it merits further attention and definition. Indeed, it compels an examination of the psychology of mass culture and the pervasive impact of media, image, ritual, dogma, and myth. In short, new realities or insights at the very least call for a reexamination of some strongly held conceptual biases. This will be the approach taken in the following chapters.

CONCLUSION

And so we come full circle:

- From rational techniques with inverted means-ends analysis relationships
- To political realities with symbolic interactions
- To legal enforcement and discretionary role playing.

Nonetheless, discrete, rational, political, and legal approaches do exist and do operate, at least theoretically, in pure form. The following six chapters will (1) further analyze each model in its pure or theoretical form and (2) further critique the theoretical model against organizational realities and in the context of its countermodel.

To set the stage for the upcoming chapters, Figure 1.3 provides a summary of this introductory chapter comparing the models in their theoretical form.

DECISIONAL MODELS SUMMARIZED

Rational: Comprehensive Model	Political: Incremental Model	Legal: Discretionary Model
1. Rational-comprehensive (root) clarification of values or objectives is distinct from and usually prerequisite to empirical analysis of alternative policies.	1. Selection of value goals and empirical analysis of the needed action are not distinct from one another but are closely intertwined.	1. Application of the rule of law is based on reliance of factual premises (stare decisis, statute, regulation.)
2. Policy formulation is therefore approached through means-ends analysis: first the ends are isolated, then the means to achieve them are sought.	2. Institutional structures (division of multiple powers or access; checks and balances; fragmented subunits) result in ad hoc policy formulation.	2. Discretionary procedures result in selective application of enforcement sanctions.
3. The test of a "good policy" is that it can be shown to be the most appropriate means to desired ends.	3. The test of good programs is whether they work; the politicized feasible program is preferred over the nonworkable ideal choice.	3. The test of effective laws is whether they are ambiguous and vague enough to allow for selective application.
4. Analysis is comprehensive; every important relevant factor is taken into account.	4. Analysis is noncomprehensive and is based on (1) neglect of important alternative policies and (2) neglect of excluded nonparticipating groups.	4. Analysis is narrowly legalist (compliance oriented) but clashes with administrative technique of overall goal achievement.
5. Theory and quantification are often heavily relied upon for legitimization.	5. The political process itself (multiple review points, open access) is said to be self-correcting.	5. Excessive discretion is tempered by mutual role playing and gamesmanship.

Figure 1.3   Source: Expansion and modification of a chart offered first in Charles E. Lindblom, "The Science of Muddling Through," *Public Administration Review*, Spring 1979, p. 81.

NOTES

1. Some formal definitions are in order A. *Social system* is a patterned collection of elements in action (operation or persistence) that involves a plurality of interacting individuals whose actions are oriented to the system, and that is capable of existing longer than its members' life spans. *Structures* are patterns (an observable uniformity) of action (operation or persistence) over time. *Functions* are consequences or conditions resultant from this action (operation or persistence) of a structure over time. See Marion J. Levy. Jr., *The Structure of Society* (Princeton: Princeton University Press, 1952), p. 76 f.

2. David Easton, *The Political System* (New York: Alfred A. Knopf, 1953), pp. 96−98, 128−34.

3. William P. Alston, *Philosophy of Language* (Englewood Cliffs, N.J.:Prentice-Hall, 1964), Chap. 2, p. 44.

4. Ibid.

5. Alvar O. Elbing, *Behavioral Decisions in Organizations: A Framework for Decision Making* (Glenview, Ill.: Scott Foresman, 1970), pp. 46−53.

6. See E. Frank Harrison, *The Managerial Decision Making Process* (Boston:Houghton-Mifflin, 1975). Chapter 9 provides a review of concepts, cases, and a bibliography. Also see Jeffrey Pressman, *Implementation* (Berkeley: University of California Press, 1973).

7. John D. Steinbruner, *The Cybernetic Theory of Decision* (Princeton: Princeton University Press, 1974), p. 16.

8. Governor George Wallace's once disdainful term for government administrators.

9. Values represent basic convictions that "a specific model of conduct or end state of existence is personally or socially preferable to an opposite or converse mode of conduct or end-state of existence." See Milton Rokeach, *The Nature of Human Values* (New York: Free Press, 1973), p. 5. Values contain a moral content of right and wrong, good and bad.

10. There are of course other decisional models, or at least other ways of classifying them. For example, methodologically there are behavioral or nonbehavior decisional theories. And there are other settings such as military institutions or church-based environments. But for our purposes business, government, and judicial settings provide an adequate base for analysis.

11. Steinbruner, *Cybernetic Theory*, p. 45.

12. Lawrence A. Gordon, Danny Miller, and Henry Mintzberg, *Normative Models in Managerial Decision Making* (New York: National Association of Accountants, 1975).

13. Charles Lindblom, "The Science of Muddling Through," *Public Administration Review* (Spring 1959):79.

14. *Contingency theories* may be defined as an attempt to understand leadership effectiveness by isolating situational factors that affect leadership success or failure.

15. Fred E. Fiedler, *A Theory of Leadership Effectiveness* (New York: McGraw-Hill, 1967); Robert J. House, "A Path-Goal Theory of Leader Effectiveness, *Administrative Science Quarterly*, September 1971, pp. 321–38.

16. V. H. Vroom and P. W. Yetton, *Leadership and Decision making*, (Pittsburgh: University of Pittsburgh, 1983).

17. See discussion in Charles Taylor, "Rationality," *Rationality and Relativism* ed. Martin Hollis and Steven Lukes (Cambridge: MIT Press, 1982), pp. 87–89.

18. Ibid., Introduction, pp. 3–5.

19. Ibid.

20. For this section, the writer relies heavily on the works of Russell Hardin, *Collective Action* (Baltimore: Johns Hopkins University Press, 1982), and Edward F. McClennan, "Rational Choice and Public Policy: A Critical Survey," *Social Theory and Practice* nos. 2–3 (Summer-Fall 1983), and on the insights provided by Professor R. Edward Freeman, University of Minnesota.

21. Ibid., p. 9.

22. George J. Stigler, *Essays in the History of Economics* (Chicago: University of Chicago Press, 1965).

23. Lindblom, "Science of Muddling Through," pp. 81–82.

24. Amitai Etzioni, *Modern Organizations* (Englewood Cliffs, N.J.: Prentice-Hall, 1964), p. 5.

25. Fremont Kast and James Rosenzweig, *Organization and Management*, 3d ed. (New York: McGraw-Hill, 1979), p. 153.

26. For this important distinction between operational goals and official goals, see Robert H. Miles, *Macro Organizational Behavior* (Santa Monica, Calif.:Goodyear, 1980), pp. 36–37.

27. Herbert A. Simon, *Administrative Behavior* (New York: Free Press, 1965), p. 5.

28. Richard H. Hall, *Organizations: Structure and Process* (Englewood Cliffs, N.J.: Prentice-Hall, 1972), p. 240.

29. The author makes no assumption that conflict is either good or bad, only that it exists. According to structural functional analysis, conflict would have both eufunctions (desirable results) and dysfunctions (undesirable results). See Levy, *Structure of Society*.

30. Oliver E. Williamson, *Markets and Hierarchies: Analysis and Antitrust Implications* (New York: Free Press, 1975), p. 20.

31. Alvar O. Elbing, "Perception, Motivation, and Business Behavior," in *Behavioral Decisions in Organizations*, ed. Alvar O. Elbing, (Glenview, Ill.: Scott Foresman, 1970), p. 353.

32. Leon Festinger, *A Theory of Cognitive Dissonance* (Stanford Calif.: Stanford University Press, 1957); Cognitive dissonance refers to any perceived incompatibility between an individual's beliefs or between an individual's behavior and his beliefs.

33. Group meetings reveal that negative review staff evaluations outweigh positive evaluations (during one quarter) by 200 to 30. Author's note.

34. David Easton, *The Political System* (New York: Knopf, 1953).

35. Ibid., p. 124. The state (as a formal institution of government) is inadequate as a focus, as politics no doubt occurs in societies where "states" do not exist, for example, in nongovernmental (nonofficial bodies). Power, as a concept, is inadequate, as power can be exercised in all social settings where one man controls the action of another. See pp. 90–124.

36. Ibid., p. 128. These terms are further refined: *policy* refers to a web of decisions that allocate values for a society. In this, policy is different from a purely or narrowly legal decision. Arriving at a decision is only the formal (legal) phase of policy. Qualities that distinguish the political system are finality, universality, and legitimacy.

37. Theodore Levitt, *The Third Sector* (New York: AMACOM, 1973), argues that there is a third sector that is neither public nor private but possesses characteristics (voluntarism/collegiality) unique to its institutional setting (unions, colleges, zoos, museums, and the like).

38. *Political activity* by this definition *does not* refer to partisanship or to the electoral activities of political parties and their adherents; nor does the term refer simply to power as any display of influence or control.

39. Lindblom, "Science of Muddling Through," p. 79.

40. Charles E. Lindblom, "Still Muddling, Not Yet Through" *Public Administration Review*, November–December, 1979, pp. 517–18.

41. See introductory material (p. 9) highlighting the work of Mardi, Cohen and Olsen by Jeffrey Pfeffer, *Organizations and Organization Theory* (Boston: Pitman, 1982) and soon to be published manuscript *Ambiguity and Command: Organizational Perspectives on Military Decision Making* by James March and Roger Weissinger-Baylon (Boston: Pitman Publishing, Inc., 1986).

42. James G. March and Roger Weissinger-Baylon, "Introduc-

tion," *Ambiguity and Command: Organizational Perspectives on Military Decision Making* (Unpublished manuscript, Boston: Pitman Publishing, Inc., May, 1985), p. 2.

43. For a general overview see Jeffrey Pfeffer, *Organizations and Organization Theory* (Boston: Pitman Publishing, Inc., 1982), p. 9.

44. Lindblom, "Still Muddling through," p. 521.

45. Theodore J. Lowi, *The End of Liberalism* (New York: W. W. Norton, 1969), p. 125.

46. The history of consumer and product quality legislation is throughly summarized in Rogene Buchholz, *Business Environment and Public Policy* (Englewood Cliffs, N. J.: Prentice-Hall, 1982), pp. 327–33. See p. 133 for the impact of law.

47. Lowi, *End of Liberalism*, p. 125.

48. Ibid., pp. 125–26.

49. George Berkley, *The Craft of Public Administration* (Boston: Allyn and Bacon, 1972), p. 369.

50. Buchholz, *Business Environment and Public Policy*, pp. 125–147.

51. Judge Jerome Frank, *Law and the Modern Mind* (New York: Tudor, 1936), pp. 6–7.

52. Summarized from Roscoe Pound, Address to the American Bar Association, 1933. Also found in idem, *An Introduction to the Philosophy of Law* (New Haven, Conn.: Yale University Press, 1922), pp. 25–47.

53. As Justice Holmes noted: "A page of history is worth a volume of logic."

54. The *common law* or *case law* (judge-made law) is distinguished from other sources of law including the Constitution, legislation statutes, and administrative rulings. Finding facts may also be a part of determining law. The facts about the parties, to which the law is applied, are called *adjudicative facts*. The facts that are used for the purpose of determining law or policy or exercising discretion are called *legislative facts*. See Davis, 2 *Administrative Law Treatise* 15:03 (1958).

55. Kenneth Culp Davis, *Discretionary Justice: A Preliminary Inquiry*, 3d ed. (Urbana: University of Illinois Press, 1976), pp. 3–4. One approach to a study of discretionary justice—not the one here taken—could be to penetrate the mental, psychological, and emotional mechanisms that operate in the making of a determination involving discretionary justice. Perhaps all choices of values are ultimately determined by the emotions, but even if that is true, the intellect may still play a major role.

*Ah-hah! if only you'll contemn
Reason and knowledge, both of them
Twin peaks of human faculty;
And stare until your eyeballs start
At sorcery's phantasmal art
The lying spirit teaches thee;
Then thou art mine to have and keep.*

                                                   Mephistopheles
                                                   Goethe's "Faust"

Chapter Two

RATIONAL MODELS

DEFINITIONS AND CONCEPTS

Although decision makers use the term *rational* to describe everyday activities, the word itself is difficult to define. At the very least the word *rational* conveys several meanings. Arguably, the word *rational* (like the words *political* and *legal*) can be understood only in the context of its institutional/interactive meanings. Nonetheless, prior to case analysis, some definitional content is relevant.

We begin with the thought that rational decision making "epitomizes the most important activity of managers in formal organizations."[1] Consider the implications: no matter what the subject matter (personnel, operations, finances, marketing, budgeting) or where (public sector, private sector, third sector), the decisional process is defined as rational. Moreover, in countless training sessions and educational programs, would-be managers are expected to be rational. Rationality (or rationalism) is thus both a goal *and* a process.[2] Chapters two and three will discuss rationality and its methodological counterpart, irrationality.

Goal-Process Elements

At the outset it should be noted that rationality (or the ideal of a rational approach to economic, political, and social problems) is a current topic and has enjoyed a revival of interest, owing in no small part to the resurgence of business school training and to the emergence of quantitative methodologies.[3] Or it may be the convergence of two events, the rise of the corporate structure and the impact of computerized technologies, that give new meaning and life to the rational model. But whether it is mere historical accident or an integral element of Western thought, rationalism is a hot topic.

In its contemporary context *rationality* (rational approach) refers both to deliberative evaluation and choice and to practical reasoning. Given the limits of the cognitive process, some writers (as discussed in Chapter One) refer to it as "bounded rationality." Edward McClennon argues that today there is a "renaissance" of rationality that finds expression methodologically in "public choice theory," which has both "positive" and "normative" components. The normative element asserts that both principles of public policy and the institutional structures that operate them can be measured by rational choice "market" criteria based on disciplines of economics, political science, and philosophy. The positive component allows an appraisal of individual rational choices within institutional settings that transcend the public or market sector and that involve nonmarket criteria.[4] Although this sounds vaguely like John Dewey's well-worn definition of the *public* and the *nonpublic*,[5] even this distinction rests on an abstraction or categorization that may not hold much water—at least not for very long. Nonetheless, it is important to recognize that the retreat from the ideal of a rational world—a retreat begun in the pessimistic encounter over several decades with power/politicized institutions—has been checked. Thus there is a reemergence of rational theory and an implicit emergence of hope in the future. But to understand this important development, we must look backwards, at least a little bit.

The notion of a rational world—the ideal of a rational approach to complex problems—is an old and recurring theme in Western thought.

Rational thinking (rationality or rationalism) has its roots in the classical Western tradition of maximizing or harmonizing human behavior.[6] In describing the essential differences between Western man (Occidental man) and Eastern man (Oriental man), Martin Buber points to the distinctive mental processes used by man to cope with his environment.[7]

Oriental man, Buber argues, is intuitive. His thought processes reflect a unified spirit and may be described as centrifugal (developing outward). The basic psychic act emanates from the soul and becomes motion. That is, an interaction with the environment begins from within as a psychic feeling or experience, one that has no tangible, structured form. Perhaps overstating the concept, Buber goes on to argue that Oriental man's mental processes result in seamless images. To Oriental man, the world appears as limitless motion. Although he perceives indi-

Definitions and Concepts 51

vidual things, he does not perceive them as separate entities. For example, to the Chinese, the highest form of being is expressed in the limitless abstraction Tao (or "the way").

Occidental man, on the other hand, is rational. His mental processes are fragmented and may be described as centripetal (developing inward). An impression is made on Western man and becomes an image. That is, interaction with the environment (physical and human) results in the experience of object or in a concrete image—a form that has specific parts and distinct shape. This is expressed in the great creative achievement of the Greeks, the *vas* with its spherical shape, limited scope, and discrete dimension. The *vas* embodies all that is valued, perfect, and desired in Western thought. It is a form or an object—not an intangible. The *vas* represents in Western tradition the highest order of cognitive processes. To Western man, guided by the most objective sense, sight, the world appears as objectified, as a multiplicity of discrete, segregated things. It was no coincidence that Plato called the essence of things *eikos* (or "form").

Rational thinking (as opposed to *intuitive* thinking) is the word that captures this newer, distinctly Western method of conceptualization. Based on the notion of maximizing things or results (the form or the object as end state), this method has generated important disciplines such as economic theory with its notions of preference, choices, goods, and desirable end results. Rational concepts allow the thinker to segregate and to objectify otherwise unlimited intangible phenomena.

More significantly, rationalism (the goal) has developed entirely new methodologies, such as system analysis, that transcend specific subdisciplines such as economics or sociology.[8]

Systems analysis has its roots in the Western notion that the intangible can be fragmented or divided into discrete parts. A *system* is a bounded region, in space and time, with functional parts that interact over time producing stresses and strains and inputs and outputs. The world as a system (as a subdivided, fragmented, discrete, and usually tangible entity) is the product of Occidental man's vision. This vision contains important theoretical and practical implications.

For example, as a heuristic device, systems theories (or objective Western concepts) are capable of dividing human phenomena into behavioral and cognitive processes. Thereby, interrelated behavioral and nonbehavioral phenomena theoretically can be isolated and explained. The purpose of explanation, via theory or generalization, is to predict, not merely to describe. If one can predict, or explain, by way of scientific (verifiable) processes, one can control behavior. And if one can control or direct behavior, one can maximize behavior toward a preferred end state.[9] This is the goal of Western thought, a thought process based on rational or objectified impulses.

The rational concept of maximizing behavior has its historical origin in classical Western theory (systems analysis) and its modern expression in behavioral theory. The modern expression or variant of the theme takes many forms. In constructing various models of rational choice, theorists construct the fictitious "Economic man" who maximizes ends through objective choices. Economic man is rational man in that he is presumed to possess a disciplined, systematic set of preferences and a skill in computation and numerology that allows him to calculate choices for voluminous alternative courses of action, thus reaching the highest possible level of attainment.

It is the interplay of maximization (of goals) and objectification (of action) that gives meaning to the word *rational* and that defines the word *rationalism* (as a goal) and the word *rationality* (as a process).

Rationalism: The Goal Element

The idealized, fictitious Economic Man seeks one goal: the maximization of his own satisfaction. He accomplishes this goal by increasing the knowledge of his environment and by weighing and evaluating various choices. This is the process element. But note the maximalist or end-state impluses present here and later projected to the firm (or the organization). Assumptions that underlie concepts of Economic man are derived from philosophies of hedonism or self-interest that argued that man calculates actions that will maximize self-interest and guide behavior accordingly. The economic doctrines of Adam Smith and others, built on this assumption, led to the theory that relations in the marketplace between organizations, between merchants, and between buyers and sellers should be unrestricted. The assumption is that the separate pursuits of self-interest would adequately regulate commercial relations. Essentially, man was assumed to be motivated by economic incentives and to take actions that would promise the greatest economic gain and concomitantly the greatest social good. This is thought to be rational, at least in the marketplace.

It is in the context of self-interested, goal-directed behavior that organizations, like individuals, are said to be instruments/participants of rational activity. Note that *rational* in this context does not necessarily mean quantitatively or mathematically demonstrable but only that the end states are the product of calculated self-interest. The mathematical formula enters the picture later and as means of insuring consistency in relating means to ends.

Historically, however, rational choice originated in the philosophical theories of Aristotle's concept of practical reasoning and in the Jeremy Bentham/John Stuart Mill utilitarian notion of the greatest good for the greatest number. As a moral imperative, rational choice theory progressed through several historical stages up to the modern era and culminated in the development of modern economic theory. A split naturally developed between those trained in social and political philosophy and those trained in mathematical and quantitative technique. Although both schools claimed rationality (and in fact shared a philosophical/historical origin), the economists assumed an air of rigor and the philosophers an air of cynicism. Arguably the fields are once again melding in the interdisciplinary public policy field with its combination of economist/behavioralist tool and philosophical/ethical applications. Thus today it is possible to think of social justice questions in the context of marked determinants. Likewise, it is possible to analyze individual self-interest as simply the prerequisite condition to broader collective maximizations.[10]

For example, just as the individual decision maker maximizes his goal-seeking behavior, so, too, the organization seeks to maximize its goals. This is not to say that an individual's objectives, though rational, are always consistent with his firm's objectives, though rational. Thus it may be in the firm's interest to maximize profits; yet it may be in the member's interest to maximize self-development via sales. These are merely different objectives. It is an irrelevant criticism of rationalism to state that such inconsistencies underscore a fallacy in the rational mode. On the contrary, the existence of different, and differing, objectives and goals at different levels (the individual, the group, and the organization) only illustrates the pervasiveness of goal-oriented (maximalist) behavior.

Underlying the concept of rationalism is the notion that human behavior, alone or in concert with others, is not random. Human behavior is caused by, and directed toward, some goal that the individual believes is in his best interests. As Edward Lawler and John Rhode noted:

> While people's behavior may not appear to be rational to an outsider, there is reason to believe it usually is intended to be rational and it is seen as rational by them. An observer often sees behavior as nonrational because the observer does not have access to the same information or does not perceive the environment in the same way.[11]

Rationality: The Process Element

But the notion of rational behavior embraces more than the maximalist or goal element; it includes as well the concept of a process, a step-by-step, discrete procedure that leads to goal maximization. The word *rationality* may be used to express this process concept. The word refers specifically to the choice method whereby preferred alternatives are deliberately (not randomly) selected from a preference ranking of universal and perhaps limitless possibilities.

Rationality, as a process, is based on two assumptions: (1) that the decision maker has a choice (or equally valid, that he thinks he has a choice) and (2) that the decision maker knows what the choice is. The first may be referred to as the *deliberative factor*; the second may be called the *informational factor*. Together these components of the process constitute the objective element of the process prong.

This is to say (assuming goal-oriented behavior, that is, rationalism) that the rational process necessitates two essential ingredients: deliberation and information, which rest on an objectified vision of the universe. Rationality as a process thus requires objectification, or the presumption of an objective (neutral, tangible, value-free) base of choice data.

Basic Concepts

Ends and Means Revisited

The concept of behavior as an end (rationalism) and behavior as a process (rationality) causes definitions of the word *rational* to be muddled. In his seminal studies, which merit reconsideration, Herbert Simon refers to the means-ends analysis of administrative behavior as an illogic process or "a seldom integrated, completely connected chain"—in short, as one that does not hold up under analysis.[12] Simon's criticism asserts the impossibility (logically and behaviorally) of separating means and ends. That is, what is an end for an organization (balanced budget) becomes a means for a subdepartment (audit). Likewise with individuals: what may at time 1 be seen as an end (a better position in a firm) becomes at time 2 a means (higher salary) to another end (more status) at time 3. It is this logical and behavioral interplay of means and ends that has caused analysts to reject means-ends analysis as a sound method for understanding decision making. Thus, over the past decades, this type of analysis has lost its definitional credibility.

On the other hand, many theorists miss the point that the term *rational* is generic and that rationalism (as a goal) and rationality (as a process) are the same basic matter; they are different marks on the same continuum, not different absolutes. Thus one may have at the same time rationalism as a goal (for example, self-satisfying behavior for an individual, profit manipulation for a firm) and yet employ rationality as a means to achieving this goal. For instance, in its simplest context rational behavior in the decisional process merely involves selecting choice alternatives based upon real or perceived preferences structured by available information. This notion carries two important elements. First, the maximalist goal or the objective may be actual or it may be psychological. Whether perceived or real, however, it exists, and therefore the presence of the goal operates to cause decisional choices or consequences. And second, the objectified means need not be based on quantitative analysis, systematic study, extended deliberation, hard data, or even deep reflection. The objectified means may derive from a hunch based upon empirical data or from the selective use of value-free information. All that is necessary to make the decision a rational one is the existence of an objective and the selection of some alternative that is viewed by the decision maker as meeting the objective. It is precisely in this context that the word *rational* equates with the word *objective*: there is an object to the content or the end result of the decision; and there is objectivity in the process of matching choice to object.

The theoretical problem with means-end analysis as a basis for rational decision making is the reality that a hierarchy of means and ends exists, one melding into the next, thus making the decision choice (the end) ambiguous, obscure, and useless as a unit of analysis.

Note again that there is a transitional or a third perspective on the rational-intuitive continuum that emphasizes the inherent ambiguity of decisions and the emergent conditions of the process of decision making. Referred to earlier as the "garbage can model," this theory argues that because of fragmentation in organizational structures and because of ever-changing preferences, knowledge of external factors is insufficient to predict action. Thus ambiguity, not rationality, prevails. It should be emphasized, however, that events within the garbage can context are understandable and in some ways predictable. These events, though, are not dominated by preferences or by rationality. Thus there exists an interim phase between the clear choice of rationality and the preferential choice of politics.

But to completely reject means-end analysis as nonrational is to oversimplify the question. We see that even the more modern fact-value distinction actually includes the same process-result elements. Facts and values operate as means and ends. The first provides the factual knowledge base for the latter valuational choice. Rational decision making, then, does not require complete knowledge but only enough to make choices based on preferences. Conceptually, this is simple enough; practically, it is what people do every day. This is rational decision making.

In terms of analysis (and case study review) it is helpful to divide the rational method into its two functional parts.[13] To repeat, the word *rational* refers sometimes to a process, sometimes to a result.

In terms of process, rational decision making may be conducted by an individual, by a group, or by the organization. In short, it may be the approach of any unit or subunit capable of making choices. The integrating motive, and the operative fact behind rationality (the process), lies in objectification or the attempt to match actual facts (choices) with end goals (objectives). *Rationality* refers to how a decision is made, and it denotes a process based on actual assessment of consequences for achievement of goals.

In terms of result, rational decision making indicates value-based choices, or choices that lead to a particular result—not any result, but one that is viewed as good or positive. The result may be psychological (intangible, long-range), or it may be practical (immediate and actual). It may be personal, or it may be organizational.

Nonrationality and Irrationality

It must be emphasized that the term *rational* is to be contrasted with the word *irrational*. The word *rational* is not to be contrasted with the word nonrational.

A nonrational decision maker, for example, is one who is incapable of either formulating objectives, gathering choice data, or both. In short, the nonrational decision maker is like the mentally ill who do not have the capacity to match means and ends. In this sense *nonrational* means "non compos mentis."

Also note that the term *irrational* does not refer to behavior that is merely mistaken or misdirected. The concept is more complicated than this. For example, a distressed soldier, attempting to commit suicide, may ignore a sentry's order to halt, thereby drawing deadly fire and thus achieving his ultimate goal, death. Is such a deliberate action irrational? Horrifying perhaps; but not necessarily irrational. Note that if the original act (defying the order to halt) was deliberate, conscious, and voluntary (that is, not compelled and not confused), arguably it was not irrational.

Thus intent seems to lie at the core of both rationality and irrationality.[14] Intent (the formation of a belief) while not the same thing as "doing an action" is "doing something." Accordingly, *wishful* irrationality (intended, desired irrationality) is to be distinguished from *accidental* irrationality (or irrationality caused by a perversion of reason).[15] In this book *irrationality* refers to both possibilities. Wishful irrationality occurs at the goal level: for example, desiring individual self-interest objectives that may be at odds with the organization's objectives. Accidental irrationality occurs when rational choice is distorted by the process of bureaucratic blockage, mishap, or accident of god.

Hence the term *irrational* refers not to a basic incapacity to make rational choices; rather, it refers to rational choice inconsistent with self-interest or to rational choice gone haywire. (This will be explored fully in Chapter Three.) Consequently, irrationality will be explored in the context of the failure of rationality both at the goal-directed stage and at the process level. Someone who attempts to make decisions regarding long-term psychological results (for instance, elimination of the intrapsychic effects of poverty) based on short-term quantitative data (for example, cost-benefit analysis of welfare procurement procedures) is acting irrationally in that means and ends will not mix to achieve the objective. Note that this is not *nonrational*, as the decision maker is employing a rational process: a conscious deliberate choice to achieve an end result or objective.

It is important to note that *rational* and *irrational* are concepts of the same order and should be viewed as extremes on the very same decisional continuum. *Rational* and *nonrational* are substantive opposites and essentially different concepts. (See Figure 2.1, which graphically depicts the continuum/contrast components of these terms.)

Figure 2.1 Rational Choice Typologies

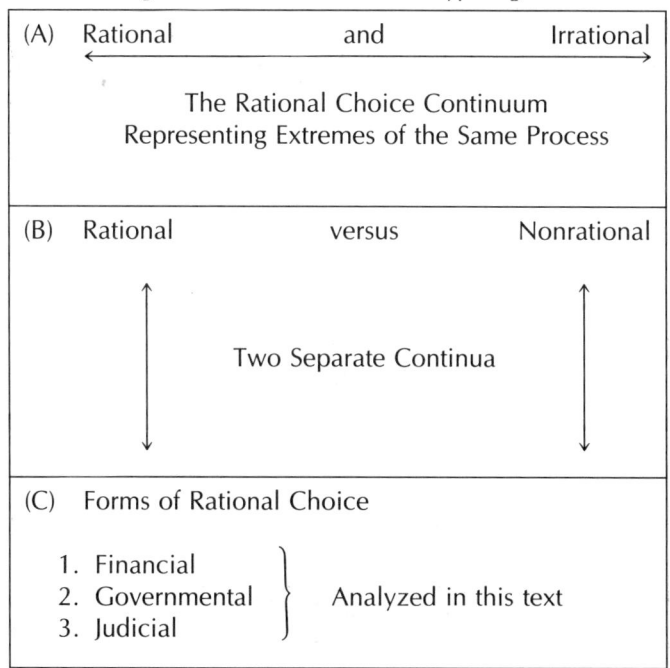

(A) Rational ←——— and ———→ Irrational The Rational Choice Continuum Representing Extremes of the Same Process	
(B) Rational ↕ versus ↕ Nonrational Two Separate Continua	

(C) Forms of Rational Choice
 	
  1. Financial
  2. Governmental } Analyzed in this text
  3. Judicial	

By this definition one distinctive feature of rationality is that the rational choice model subsumes political approaches and legal approaches. That is, these latter are merely another form of rationality with a different criterion of rationalism. This is naturally so, since these forms of decision making (political and legal; see Chapters Four through Seven) are hardly nonrational. Definitionally they belong to the same order as *rational*; they are simply a different subspecies. However, it is argued in Chapters Four and Six that the criteria of decision making of the political and legal models (the institutional determinants, the process conditions, the distinct objectives, and the resultant consequences) make these subforms of rational choice unique to some degree. Hence, they will be treated below as separate methods, at least for analytical purposes.

A distinctive feature of rationality is that it represents a value in and of itself. That is, rationality has a high priority in our culture. As a people we seek objectivity; decision makers strive for rationality (at least publicly).[16] Even public sector decision makers are reluctant to admit that they make "political" or "irrational" decisions. This would suggest that they make decisions in an unjustified, nonobjective, undisciplined fashion, which of course, would be publicly unacceptable. All decision makers feel the pressure of the rational choice model. This is clearly seen in the management world, regarding decisions that can be objectified[17] and involving processes that can be internally controlled.[18]

Within this definitional construct what does the rational decision maker actually do? In the pure form he would take the following steps:

1. Identify the problem;
2. Clarify goals and then rank order goals as to their importance;
3. List all possible means, or policies, for achieving each of the goals;
4. Assess all of the costs of and the benefits that would follow from each of the alternative policies; and
5. Select the package of goals and associated policies that would bring the greatest relative benefits and the least relative disadvantages.[19]

CASE IN POINT

Rational Models: The "Hard" Case—Higher Education

Perhaps the best case to illustrate the rational model is the "hard" case, that is, a case that applies hard-core management techniques to a decisional area that is not traditionally or easily given to objective, quantitative cost measures or techniques. What better area than higher education (academia), which for centuries has defied modern management techniques?[20] The argument by academics is that higher education is not a business; therefore, college-level activities should not be assessed or evaluated by traditional businesslike methods. How, for example, does one objectively measure the long-range costs and benefits of value-based philosophy courses? If there is no immediate financial return on the course, does one pull it off the shelf like some unmarketable product?

Nonetheless, today modern management tools are applied even to this most resistent decisional area. Does the application work? First, a brief case will be presented to describe the approach. Second, an analysis of modern management tools as applied to higher education will be reviewed.

THE CASE: MODERN MANAGEMENT APPLIED TO ACADEMIC DECISIONS

In Illinois, the conflict [between rational management and academic decisions] arose when the state coordinating board* in the early 1970s applied an economic model for resource sharing [called Collegiate Common Market] to several public junior and senior institutions. The purpose of the plan was to save money for the state in a time of tight dollars. The academic community responded by saying that rational economic models of economy and efficiency were irrelevant to academic purposes, which could not be measured in money terms alone and which had almost metaphysical social benefits. The state officials argued that the academics were fiscally irresponsible. The faculty countered that the board staff was destroying higher education in Illinois. The issue was joined.

The Illinois case is only one example of the larger conflict between management techniques and academic purposes. The case represents the deep tension between a model of decision making based on criteria of economy and efficiency and a model of decision making based on abstract values. The issue is not whether the sci-

---

This case was first prepared by the author and in longer form printed in *Academy of Management Review*, 1., no. 1, January 1976: 79–88.

---

*The Illinois Board of Higher Education (IBHE).

ence of management has helped practitioners to cope with physical realities and to plan operations of almost unimaginable complexity. This is not debated. The issue is whether modern management techniques may have retarded our capacity to cope with ethical issues, to think systematically about values, and to deal with nonquantitative, nonmaterial but nonetheless critical questions.

THE QUESTION: INHERENT CONFLICT?

The purpose of this (case) is to examine this larger conflict by focusing on the specifics of academic management. A focus on academic policy-making represents a classic study of the tension between technique and purpose. The value of intangible and metaphysical results is protected and cherished in higher education, perhaps more so than in other institutions. At the same time almost nowhere is there greater pressure to assess outputs and produce disciplined budgets. Modern management has arrived in academia.

It is possible to express this conflict between sophisticated management tools and intangible educational benefits by contrasting the major objectives of each.

Academic Policy-Making— Values	Modern Management— Purposes
1. Academic freedom	1. Measure of efficiency and economy
2. Institutional autonomy	2. Maximization of efficiency and economy
3. Long-range social benefits	3. Production of demonstrable results
4. Intangible, nonmaterial products	4. Cost accountability of institutions
5. Ambiguous, changing objectives	5. Rational coordination of resources

Chart 1

Obviously, Chart 1 represents an idealized contrast. Academic institutions are not concerned with nonmaterial matters alone. Nor are modern management tools applied without consideration of broader purpose. But the theorized conflict permits us to explore actual cases of conflict.

It might be helpful to recount some of the historic pressures for "better" management in higher education. The factors and pressures involved can be reduced to one element: money. That is, underlying all of the attempts to modernize and rationalize higher education planning, programming, and policy-making is the pressure to make the institutions "cost effective" in a time of limited resources. Consider these factors:

1. Vacillating enrollments have caused governing agencies (legislatures and boards) to question expensive research, service programs, and teaching techniques.
2. Competition for limited dollars by other social institutions has caused private donors and public officials to seek more control over budgeting, accounting, purchasing, and personnel activities within the university system.
3. The financial crisis, reinforced by inflationary trends, has caused academic governors to question the values of higher education, especially in periods of campus unrest and apparent wastefulness of resources.
4. All this has enhanced the applicability of modern management tools, especially in the areas of fiscal administration, program planning, and budgetary controls.

It is this concern with money matters, coupled with academia's inability to articulate the intangible values of higher education, that underlies many of the present conflicts in higher education.

Definition of Terms

The phrase *modern management* as used in this case refers to a variety of innovative techniques including systems analysis, linear programming, and budgetary tools that are being applied to traditional management functions such as planning, coordinating, staffing, financing, communicating, and decision making. Modern management, like its predecessor term *scientific management*, refers to the discovery and application, through use of the scientific method, of basic elements of administration to replace human "rules of thumb."

The term *academic decisions* is used to refer to the decisional structures and processes that affect the operations of postsecondary educational institutions, junior and senior, public and private. This (case) will examine only senior institutions and only selected governance activities such as budget policy, personnel questions, and program definition. To give added scope to the study, both internal and external governance issues will be considered, and examples will be drawn from both public and private institutional settings.

MANAGEMENT OF ACADEMIA: A SURVEY OF POLICY ISSUES

There are five key focuses for decision making in higher education: the budget, the curriculum, the faculty, the students, and the physical plant. In each of these areas there is a built-in conflict between the way management technology approaches the issue and the way academic decision makers define the problem.

The Budget

Academics generally assume that the budget is a way of implementing educational decisions and not a way of arriving at them. However, this rule is more often ignored than honored by the budget officer who is making fiscal decisions for academic institutions. And this is the rub. The encroachment of economics and the criterion of efficiency into what is intrinsically a noneconomic value set of questions generally horrifies academics and scholars, who fail to understand the relevance of concepts like optimal resource allocation. How, they ask, are truth and scholarship reduced to a negotiable or optional value?

In private institutions in a time of fiscal contraction, budget tools such as the program planning budgeting system (PPBS) are utilized, to some degree, to compare different levels of expenditures between units on a campus, to make decisions concerning undergraduate versus graduate expenditures, and to aid in determining student-staff ratios. In short, the budget process is used to determine the new economic "mix" and to allocate resources accordingly.

In public institutions the same internal problems exist, with one additional complicating factor. Today, with widespread inflation, with the "strings attached" impact of federal funds, and with academic unrest and public disenchantment with academia, more governors and legislators are entering a budgetary process formerly conducted by administrators and trustees.

Thus, in addition to questioning the wisdom of applying technical methods to nonquantitative problems, there is growing concern over the opening of budgeting to the political process. Instead of resolving administrative problems, this might add a new element of uncertainty and might make long-range planning even more difficult. On the other hand, the net effect of politicizing the process may reintroduce a "nontechnical" element into the calculus of decision making, thus moderating the impact of a totally quantitative economic approach.

The Curriculum

Form follows function, and in many cases, curriculum follows budget. In recent years curriculum, the last bastion of faculty decision making, has been influenced by nonacademic managers and by their tools of management. This is reflected in the lightning quick shift to courses and programs in "evaluation" as a result of shifts in federal grants and in the new emphasis on "assessing" projects (which can no longer be funded). It is the academic shift that is fascinating in this case; not the federal shift, which is explained by the forces of politics. At any rate, it is obvious that curriculum has been affected. This example reveals the character of the relationship between the management tool and the academic policymaker. Even in the private sector, higher education is becoming more passive and reactive. Designs for curriculum follow federal funding guidelines, printouts of enrollment trends, and efficiency standards.

The major external curriculum management techniques derive from a response to social pressures and societal responsibilities that characterize many public institutions. In part, externally imposed management techniques are a result of the growth of coordinating and governing boards of higher education, who have an unofficial but significant influence over public institution curriculum. Once a function of legislative policy (usually characterized by a hands-off approach), public institution curriculum priorities are more and more reviewed by government professional staffs. In many cases this professionalism is moderated by a strong input of political policy from either the legislative or executive branch.

The Faculty

Academic management concerns embrace faculty-related issues including salaries, time, and projects. With less financial support and with costs rising, operational efficiency techniques have focused on the faculty as the quickest, cheapest way to improve higher education's financial position. Different plans reflect different management/production techniques and concern teaching load, class size, faculty quality, space utilization, course load, and extracurricular activities. Always the technique calls for measuring efficiency in terms of output and costs. The consequence is greater control and constraints on faculty.

This is a new twist in higher education planning. In the past, personnel administration and workload were left to professional groups (the guilds as expressed through the department model). Now with personnel questions deriving from the compensation-productivity model, and with the application of industrial engineering techniques, the guilds no longer have control.

In both public and private institutions, demands for greater productivity are met by decreasing costs, cancelling sabbaticals, increasing class size, deferring raises, and optimizing time schedules.

In private institutions, with somewhat more freedom of action, the administration sometimes must phase out programs and eliminate faculty. Putting junior and middle-level faculty on time contracts is another way of controlling tenure and productivity.

In public institutions, bureaus of the budget and coordinating boards generally have not interfered with faculty "hire-fire" issues except indirectly by freezing programs or ending program support.

Students and Recruiting

There is some evidence that universities and colleges are employing high-powered and sophisticated marketing techniques to attract and recruit students. On some campuses, the activity is more explicit than on others, but often the admissions officer is responsible for "income production" and the business officer responsible for "income control."

Whether on a public or private campus, admissions policies oriented toward sales may create a negative, counterproductive image of an institution of higher learning. To be sure the business approach has many lessons for higher eduction in terms of research, management planning, budgeting, strategy, and implementation. The bottom line profit motive, however, may be inappropriate in admissions and counseling in the college environment generally.

Some accepted means for meeting the needs of potential students include: informational advertising, public relations, improved publications, visual presentations, college information sessions, and the "open house" day.

Students are also being treated in terms of markets, yields, or quotas by the pervasive "head count" as the base unit for program planning, faculty recruitment, and long-range planning. However, few institutions have explicit ongoing long-range planning. Usually this function is performed by the budget staff or by an ad hoc faculty committee. Nevertheless, the important activities of planning (setting goals, forecasting trends, analyzing alternatives) generally use head count for baseline data.

Physical Plant

One of the most difficult aspects confronting "management" is the planning and operation of the physical plant. Ironically, although management of the physical plant is the most tangible managerial responsibility, it is perhaps the area least susceptible to management science. In higher education, management of the physical plant has always been a "poker game" with faculty office assignments and classroom space allocations a mysterious, "chancy" process. Traditionally the campus office, which has made physical plant decisions, has also made substantive program decisions. That is, planning as a programmatic activity, where it could be found, usually has been linked to facilities planning. The latter was based upon physical, technical "operational criteria" as opposed to substantive, abstract long-range criteria: a strange case of the tail wagging the dog.

APPLYING MANAGEMENT TOOLS TO ACADEMIC DECISIONS: SOME ILLUSTRATIONS

Examples illustrating the actual application of management tools in higher education policy areas are drawn from both private and public institutions. In the private sector the emphasis is on "internal" management techniques. With state-supported schools the focus is on "external" management methods.

The reason for this internal/external classification is the thesis that the application of modern management tools does not differ in practice between private and public schools. What differs, via policy decisions, is the actors. With inflation, federal funds, academic unrest, and public awareness of educational cost in the large public systems, more governors, legislators, and professional state staffs are now entering the process formerly conducted by administrators and trustees. In the private sector the principal actors are still administrators and trustees.

Important distinctions are not in the application of the tools but in the source. Consequently, the illustrations on internal management decisions (as provided by private institutions) could equally apply to any institution, public or private. Likewise, the impact of externally imposed tools could apply to private schools, particularly where they must deal with external governmental and funding bodies.

Internal Management Decisions

The University Administration

Modern management techniques have not been accepted as readily in academia as in business or government, mainly because of the values of university and college administrators. The route to key university administrative posts is along the traditional educational lines of teaching and research. Few academic administrators are trained in budgeting, accounting, finance, managerial economics, administration, and operations research. Even fewer are grounded in the underlying fundamentals of economic theory, information systems, decisions theory, and quantitative analysis. Hence there is a lag in the application of modern management at the point closest to the operation. This may account for the extraordinary impact by managers outside the system.

Although modern management tools have not gained wide acceptance even by the university administration, some of the management tools that have been applied are:

1. *PPBSs.* Although few institutions (including the Defense Department) have total progam planning and budgeting systems (PPBSs), there have been attempts on many campuses to institute the logic of PPBS, which is to impose some standard of cost-benefit relationship between inputs and outputs and to measure outputs in terms of overall goals. A move toward output-oriented budgets is occurring on some campuses.

2. *MIS.* A management information system (MIS), which is a computerized collection, storage, and retrieval system of information for planning and control (especially financial and budgetary), is a costly, complicated arrangement and exists in comprehensive form on only a few (mainly public) campuses.
3. *Resource Allocation Models (RAMs).* Mathemtical models aimed at relating the inputs of the educational process to resources required are used on most campuses, usually in the areas of translating enrollments into demands for courses, faculty, facilities, and support activities.

In each of these areas, the trend is toward more valid and quantifiable measures of university outputs.

Board of Trustees

Moving further from the center of operations, the next level of administrative impact is the institution's board of trustees. At this level, the attempt to apply the businesslike economic models of decision making to academic activities becomes most obvious. There is no single explanation for this "businessperson's mentality" on boards of trustees.

Background of trustees is certainly a factor, as is the general societal trend toward greater institutional accountability, especially when public funds are in question. The profit-loss statement is the acceptable gauge of accountability in our society.

Trustees are primarily concerned with the financial management of their colleges. As Morton Rauh notes, "[S]uch matters constitute a major part of most meeting agenda." This "almost universal concern" derives from two sources: the fact that financing is a constant and pervasive problem for all institutions and the traditional belief that nonacademic matters, such as management, fall within the competencies of most trustees.*

Given the pervasiveness of the money crunch, one management tool being applied to campus activities is the resource-sharing or "merger" technique. The theory is that with scarce resources (money, faculty, facilities) but with constant or increasing enrollments (hopefully) the institution can retain quality programs by more

---

*Morton A. Rauh, *The Trusteeship of Colleges and Universities* (New York: McGraw-Hill, 1969), p. 37.

effectively utilizing existing resources through integrated programs and other resource-sharing techniques.

While sometimes rationalized as another way of rearranging the boxes on the organizational chart, interdisciplinary, intercampus reorganizations have significant curriculum and research implications, positive or negative depending on one's point of view.

External Management Decisions

Boards of Governors and Coordinating Agencies

A step further removed from the operation of the campus is the coordinating board or governing board, which oversees the activities of public junior and senior institutions. Theoretically, a fine line separates the functions of such boards, agencies, or commissions and the functions of the university administration. In many cases the fine line disappears.

For example, questions of "governance," such as capital financing, budgetary review, and broad policy matters (growth and mission of a campus), were traditionally the bailiwick of the board of governors. Internal administrative matters having to do with faculty salaries, promotions, personnel questions, and curriculum were delegated to university officials. In recent years, the external governing board has increased its influence not only through enhanced budgetary powers, collaterally reinforced by growth of budgetary power in the governor's office, but also by tying program review (including old and new programs) to the budget process. Few states remain without some form of governing or coordinating board. Obviously, the issue of who reviews programs affects the sacrosanct areas of curriculum and faculty control.

The Bureau of the Budget

Given the growth of executive powers in state government in recent years, there has been a shift in the budgetary process from the legislature to the governor's office. A general index of gubernatorial power shows strength in the budgetary area, especially in the most populous urban states. Through a bureau of the budget or through a division of the revenue or finance office, gubernatorial influence is more and more felt in higher education circles. To be sure, this influence varies from state to state. In some cases, the bureau of the budget's control over institutional dollars is moderated by a strong and independent coordinating board. In other states the legislature still plays a significant role.

One significant increase in state executive power has occurred in budgetary areas. This budgetary influence is being used to influence higher education program planning and capital development and is especially noticeable in large multicampus states where the effect of budgetary review is to put the variety of state institutions (junior and senior, urban and rural) into a competitive position.

The stated purpose of budget bureau analysis is to protect the public purse. The result places academic programs in competition with mental health or highway trust programs. In some cases, state budget officers make programmatic decisions on a comparative basis between institutions, which may include the resources of private institutions in the calculus of decision making. For example, the state budget officer might look negatively upon a proposal for a new degree in business education in a city where three or four private institutions already offer business degrees. To cite a more blatant political choice, the budget officer might compare one university's day-care program against a neighboring university's program for a police training institute. Budget officers, too, are a part of the political system and are subject to political influence.

The Legislature

In many states the increase in executive power has been at the expense of the legislature, particularly in the budgetary process. In days gone by, the legislative technique for funding colleges and universities was the tradition-honored "money on the stump" method. This is, the legislature would earmark X amount of dollars for higher education and "put it out on a stump," and the separate institutions would have a foot race (that is, lobby the legislature for specific allocations). Today these decisions are often made in the budget offices by professionals who are capable of examining the most minute details of a university's budget.

Given the growth of state coordinating boards and the emergence of bureaus of the budget, the days of university "lobbying" may be over. On the other hand, legislatures are beginning to enhance their own powers and staffs. In a time of post-Watergate disenchantment with the executive branch, they may return to their former position of institutional and constitutional preeminence.

SUMMARY AND CONCLUSION

Given the variety of management tools used in higher education, plus the range of actors involved in the process, one safe statement can be made: It is difficult, if not impossible, to draw any firm conclusions about the impact of modern management on academic policies.

At the same time, it is possible to recap some of these "impacts," gain an overall perspective on them, and suggest some possible implications and areas for further study.

CASE REVIEW

What do we learn from this case wherein highly rational methods are applied to measure extraordinarily subjective or nonrational ends?[21] There are both general and specific lessons or conclusions.

General Thoughts

After reading and reviewing this case, one is left with at least these basic thoughts, which are outlined below.

Rational Models and Elitist Jargon

Perhaps it is true of any new venture or of any specialization (medicine and law are examples), but it is clear that rational modeling (including computer applications) is characterized by a polysyllabic rhetoric (cost-systems, data base units) and an alphabet soup blather (MIS, PPBS, RAM) that is inaccessible to most laypersons. Like modern art or sculpture, rational modeling has little apparent meaning to most outside observers. The language (the art form) itself is inaccessible, although it conveys great meaning to the insider or practitioner.

The Imperialist Impulse and Collision Courses

Rational thinkers are imperialists; that is, nothing is to be "unthought." To put it another way, there is no problem that cannot be conceptualized as a rational problem. Note in this case the built-in collision course. Rational modeling recognizes no conceptual boundaries. Any decisional area (even philosophy) is susceptible to rationalizing techniques. But academia also is imperialistic. That is, academia recognizes no legitimate bounds on its thinking or truth-seeking purposes. Academia chokes under constraints of any sort. Yet the directions of the two entities are inapposite. Academia seeks to expand, to push back the darkness—to grow. Rational modeling, with its cost accounting, efficiency-oriented, evaluative measures, seeks to control and to contain—to manage. That a collision course exists is obvious. It is not so obvious that positive intellectual or practical results are a by-product of this collision.

Controllable Quantitative Processes

The techniques and step-by-step processes in the above case flow from one critical assumption: If it cannot be counted, it cannot be measured and therefore it cannot be used. In short, policy choices must be controllable (must refer back to a measurable data base) or else these policy choices will not only be discarded; they will not emerge in the first place. This is very safe for the decision maker since he is always at anchor; it does not, however, take one very far into uncharted waters. Since there is much to be discovered and developed, especially in higher education, a safe-berth approach is not always a wise approach.

Focus on Budget Issues

It is clear that modern management tools increasingly are being used on public and private campuses—but only in selective areas. The area of budgeting and fiscal administration has become the central focus of campus administrators and of institutional governing agencies (public and private). A close second, in terms of applying management tools, is physical planning, and particularly the relation of building programs to enrollment projections. Management tools have been applied to curriculum questions only indirectly; although, as in the case of budget bureaus, this influence can be significant. Personnel administration techniques have not cracked the guilds of faculty control and may not, with the added shield of unionization, even though management concepts are questioning the once-sacrosanct tenure issue. Students are affected by management techniques, especially in the admissions process with the use of marketing and recruiting techniques. But by and large, student affairs issues have been left to university administrators, who are not yet oriented toward management sciences.

Lack of Management Alternatives

Modern management tools are being utilized not so much because they are effective, or because the user is schooled in the discipline of management, but because there is no alternative. On the one hand, there is a tremendous pressure for fiscal accountability. On the other, there is a lack of alternative (nonfiscal) measures of benefit. There is an almost inevitable drift toward the business-oriented management tool. In this context the irresolute application of management techniques in higher education is seen as threatening or "unsatisfactory," not merely because the techniques are inherently unsound but because they result in the exclusion of faculty members from decision-making processes.

Specific Implications and Trends

Making the Problem Worse?

Modern management tools and concepts are grounded in mathematical models, in economic theory, and in a technological conception of problems. Higher education's purposes, however, have to do with abstract, long-range, and sometimes metaphysical social benefits. This is the central conflict and danger:

> [A] technological conception of a problem limits the focus to those aspects which can be expressed quantitatively and which fit certain models. The technological solution which results may be satisfactory from the engineering point of view, but because it has encompassed only select facets, vital dimensions have been neglected. Such violation of the essence of problems may, in the long run, exacerbate rather than ameliorate the troublesome condition.[22]

Limits of Management Tools

In addition to the danger of overlooking substantive questions, each management tool carries its own defects. For example, the general approach of simply reducing expenditures may have a negative effect on productivity. Unless faculty are involved in the process, they may become bitter and may even sabotage efforts. With regard to the most popular

Summary and Conclusion 73

tools, PPBSs and other MBO (management-by-objectives) techniques are helpful, but sometimes the side effects of internal resistance—(1) focus on cost models and (2) evaluation by quantifiable outputs—produce short-term negative results. Some studies have found that the net effect of PPBSs is to restore authority for decision making to originally powerful units by reducing uncertainty. Although the long-range university objective is to encourage innovation, change, and responsiveness, the actual impact of PPBSs could be just the opposite.

Failures of Academic Leaders

Another theme throughout this case has to do with the unwillingness or the inability of academic administrators to articulate the elusive values of higher education for society as a whole. It is difficult to express intangible benefits in terms of quality-of-life standards and long-range assets. Nonetheless, this is the job to be done if management tools are to be used wisely and appropriately. The paying public has little stomach for costs that have no obvious tangible benefits. The burden of proof is on the academic community. In part, this is a marketing problem. The fact is that the marketing of educational values is itself foreign to the academic community—thus the one-sided contest where the relentless technicians, with their obtuse jargon, define the issues.

Depoliticization of Decision Making

The promise of modern management in higher education is to remove politics (in the self-interest sense) from academic questions, or questions of substance. Internally, management tools might encourage change and innovation by questioning the real value of outmoded but powerful disciplines and departments. Externally, coordinating board staffs and professional bureaus of the budget might help to minimize the sometimes inequitable decisions of the legislative process. The hope is that the criteria of merit and quality would outweigh the criteria of status quo and political strength.

Professionalization—The Emerging Danger

However, the introduction of management skills carries its own problems, namely, the substitution of remote, "scientific" decisions for close-to-home and accountable "political" decisions. Professional management in academia, with its heavy emphasis on business credentialism, could serve to further remove the academic community from social responsiveness. This drift toward objective professionalism could be offset by recent trends to strengthen legislative bodies. There are some signs, in the wake of Watergate and the consequent weakening of executive power,[23] that Congress and state legislatures are recovering their strength and reintroducing political criteria into policy-making.

Governance by Nonacademics

With management professionalization comes a bitter pill: the exclusion of faculty members from decision making in key areas concerning student life, curriculum, facilities, and budget. If the faculty role is diminished in these key areas, governance of the institution no longer rests in faculty hands. These policy areas represent the key governance questions. Those who see the academic community as elitist, remote, aloof, and arrogant will cheer this result. Those who see academia as the last bastion of freedom of thought and action in a technological society will mourn the result.

Dealing with Stereotypes

One of the pervasive and annoying problems with this issue—and with this study—is that the parties involved think in terms of stereotypes. Management science people view academic decisional process as soft, ad hoc, and wasteful. Academics see modern managers as "technipols," or worse. There is almost no middle ground. If there are benefits to management techniques, few purist academics see them; their view is clouded by the alarming threat to their autonomy. If there is an inherent value to be preserved in academia, nonacademics have difficulty understanding the elusive metaphysical value.

New Forms of Management

In sum, there seems to be some merit in both camps. Looking into the future, it is probable that neither side will win. Higher education will make philosophical adjustments; modern management will adapt to the expansionist impulse of academia and will probably wind up supporting that impulse. What will emerge in the next few years—and is already emerging in the no-man's land separating the camps—is mutated forms of modern management and new styles of administration on the campus. With the faculty member and the technipol checking and neutralizing each other, a new style of administrator will emerge. This style is seen today in the "political"-type chancellor or academic manager—one who is accountable in the sense of being responsive but whose authority lies in external (noncampus) constituencies. New forms of administrative structures are emerging in the gray area between the faculty department and the cost-accounting office. Already, outside boards (community leaders, bureaus of the budget, coordinating staff, religious organizations), each with political values, are beginning to benefit from the standoff.

The Shape of the Future

The shape of future academic management is emerging. Although somewhat nebulous and amorphous, it has two discernible features. First, the character of academic management will be political, not in the partisan sense but in terms of being shaped by pressures and criteria involving external needs. Second, the location of academic management will be off campus in the sense that it will become more and more an external function or activity.

Winners and Losers

Both academics and technipols have to worry about these trends because they indicate that both have lost the game. Modern managers have lost nonpolitical decisional criteria as the modus operandi. Academics have lost internal autonomy. This is the net result of the current standoff, and the long-range result of modern management techniques applied to academic issues and institutions.

CONCLUSION

The case "Modern Management Applied to Academic Decisions" was selected to illustrate the process (or means-ends technique) of rational decision making when applied to a nonrational subject area. Although it is easy to describe the rational process, it is difficult to answer the question, Where ultimately does it lead us? The analysis shows that there are general and specific results. Yet the question remains, In the long run, where are we heading with this method of decision making?

It is necessary in this context to recap the choices and the tools. Academia has its values; modern management has its tools. Are they compatible? A focus on academia as an institutional example of rational policy-making represents a classic study of the tension between technique and purpose. The value of intangible and metaphysical results is protected and cherished in higher education, perhaps more so than in other institutions. At the same time almost nowhere is there greater pressure to assess outputs and produce disciplined budgets. Modern management has arrived in academia.

It is possible to express this conflict between sophisticated management tools and intangible educational benefits by contrasting the major objectives of each as expressed in Chart 1 of the case (p. 60).

Obviously, Chart 1 presents an idealized contrast. Academic institutions are not concerned solely with nonmaterial matters. Nor are modern management tools applied without consideration of broader purpose. But the theorized conflict permits us to explore actual cases of conflict hypothetically. A brief quote from the Illinois case may further illustrate the tension:

> "The King is dead, and now they've killed the Queen," charged a Professor upon hearing that the Illinois Board of Higher Education had first eliminated a Physics Ph.D. program and then put a moratorium on graduate programs in Philosophy. The quote illustrates the painful conflicts which arise when modern management techniques are applied to academic decisions. Although many people feel that the "Management Science" models now being applied in education are the salvation of the system, they are more often than not the source of great difficulties.[24]

As noted, the Illinois case is only one example of the larger conflict between management techniques and social purposes. The case represents the deep tension between a decisional model based on criteria of economy and efficiency and a model based on abstract values. The issue is not whether rational management has helped practitioners cope with physical realities and plan operations of great complexity. As the case noted: "The issue is whether rational management actually may have retarded our capacity to cope with ethical issues, to think systematically about values, and to deal with nonquantitative, but nonetheless critical questions." Perhaps the problem is best stated by the fear that rational management represents "the triumph of technique over purposes." Or as Bertram Gross suggested: decision making by technipols, achieved through the rationality of efficiency, "could ultimately promote disorder and discontinuity instead of the social systematization and order purported to the objectives."[25]

Chapter Three will examine these potential irrationalities of the so-called rational model.

NOTES

1. E. Frank Harrison, *The Managerial Decision-Making Process* (Boston: Houghton Mifflin, 1975), chap. 3, p. 59.

2. The *goal-process notion* in this context is to be distinguished from the word *political*, which describes a process rather than a desired end state or objective (see Chapters Four and Five of this work).

3. For this prefatory section the writer is indebted to Edward F. McClennon, "Rational Choice and Public Policy: A Critical Survey," *Social Theory and Practice* 9, nos. 2–3 (Summer-Fall 1983): 336–43.

4. Ibid.

5. The *public* is that group or element in society that is indirectly affected by the transactions of policymakers. See John Dewey, *The Public and Its Problems* (New York: Henry Holt, 1927), pp. 15–16.

6. Plato, *The Republic*, bk. 10, 590-D (New York: Bollinger Foundation, 1969).

7. Martin Buber, *Drei Reden über das Judendentums* (Frankfurt am Main: Rutten & Loening, 1916).

8. Note that economic theory studies subsystems or subunits (based on systems analysis), and sociology (parent of the social sciences) studies specific groups and appropriate/deviant behavior.

9. The maximization of human behavior (toward a desired or desirable end state) has many expressions and techniques in Western life, ranging from Goethe's eighteenth century poem expressing choice and action to B. F. Skinner's contemporary behavioral modification studies. See B. F. Skinner, *Beyond Freedom and Dignity* (New York: Knopf, 1971).

10. McClennon, "Rational Choice and Public Policy," pp. 338–39.

11. Edward E. Lawler III and John G. Rhode, *Information and Control in Organizations* (Pacific Palisaldes, Calif.: Goodyear, 1976), p. 22.

12. Herbert A. Simon, *Administrative Behavior* (New York: Free Press, 1957), p. 64.

13. Note that these "parts" are functional in that they entail significant consequences.

14. David Pears, *Motivated Irrationality* (Oxford: Clarendon Press, 1984), esp. chap. 6.

15. Ibid., pp. 102–11.

16. Ira Sharkansky, *Public Administration: Policy Making in Government Agencies* (Chicago: Markham, 1972), p. 43.

17. That is, reduced to empirical, objective, quantified data (for example, profits and losses as opposed to racial inferiority issues).

18. That is, the external (nonsystems) factors (inputs, constraints, and distractions) can be comparatively minimized. Note that not all external factors can be completely eliminated. There is no such thing as a pure "subsystem"; the universe is interrelated. But some areas (internal budget issues) lend themselves to the pure form of rational choice.

19. Charles E. Lindblom, *The Policy-Making Process* (Englewood Cliffs, N.J.:Prentice-Hall, 1965), p. 13, as quoted in Sharkansky, *Public Administration*, p. 43.

20. In addition, the subject matter and the institutional context of this case (academic decisions) should be familiar to most readers whether students, professors, or graduates of schools of business, administration, or law.

21. Michael A. Murray, "Modern Management Applied to Academic Decisions," *Academy of Management Review*, 1, No. 1., (1976), pp. 79–88. Several of these concepts were outlined in the earlier article.

22. Ida R. Hoos, *Systems Analysis in Public Policy* (Berkeley: University of California Press, 1972), p. 26.

23. The Supreme Court recently reversed the long-standing procedure whereby Congress was allowed to exercise a "legislative veto," thus giving the executive branch the initiative in key policy areas. See *Immigration & Naturalization Service* v. *Chadha et al.*, 462 U.S. 919, 103 S.Ct. 2764 (1983).

24. Murray, "Modern Management Applied to Academic Decisions," p. 79.

25. Quoted in Hoos, *Systems Analysis*, p. 76.

{I}t is my last duty to state: there is nothing to stop unleashed technology and science from completing its work of destroying man which it has so horribly begun in this war. . . .

The nightmare shared by many people . . . that some day the nations of the world may be dominated by technology—that nightmare was very nearly made a reality under Hitler's authoritarian system. . . . {T}he more technological the world becomes, the more essential will be the demand for individual freedom and the self-awareness of the individual human being as a counterpoise to technology.

Albert Speer
"Final Speech" at Nuremberg

Chapter Three

IRRATIONAL MODELS

DEFINITIONS AND CONCEPTS

Rationalism and *irrationalism* (as methodological phenomena) are variants of the same constant. That is, they are members of the same family or order of deliberative processes; they are merely logical opposites or extreme ends of the continuum.

Rationality represents a conscious, deliberative choice model based on analysis of means and ends. A rational choice seeks to maximize ends, and it proceeds according to logically related causal factors (means-ends analysis). Irrationality, as opposed to nonrationality, is a variant or derivative of rationality. To an outsider or to an observer, irrational behavior may appear to be random or pointless. It usually is not. There is reason to believe that behavior usually is intended to be rational (goal oriented, logically causal) and is viewed as rational by the actor. The observer sees behavior as irrational because the observer does not have intrapsychic access to the motivations of the actor. Thus, as emphasized in Chapter Two, irrationalism is more complex than mere accident or mishap; it usually connotes behavior linked to some intended purpose.

It is in this context that David Pears titled his recent book *Motivated Irrationality*.[1] Pears points to an intended behavior that looks crazy (irrational) to an outsider. One is irrational when one acts against one's own self-interest. One is irrational when one's intended choice is (1) inconsistent with some individual or organizational goal, leading to difficulties, or (2) when the intended choice is misdirected or wrecked along the way because of process factors.

For example, Johnny, an eight-year-old boy, is forced by his mother to take piano lessons during the summer holidays. He would rather be playing baseball. When Johnny is marched off to the piano, instead of playing the keys with his fingers, he bangs on the keyboard with his head! Rational? Irrational? The behavior is certainly rational in the sense that Johnny chooses the head-banging strategy as a means of communicating displeasure and anger. Johnny wants to get his way; his goal is to play baseball. The choice (head banging) may not result or lead to goal maximization, however, and in this sense the behavior departs from pure rationality. Clearly, however, irrational behavior is related to rationality; it is a form of rationality gone haywire.

Likewise, Mother Theresa, the epitome of Christian altruism, is not acting irrationally (against her self-interest) by self-denial and by choosing a life among the wretched of the earth. She has her reasons—and her rewards. Thus irrationality must be analyzed as a rather complicated topic, with clarification of definitional elements the first step.

Irrational behavior need not necessarily or ultimately lead to dysfunctional or undesirable results. (Just as rational activity does not always lead to eufunctional or desirable results.) However, irrational behavior does lead to results that are inconsistent with either an external organization's/entity's goals (Mom's wishes to have Johnny be a concert pianist) or the actor's goals (getting a headache from banging on the keys). It is, however, the element of breakdown, inconsistency, or dysfunction that earmarks irrationality as a concern for management and business. It is the dysfunctional quality that causes us to probe irrationalism. It is the dysfunctional character of the process that compels our attention.

We begin with the notion that irrationality is to be contrasted with nonrationality. *Nonrationalism* is a word or concept that refers to the absence of rational content, either as a goal or a process. Unfortunate individuals who are mentally incapacitated or psychologically disturbed are psychologically and mentally incapable of thinking or behaving according to rational (or irrational) processes. Intent, deliberation, and causal analysis are elements that are not present in nonrational behavior. These elements are, however, present in irrational behavior, although in a distorted, dysfunctional way.

So irrationality as a derivative process *does not* represent a complete failure of rationalism. Irrationality is merely a breakdown or misapplication of rational methodologies. For example, philosophers of science express concern over the inability of the scientific method to solve deep-seated social and behavioral problems.[2] That is, science can deal effectively with the "hard" mathematical questions of physics and chemistry. But answers to the "soft" fields of inquiry (sociology, economics, anthropology) elude science. Does this mean that science has failed? Not at all. It means that new scientific approaches need to be attempted.[3] Likewise, irrationality represents not a total failure or fruitless activity but a misapplication of a basic tool or a temporarily inadequate causal analysis. In this context it is worthwhile to pursue and to investigate irrationality as a process (we learn from mistakes) and to understand its essential linkage to rationalism.

Science, Systems, and Rationalism Revisited

The scientific method, through rigorous causal analysis, seeks to "push back the darkness of ignorance," to make the universe more understandable to its human occupiers, and perhaps to make the world a better place in which to live.

Systems theory, which postulates that there are artificially bounded regions that can be analyzed in space and time, is a logical derivative of this scientific approach. Systems theory, in its reductionist approach, seeks to break down the universe into manageable, analyzable parts. Systems theory allows the analyst to hypothesize that there are discrete and distinct physical *and* behavioral phenomena or units (bounded regions) that exist in tangible, separate form, and that have inputs and outputs that can be observed and even to some extent measured.

There is no question that there is a heuristic beauty to this scientific/systematic formulation. For example, it permits us to isolate phenomena and relationships that are distinct and unique. Thus, theoretically, we can look at the "public" sector or at the "private" sector as if they existed in hermetically sealed bubbles. It permits us to examine relationships between selected and separate variable such as automation (independent variable: the presumed cause) and productivity (dependent variable: the response measured). It permits us to isolate behavioral factors (interactive social phenomena) from physical factors (size of plant). It forces us to acknowledge the dynamic interchange between the unit (sales department) selected for analysis and its external environment (the marketplace).

There is a great deal of merit in this approach. Systems theory, while hardly a profound insight, offers significant heuristic advantages.

Rationalism, as noted, is a logical part of this scientific/systematic approach to problem solving. The rational approach, based on causal analysis between means and ends, seeks to maximize goals (productivity in a plant, the bottom line, social good). There is much to be said in favor of this approach. But that is not the issue. Today academics and practitioners alike are more than enamored with the scientific/rational model. Today the problem is that we have forgotten the theoretical and the practical limitations of the model. This chapter seeks to explore and restate some of those significant limitations.

Limits of Rationality

Rational methodologies, based on the causal concepts of science and systems theory, are relatively simple and straightforward. Rational thinking actually involves only the development of a new viewpoint (interacting parts or interrelated variables) on the part of the decision maker. Rational thinking is not something technological (mechanical) in itself. Rather, it is a new way of looking at the world and at ourselves. It may derive from intellectual technology (systems theory, economics, mathematics), but its application is not necessarily dependent on machine or technical competence (computer technology).

Nonetheless, in their applied form, rational models deviate from the logical imperatives of the theory on which they are grounded. Rational models assume an exaggerated dependence on the technology with which they are associated. This is to say that the general limitations of rationalism are both theoretical and procedural.

Theory Deficiencies

Ida Hoos[4] notes the intellectual, sometimes semantic origin of the limits of rational modeling:

> With such key concepts as system and model illusive of articulation and subject to marked latitude of interpretation and semantic slight-of-hand, the ascription of "scientific precision" to the method built on them constitutes a striking paradox. Precisely because systems analysis is a technique in which form takes precedence over and even determines content, the reliance on language becomes treacherous. It encourages lack of careful formalization

and formulation. This leads to a chain reaction of poor conceptualization, gathering of data more because they are available than indicative, and dependence on factors only because they can be counted in the on-going analysis and not because they are known to be important in the final analysis.[5]

In the soft sciences, that is, in the organizational and social sciences (law, management, politics, and so on), rational modeling represents the classic case of applying scientism (modern management principles) to social and organizational decision making. No doubt the rush to rationalism arises owing to the complex nature of our society and to the need to formulate solutions without great cost or unusual disruption of institutional forces. In the rush to a solution, however, lies the intensification of the problem and the exaggeration of the limits of rationalism. There are three basic limitations.

Simplicity versus Complexity. The engineer or physicist with his scientific, system-based models is able to see the physical world as composed of small, discrete elements configured in linear deterministic patterns. The social, or organizational world, however, is composed of an infinite array of intangible, interrelated, and nonlinear organic parts that react and respond to external stimuli of all sorts. Kick a small rock and it will move; to be sure, there is a reaction. Kick your supervisor and he will move; but that will not be the end of it. An intangible, nonphysical, unpredictable human chain reaction will likely occur. There is no simple mathematical equation that will cover this complex causal interaction. In fact, models that reduce human interactions to 5 or 10, or to 50 or 100, elements are naive.

Organization versus Disorganization. Statisticians, program planners, and other "futurologists" see the world in terms of linear, orderly, fixed variables rather than in terms of nonlinear, individually erratic, ever-changing variables and forces. Consider two of the most modern and most scientifically legitimate rational approaches to problem solving: PPBS and MBO. Each managerial technique, seeking greater effectiveness through scientific cost-benefit analysis, rests on the notion of predetermined interactions—that is, on the silly idea that everything important can be factored in and then controlled. As we now know, PPBS, MBO, linear programming, operations research, and other techniques derived from an organized view of the world hinge more on imponderables such as personality or politics than on anything else.

Statism versus Organism. An organic body is one that responds to change or to stimuli.[6] A static unit (a pile of bricks and mortar) is fixed and nonresponsive. Organic units are those that respond simultaneously to many factors and variables that are constantly interacting. Managers, decision makers, planners, and others who use rational models *necessarily* see the world as fixed in time and space, because to factor in the rational equation means to fix elements at some point in time. This is logically fallacious, as the world is not static. And yet this is what occurs when corporate planners project the future. Variables are fixed on a chart and projected out. Certainly crisis planning and contingency planning are coming into vogue. But even these adaptive approaches have a fixed or limited quality.

Data Deficiencies

As Ida Hoos has argued, a mathematical, systems-based, or rational conception of a problem limits the focus to those aspects that can be expressed quantitatively and that fit certain models. "The technological solution which results may be satisfactory from the engineering point of view but, because it has encompassed only select facets, vital dimensions have been neglected. Such violation of the essence of problems may, in the long run, exacerbate rather than ameliorate the troublesome condition."[7] Phrased even more strongly:

> Carried to logical extremes emphasis on quantification could so limit and bias perspectives as either to distort and violate the essential nature of social problems by forcing them into a tractable soluble state or to institutionalize and legitimize neglect of them or their vital parts.[8]

What does this disturbing critique mean in a real-world, day-to-day context? It means that contrary to being an instrument of progress and innovation, the rational approach to problem solving (grounded as it is in mathematical, quantitative data) is essentially problem causing. By defining problems in terms that fit existing tools, rational models factor out variables that may be crucial to ultimate problem solutions but that do not fit the tool. There are three basic concerns, outlined by Hoos.

Misuses of Data. Implicit in the rational conception of a problem-solving model is the presupposition that facts, data, or information exist in some "pristine" discrete state. These data need only to be found and then factored into the calculus of decision making.[9] Naturally, the gathering, selection, and use of data derive from some preconceived and value-laden formula that necessarily negates the presupposition of a pristine or value-free solution. This fundamental preconceptual step is ignored as decisions makers willy-nilly use so-called value-free data.

Dominance of Tools and Machines. If the data do not fit the mechanical or technological tools designed to ingest quantitative data, then the data are rejected. Although these data *may be* absolutely critical to intelligent problem solving, if they do not fit our machines and models, they are ignored. For example, the profit-loss sheet of a large corporation may be able to factor in (via computerized technology) great amounts of hard data in order to assist management. But can the same computer factor in long-range, intangible social or political data that are not available in hard mathematical form? Probably not. And so these data will be ignored. In short, if the data do not fit the technology, they are not considered "data." Tools and models dominate, not data and solutions. The tail is wagging the dog.

Measures of Success and Cycles of Defeat. Professional decision makers (managers who rely on rational models) often become victims of their own methodologies. That is, if the data are deterministic, albeit limited, then success is measured when the data are gathered and the formula solution implemented. The decision maker's time frame is often limited to this time frame and not to any evaluative follow-through. Follow-up, or postdecisional, analysis would involve gathering new data unforeseen in the original formulation, thereby casting doubt on the original model. Thus success is not measured by a long-term postimplementation review. For the professional manager it is measured by the next case or the next problem to be solved. This reality is not to be characterized as classic short-run versus long-run conceptualization. It is much more serious than this and leads to a hopelessly circular set of forces: the more that rational decision makers decide (and the pressures and incentives on them *are* to decide), the more is fixed in place and the worse things may become. The worse things become, the more the manager is tempted to act. And the cycle begins again.

CASE IN POINT

Irrational Models: The "Easy" Case—Automobiles

Perhaps the best way to illustrate the above processes and results is to focus on a classic case of applied rational modeling. What better area than assembly line planning, which for generations has exemplified the dominant form of modern production technology? Today of course, the validity of purely rational decision making even in this area is seriously questioned. The following case explains why and in doing so tells us much about irrationality.

THE CASE: THE LORDSTOWN FIASCO

Every thirty-six seconds, the Vegas glide forward on the assembly line, and each worker performs his prescribed duties, going through motions he will repeat 800 times in the course of his shift. The next day he will return to his place on the line and the same thing another 800 times. And the day after and the day after. For him, there is little else but the next car down the line. This is the General Motors Vega assembly plant at Lordstown, Ohio, fifty acres under roof, eighteen miles of conveyor belt, 2,000 new cars a day, 2,800 people on the assembly line. The men and women on the line are prisoners of the industrial system; doing their job on car after car, like so many sinners in hell consigned to a single task until eternity to pay for their transgressions. But unlike those in hell, they can rebel.

Last winter, the Lordstown factory reverberated with troubles that threatened a crisis in the American automobile industry. At Lordstown, General Motors' determination to increase productivity through the use of the industry's most automated facilities and a reduction of the workforce ran headlong into the opposition of workers fed up with the drudgery of their jobs. Event followed event in rapid succession: layoffs; a disciplinary crackdown; complaints of a speedup; worker sabotage of Vegas; high absenteeism;

Robert H. Miles, *Macro Organizational Behavior* (Santa Monica: Goodyear, 1980), pp.86–89. Agis Sapulkas, "Young Workers Disrupt GM Plant," The N.Y. Times, 23 Jan., 1972, p.1; "Sabotage at Lordstown", *Pine*, 7 Feb. l972, p. 76; "The GM Efficiency plan that backfired," Business Week, 25 March 1972, p.49; "GM Resumes Output at Lordstown, Ohio as Striking UAW Local Ratifies Accord," Wall St. Journal, 27 March 1972, p.2; Ronald K. Boyer and Richard L. Shell, "The End of the Line at Lordstown," *Business and Society Review* (Autumn 1972), pp. 31-35; and James O'Toole, "Lordstown: Three Years Later," *Business and Society Review* (Spring 1975), pp. 64-71.

slowdowns; a strike lasting twenty-two days; and finally, a settlement that was approved with only 70 percent of the union members voting.

GENERAL MOTORS' LORDSTOWN PLANT

General Motors' Lordstown, Ohio, plant is a hub of superlatives. Its assembly line is the most highly automated one in the industry: it has twenty-six bellows-like armed robots that can bend around corners and that make some 520 welds in each car. The line is also the fastest in the United States, capable of producing 100 cars per hour (compared to an industry average of 55-60 per hour). The labor force—long-haired, pigtailed and bell-bottomed—is the youngest of any GM plant with an average age of twenty-four to twenty-five. Now Lordstown, the only U.S. plant that turns out subcompact Vegas, has the industry's worst labor problems, and so far it has cost GM about $40 million in lost production.

Through better design, a variety of new types of power tools, and other automated devices, much of the heavy lifting and hard physical labor has been eliminated in the plant. Even the parking lots were planned in such a way that the long walk to one's car has been done away with.

THE EFFICIENCY EXPERTS TAKE OVER

About a year before the strike, the Lordstown workers had received awards from GM recognizing the high quality of their work. Shortly after the awards were presented, GM turned the plant's management over to its tough Assembly Division—one of the last management teams in the United States still to practice an undiluted version of Taylor's scientific management. . . . This no-nonsense team concluded that although the line in the Lordstown plant was fast, . . . it could go still faster. After all, productivity is the name of the game.

. . . .General Motors Assembly Division (GMAD), a management team that developed a reputation for toughness in cutting costs and bettering productivity took over . . . and began to consolidate the operations.

A major reorganization of work began. According to management, it consisted mostly of changing jobs to make them more efficient, although management conceded that about three hundred jobs had been eliminated and some workers had been given additional work. . . . Mr. Anderson [the plant manager] explained that changes had to be made to bring the assembly line . . . up to the potential it was designed for.

In order to increase productivity, the Assembly Division did the two things that industrial engineers always do: They cut back the manpower on the line, and they increased the number of separate operations for which each worker was responsible. For example, by bringing his stockpile of parts within easier reach, a worker could double the number of parts he could install, screws he could turn, and bolts he could fasten in the thirty seconds or so he had with each car.

Many workers couldn't keep up with the increased pace. Some fell so far behind that they ended up riding down the line trying to complete their tasks and having to run back to their stations to start the cycle again. Workers complained, but management held its ground. Joseph E. Godfrey, general manager of the Assembly Division, stated his position succinctly: "We can occupy a man for sixty minutes, we've got the right." The workers answered Godfrey in kind.

EARLY WORKER REACTIONS

Hardly anybody called it sabotage—yet. But . . . somebody deliberately set fire to an assembly-line control box shed, causing the line to shut down. Autos regularly roll off the line with slit upholstery, scratched paint, dented bodies, bent gear-shift levers, cut ignition wires, and loose or missing bolts. In some cars, the trunk key is broken off right in the lock, thereby jamming it. The plant's repair lot has space for 2,000 autos, but often becomes too crowded to accept more. When that happens, as it did last week, the assembly line is stopped, and workers are sent home payless.

. . . .[A]cross the Ohio Turnpike, Gary Bryner, the twenty-nine-year-old president of Local 1112, in an interview in his office in a modern brick union hall, said that about seven hundred jobs had been eliminated and that much of the extra work had been shifted to men who had no time to do it.

He said that before the new management team (GMAD) took over, there were about one hundred grievances in the plant. Since then, he said, grievances have increased to five thousand—about one thousand of which consist of protests of too much work added to a job.

Led by its angry young, the local . . . threatened to take a strike vote . . . unless GM makes concessions. Money is not the issue; the workers earn about $4.50 an hour, plus $2.50 fringe. What the union wants is a redefinition of work rules that will result in some rehiring and elimination of extra chores, which workers claim rush them as the autos move by at an average of one every thirty-six seconds. GM added some of these chores partly in the hope of alleviating the mind-numbing boredom of endlessly doing just one task.

MANAGEMENT'S ATTEMPTED CONCILIATION

Management has attempted conciliation and has instituted sensitivity sessions with groups of workers to find out what the complaints are. But the overall management strategy so far has been one of toughness, of hoping for results from the smaller paychecks that are issued when workers are sent home early when there is a slowdown and from foremen's disciplining workers by sending them home without pay.

THE STRIKE

[These token attempts at appeasement were to no avail, and the strike that is now history commenced. After extended negotiations, which amounted to a very costly delay in Vega production, management agreed to restore many of the abolished jobs and settled most of the grievances, especially those regarding overwork. But, the basic managerial strategy remained, and differences in worker and management attitudes were apparent. As one reporter observed, "[I]t isn't certain the strike settlement will end labor discord here. Labor sources said the 70 percent approval margin was relatively low for such votes, indicating more than a little dissatisfaction with the settlement."]

SUBSEQUENT "BEATING-THE-LINE" TACTICS

What is particularly bothersome to the company is that workers have taken to looking for ways to "beat the line": As management is trying to re-engineer the jobs on the line, the workers are responding by redesigning their own jobs. Their favorite method is "doubling."

Under this invention, four workers might agree to become an informal team, and for a set period of time (fifteen minutes to half an hour), two of the team members will work like the devil doing the work of all four, while the other two workers rest, smoke, or chat. The workers claim that this method improves the quality of their work because it forces them to concentrate on what would otherwise be routine tasks, gives them the opportunity of socializing with coworkers (the latter being an important element in job satisfaction for blue-collar workers, but one that is all but impossible on a fast and noisy assembly line).

Doubling drives the Assembly Division managers up the wall. Workers are paid to work, not to stand around chatting, they say. So, when workers engage in doubling, the managers respond by disciplining them, sending them home for a day or more without pay. The workers then file grievances, and when this sequence escalates to an unbearable level, the workers strike for a few days. That was how matters stood on November 15, 1974, when the plant was first closed due to the recession.

BRIEF ASSESSMENT

At Lordstown, two trends in American industry had their inevitable collision: an increased level of automation, which requires less skill of workers, and an increasingly young and well-educated labor force, which demands more satisfaction from its work than ever before. Technologically, Lordstown is in the vanguard of industry, holding title to the world's fastest automobile assembly line. It has been hailed as "the wave of the future" in auto production. Lordstown suggests a future, however, not of industrial efficiency but industrial strife pitting labor against management, and man against machine.

Most automation development in the United States has stressed machinery, computer control, and other technical aspects of the system while ignoring human problems. Workers have always groaned about the dreariness of assembly-line routine. What is new is the number of workers, particularly independent-minded young workers, who are refusing to submit to the mind-numbing discipline their jobs demand. A new breed of workers prevails at places like Lordstown, where production workers average just twenty-four years in age. Worker resistance to the dehumanizing effects of automation is growing and poses a serious threat to the need for increased productivity in the American economy. Today the educational level

Case Review 93

of the young blue-collar workers is a good deal higher than in the past, and their vocational expectations greater. Yet blue-collar work is becoming even simpler and more monotonous as technology seems to be squeezing out the last vestiges of skill.

. . . . [T]he basic relationship between management and labor has remained the same. Management determines the technology, and the workers make it work or perform the tasks they cannot. In semi-automated assembly, the worker is still viewed as an extension of the machine, just as he was forty years ago under Frederick Taylor's original conception of "scientific management." The worker is to be told what to do and when to do it. Standard technology makes no allowance for the changes evident in today's workers, their need for more rewarding and interesting jobs. The demands of the machine remain supreme; the worker, who runs a poor second, knows it and is resentful. So long as union and management make no attempt at fundamental accommodation of man and machine, there can only be continual conflict in the auto industry.

Despite the advances that GMAD claims, the question now facing GM's top management is whether good labor relations have been sacrificed. There is a feeling among some GM executives that they should have moved more slowly. Getting tough with a younger work force that is more ready to fight back may work to the detriment of GMAD and its parent. Admits one top GM executive: "They may have acted too quickly. We didn't need the Lordstown strike. A slower approach might have worked out the problems. Now the corporation has lost more in the strike than it could have saved by laying off all those workers."

CASE REVIEW

What lessons or thoughts might be drawn from this case of seemingly irrational behavior on the part of the workers at Lordstown?

General Thoughts

Behavior is Not Random

Among organizational behavioralists, it is generally agreed that behavior is not random. Rather, human behavior is purposive or goal oriented. While an outside observer may view someone's activity as nonrational, generally just the opposite is the case. As in the Lordstown case the behavior of the workers in sabotaging production was not without rational content; nor was this seemingly destructive behavior random. On the contrary the worker's behavior represented a deliberate attempt to communicate anger, frustration, and disgust to the GMAD planning staff.[10]

Technocratic Monopolism

Referring to the power of technology, Albert Speer, infamous architect and Armaments Minister in the Third Reich, has argued that the origins of Nazism reside in the German tradition of nonhumanistic education, that is, with the emphasis on engineering, the physical sciences, and mathematical formulas. Speer theorized that after World War I, the German people ignored studies in philosophy, the humanities, and the social sciences, thus building the base for an authoritarian leadership.[11] Today, Bertram Gross makes the same argument.[12] Monopoly by technocratic orientations, according to Gross, might ultimately promote disorder and discontinuity instead of the social systematization and order that were the objectives of the GMAD planners.[13] The failure of the GMAD planners to include sociopolitical variables in their schema represents not just a short-range, one-time shortcoming but a long-range, systematic failure to include nonphysical, nonquantified data. The results were disastrous.

Technical Thresholds and Behavioral Acceptability

The GMAD planners saw a problem (underproduction), and they fixed on a solution (automation). In doing so, they no doubt considered one important criterion of decision making (technical quality) but ignored a second critical factor (behavioral acceptability).[14] These two criteria—technical quality and behavioral acceptability—are often confused in decisional processes, but they are really quite different. In some technical decision situations (installing a machine, choosing office furniture) there is minimal influence on the lives of the work force. Hence the acceptability of a solution is of little concern in choosing alternatives, and only the technical quality of the decision needs to be observed (does the machine operate, does the furniture fit). In most organizational settings, however, even the most technically superior solution (automation) may be a disastrous choice if it is unacceptable to those who are affected by it. Even though GMAD was sufficiently motivated to implement the decision (it was acceptable to management), the solution was behaviorally rejected by the workers (it was unacceptable to them). People care very deeply about what is done to them;

humans are capable of possessing passionate preferences. Behaviorally, humans may accept or reject solutions. Unlike the machinery itself (the robots) the workers at Lordstown cared deeply about being manipulated. Thus the highest quality technical solution will fail if it is not acceptable to those affected by it.

Decisional Blinders and Anticipated Responses

The case suggests that an effective rational solution (accelerate production) must somehow produce a desired behavioral change or at least a consideration of "human behavior," which is at the core of the problem (underproduction). Clearly, the GMAD approach to robot acceleration did not produce the desired behavioral change (productivity). In fact it produced a decidedly undesirable change (sabotage). Why? Is it because the planners/managers were more concerned with *their* behavior (what should *we* do) as opposed to concerned with the critical questions, What will the responses be? and How will the proposed solution bring about the desired behavior?[15] To answer these questions competently the decision maker must necessarily predict behavior. Or at the very least he must attempt to make behavioral assumptions. That is, he must somewhere calculate in his decisional framework anticipated responses to his solutions. Humans will react to a change. The question is, *What* will their reactions be? Was Ford Motor Company, one of the *Fortune* 500 and one of the largest firms in the world, absolutely blind as to anticipated responses? Or did the planners/managers simply not care what the responses would be? The latter possibility is beyond mere cynicism and hence is not realistic. Thus decisional blindness becomes a serious issue in rational modeling.

Incentives and Disincentives

The case suggests another disturbing but less conspiratorial possibility—namely that there is an almost perverse incentive system operating in the rational world that leads decision makers to select solutions that have short-run, quantifiable results capable of objectification (accelerated productivity) but that lead to long-run, nonquantifiable but disastrous results (psychological hostility or organizational resistance). The short-run incentive can be objectified and possessed; therefore, it is sought by decision makers trying to climb the corporate ladder. The long-run disincentives (to a solution) cannot easily be quantified; thus they can conveniently be ignored. The pressure is on to make a quick decision.

Specific Implications and Trends

Risk Calculation and Segregated Decisional Structures

In addition to the existence of an almost perverse hierarchy of incentives and disincentives, there is a curious interaction between rational decision making and risk displacement. There are two types of risks when one is offering and implementing solutions: the risk of failure (well known) and the risk of success (less familiar). If a decision fails, the risks are obvious. If a decision succeeds, however, there are also risk consequences. As there are no doubt several possible solutions, one prevails, the others fail. Thus there are winners and losers. In a highly competitive, departmentalized corporate structure such as Ford Motor, there will be obvious winners and losers. This behavioral reality interacts in a powerful way with departmentalized structures. For example, the GMAD staff represented the purely rational approach to the problem of underproduction. Is it possible, within the entire Ford Motor Company, with its many subdivisions and departments, that no unit or individual considered the behavioral consequences of automation? Probably not. The reality is that somewhere in the system the process considered consequences of failure as well as the risk of success. The fact that no one pointed out the dangers is mute testimony to a disturbing dynamic of noncooperation encouraged by the competitive drive of the corporation and by the GMAD unit in particular. Segregated specialization (as a function of systems analysis) has disadvantages as well as advantages. Risk calculation or avoidance is only one example of this phenomenon.

Competition and Rationalism

Chris Argyris has argued that rationality and competition are inapposite; that is, they pull in different directions. According to Argyris, the rational manager is not governed by competition; likewise, the competitive manager lacks rationality.[16] This case suggests that contrary to Argyris's theory, rationality and competition are mutually supportive. Departmentalization of decisions is only one structural manifestation of rationalism through specialization, which in turn fosters, and is fostered by, competition. But specialization that induces competition among departments carries other side effects. For example, "restricted commitment" to a solution or policy is a consequence of specialization. "Subordinate gamesmanship," or the norm of not feeding up negative information, is another consequence of departmentalization and of strict superordinate-subordinate relationships.[17] Such realities not only lead to the suppression of risk calculation but over time produce intradepartmental/intragroup norms of distrust, noncommunication, covert noncooperation, and other irrational behaviors.

Automate the Line: The Tendency to Equate New and Old Experiences

St. Augustine is reported to have said: Time is a threefold present: the past as present memory; the present as currently experienced; and the future as present expectation. The point is that because our past experiences seem so clear to us, we often us the past as the basis for approaching future decisions.[18] For Ford Motor Company there is no question that the invention of modern automation (the assembly line) was a brilliant and significant past accomplishment. But to extend this automation principle into and beyond the limits of the twentieth century was shortsighted. Even though a prior experience may have been a good and productive experience, similarities between a present situation and a past experience are few, and comparisons often are misleading. At the very least the second situation will differ from the first in at least two basic regards:

1. The two experiences occur at different times, with whole new sets of variables present; and
2. The actors are different and bring different needs, values, and skills to the situation.[19]

The Sunk-Costs Syndrome

Related to the historical logic of extending the assembly line principle is the habit of using available solutions. Having acquired automated machinery over the decades, and having invested in a costly preplan operation of new-age machinery, the GMAD decision makers were compelled to use the available solution, or the machinery, into which so much cost had been sunk.

Rational Analysis and Taking Action

The pressures—and the incentives—among decision makers in modern Western corporations are to *do something* about problems. That is, corporate decision makers are paid to take action—not to debate or to deliberate. The rational method (with its heavy reliance on decision theory, operations research, and linear programming) compliments the action impulse as opposed to a more analytical diagnostic approach. For example, numbers, data, and quantified variables are selected to help make a choice. Data are not gathered to exhaust all possible choices, to examine nonquantifiable causal variables, or to spur further investigation. The incentives and the tools are aimed at doing something.

Simple Goals, Single Goals

Very often, even though a complex organizational problem exists, a manager reduces action or choice to a single goal. If the question is simple (what must be done), the answer is often singular (this must be done). Methodologically, rational models support this singular approach by gathering data aimed at doing something: making the "right" choice. Behaviorally, it is easy and comforting to think of one goal at a time (or even of only one goal). The result, however, is to ignore other variables, complex choices, and multiple solutions to a multifaceted problem.

Participative versus Authoritarian Approaches

In the literature and in the organization the debate continues regarding the appropriateness and effectiveness of participative democratic styles of management (Theory Y) versus nonparticipative directive approaches (Theory X).[20] The debate will not be resolved here (or perhaps anywhere else). But a few comments are appropriate. First, it must be assumed that managers are aware that employees being human, have feelings about what they do in the workplace. Second, it seems sheer folly to ignore some calculation of these feelings. Perhaps an all-out participative/nondirective style of management is not appropriate or desired. But in-between, nondirective managerial techniques of social analysis, feedback mechanisms, group consultations (formal and informal) seem to represent a minimally intelligent approach to radical, drastic change.

New Styles of Management/Leadership

The traditional and dated literature on management and leadership is replete with many theories and models: Douglas McGregor's Theory X−Theory Y;[21] Fred Fiedler's contingency model of leader-member interactions;[22] and Robert Blake and Jane Mouton's managerial grid.[23] Despite internal variable distinctions these and other models fall essentially along a democratic-autocratic continuum. Is it possible that a new form of management decision making/leadership is emerging—one that does not fall along this continuum and that transcends the participative/nonparticipative approach by ignoring ab initio any concern for employee feelings? That is, does the GMAD approach itself represent a total lack of concern with employee reaction or with human response? Just as doctors and lawyers and other helping professionals seem to be concerned in some cases with results rather than with human feelings, is it not possible that a new breed of technocratic elites simply does not care about human consequence? Malice is not intended; the human variable is simply not emergent. Behavioral considerations are considered irrelevant.

The Twilight of Rationalism

If this analysis is correct, if the Lordstown case is a window on the future, then rationalism as the hope of tomorrow is finished. Rational models promise objectivity, intelligence, and effectiveness in quicker, better, and wiser decisions. But if rationalism or rational approaches spit out, or factor out, nonquantifiable human responses, then rationality fails to live up to its promises. Note in this context that it is assumed that rationalism means more than mere improvement of data-gathering skills. At the heart of the rational model lies the hope of a better result, a better world as a result of better decisions.

Winners and Losers

Both employers (management) and employees (workers and union) have to worry about these consequences, as the case reveals that both parties are in a no-win situation. Management loses both the short-run objectives of productivity and the long-run essentials of stability and control. Workers lose faith in management and satisfaction with work. With today's legal and social protections, worker dissatisfaction will take new and perhaps more threatening forms of expression. The bottom line of the rational model is that it may be unhealthy for all.

CONCLUSION

The "Lordstown Fiasco" case was selected to illustrate the irrational elements of rational approaches and the inherent limitations of rational modeling even when applied in a highly rational manner (automation) to a problem given to rational analysis (productivity). The conflict between sophisticated, remote management tools (planning, design) and crude worker responses (sabotage, physical destructiveness) is obvious. What is not so obvious is that these behaviors—rational planning, on the one hand, and irrational destruction, on the other—are not problems in themselves but reflections or symptoms of a more deep-seated set of circumstances. The circumstances suggest a drift in our organizational society toward two worlds: one rational, the other not. The rational world, composed of GMAD-type techniques, rejects tools for evaluating human response. More disturbing perhaps, there is no incentive or value to calculate human response. The intuitive world is composed of those untrained and unschooled in rational (objective) approaches. Their world is evaluated according to traditional values and norms derived from human experience. The clash was predictable. The question is whether it was *inevitable*. The answer depends in part upon whether there are other ways to go about solving problems in organizations. In short, are there other more viable approaches?

Chapters Four and Five will examine a second generic approach: the political model, with its derivative, the administrative approach.

NOTES

1. David Pears, *Motivated Irrationality* (Oxford:Clarendon Press, 1984).
2. "Is Science Stymied by Today's Complexity?," *New York Times*, June 28, 1983, p. 19.
3. Pragmatic reductionist approaches are beginning to emerge. Note attempts to pose questions on a simple hierarchical level where interactions are more fundamental and traceable.
4. Ida R. Hoos, *Systems Analysis in Public Policy* (Berkeley: University of California Press, 1972).
5. Ibid., p. 8.
6. In this sense certain institutions (not the building but the social unit) and certain concepts (like the U.S. Constitution) are organic. They change in response to external stimuli.
7. Hoos, *Systems Analysis*, p. 26.
8. Ibid., p. 241.
9. Ibid., p. 198.
10. A serious question is whose behavior (management's or workers') should be characterized as irrational. It is only in the strict definition of terms that GMAD was acting according to rational policies. That is, it

was highly irrational to ignore deep-seeded social and cultural circumstances.

11. Albert Speer, *Infiltration* (New York: Macmillan, 1981) p. 84, and *Inside the Third Reich* (New York: Macmillan, 1970) pp. 8,33.

12. Bertram Gross, *Friendly Facism: The New Face of Power in America* (New York: M. Evans and Company, Inc., 1980) pp. 206, 384.

13. Hoos, *Systems Analysis*, p. 76, from "The New Systems Budgeting" (paper presented at the American Political Science Association, Washington, D.C., September 5, 1968), p. 18.

14. Alvar Elbing, *Behavioral Decisions in Organizations* (Glenview, Ill.: Scott, Foresman and Company, 1970), p. 133.

15. Ibid., p. 137.

16. Chris Argyris, "Interprersonal Barriers to Decision Making." *Harvard Business Review*, March-April 1966, pp. 87−88.

17. This key point is not specifically made in the Argyris study on "Interpersonal Barriers." Ibid. pp. 88−89.

18. Daniel Bell, "The Year 2000—The Trajectory of an Idea," in *Toward the Year 2000* ed. by Daniel Bell (Boston: Houghton Mifflin Company, 1968), p. 1.

19. Elbing, *Behavioral Decisions in Organizations*, pp. 50−51.

20. Douglas McGregor, *The Human Side of Enterprise* (New York: McGraw-Hill, 1960). McGregor argued (Theory X) that workers required relatively strict direction and supervision.

21. Ibid.

22. Fred E. Fiedler, *A Theory of Leadership Effectiveness* (New York: McGraw-Hill, 1967).

23. Robert R. Blake and Jane S. Mouton, *The Managerial Grid* (Houston: Gulf, 1964).

{S}ystematic research . . . has repeatedly called attention to wide gulfs between our solemnly taught, common sense assumptions about what political institutions do and what they actually do.

Murray Edelman
The Symbolic Uses of Politics

CHAPTER FOUR

POLITICAL MODELS

DEFINITIONS AND CONCEPTS

The comingling of fact and value, as suggested by the distortion of value-free models (Chapter Three) is distressing to many methodologists and to adherents of a value-free scientific approach. At the same time, "goallessness," or the absence of values (read *ethics*) in management practice, represents to others one of the most disquieting aspects of administrative theory. Chapters Four and Five will explore the development of policy science in its "pure" and in its "actual" forms. Again, we begin with definitions and concepts.

Management versus Administration

Popularized word usage suggests a distinction, if not a difference, between the terms *management* and *administration*. For example, *management* is the preferred term in the so-called private sector.[1] Thus in a college of commerce the department focusing on organizational activities (operations, behavior, planning) is called a "management department." Likewise, matriculated graduates who enter corporate life in the business world refer to themselves as management. Whether a process or a status, the term *management* in the private sector refers to the optimum attainment of organizational goals.[2] Even though managers in the business sector are involved in the generic process of administration, ideology and personal preference dictate the use of the term *management*.

Administration is the word used to describe the managerial process in the public sector, that is, in legally constituted government activities. *Administration* (like *management*) in any complex organization refers to the activities of defining purposes and objectives; planning and organizing; selecting personnel and motivating people; controlling and measuring results; and using a variety of analytical, problem-solving, and managerial techniques.[3] Although certain business-oriented management schools might prefer the term *public management* as a way of diluting overtly public sector focus, the government is still referred to as the "administration," and most scholars refer to the field of public sector analysis as *public administration*.

The contrast between the terms reflects not a substantive difference but a distinction based on ideological viewpoint. Perhaps to the business executive the term *administration* has a pejorative connotation of inefficiency and incompetence. Likewise, to the public practitioner, the term *management* conjures notions of corruption and memories of management-labor conflict.

The point is that even absent a clear methodological difference the different terms are used in different contexts.[4] This is because there is presumed to be an important difference between the private sector rational model of management and the public sector political model of administration. The next two chapters will explore and detail the political model in its pure[5] and in its applied form.

Public versus Private

As noted, the concept that there is a discrete and unique public sector and an equally discrete and unique private sector belies reality. The reality is that most private institutions interact heavily and regularly with government agencies. And most government agencies are supported by, or interact with, private institutions. For example, even so-called private institutions of higher education are heavily subsidized and regulated by the "feds." The same is true with regard to airplane manufacturers, automotive manufacturers, banks, railroads, and so on. Even the largest and most visible public bodies (for example, the Pentagon, the National Aeronautics and Space Administration [NASA], the prisons) are dependent upon interactions with private vendors, managers, and consumers.

The academic (and ideologically reassuring) fiction of separate, discrete planets orbiting at different but parallel levels is strictly science fiction.[6]

At the same time, there are significant conceptual differences between the words *public* and *private*. For example, John Dewey observed that the public consists of all those who are affected by the indirect consequences of transactions to such an extent that it is deemed necessary to have those consequences systematically cared for.[7] That is to say, the line between public and private "is to be drawn on the basis of the extent and scope of the consequences of acts which are so important as to need control."[8] Consequences that affect only those directly involved in the transaction or activity are private. Consequences that affect others beyond those immediately involved are public. The latter need to be regulated and are societal in scope. Society in the form of government thus enters the picture.

Dewey's enduring conceptualization embraces more than a simplistic application of the modern science of sociobiology[9] and other esoteric disciplines. Dewey's formulation of the public transcends a mere temporal and spatial relationship and introduces new concerns (reviewed in Chapter Five) dealing with responsibility, accountability, and ethical measures.

To understand Dewey's use of *public* is to discredit the monopoly of economic theory and the encroachment of the criterion of efficiency into what is essentially a noneconomic set of value questions. Dewey proposes that human acts have consequences—that when these consequences affect others and when it is perceived or agreed that they need to be controlled, then a public is born.

Note the important distinction between *public* and *government*. The public is that body or force that intervenes between a perceived problem and the governmental outcome. For example, the public is a group of affected parties or individuals aroused and engaged in interventionist activities for ethical, moral, societal, or political reasons. Note also that the public need not be a legally constituted body. The metaphysics of formalism should not prevent recognition of publics. The essential point is that the public emerges around consequences, and these consequences transcend mere procedural or administrative matters (policy formation, coordir tion, regulation planning, and so on). The concept of the public also raises new criteria of measurement: the criteria of compromise and consensus (collective action), which are different from the economic criteria of efficiency (corporate goals).

Policy versus Administration

Even since Woodrow Wilson's powerful promotion of a cultured and decent civil service,[10] decision science scholars have labored under the burdensome policy-administration dichotomy. Aside from its obvious teaching tool merits, and apart from the context of apolitical reform in which it was offered, the Wilsonian ideal does little to advance our thinking. Rooted in John Austin's positivistic[11] philosophy, *policy* is that which emanates from a legal (preferably constitutional) body, namely the legislature. The source is all-important: policy derives from the formal sovereign, as a binding rule. *Administration* consists of the application of values (set by policymakers) to neutral facts, as determined by a value-free objective corps of administrators. Clearly, the importance of an apolitical corps of administrators was central to Wilson's reform-minded civil service. But the intellectual dichotomy between policy and administration was overblown.

First, the distinction is a legal one, based upon constitutional precepts, not upon workaday realities. Most interpreters of Wilson, not being lawyers, missed this fundamental point. Second, the dichotomy is pure formalism with all the substantive limits that positivism implies. For example, a constitutionalist or positivistic view sees policy as only issuing from a sovereign, legally constituted government with its official sanctions. This view ignores all the policy (binding values) allocated through nongovernmental bodies (labor unions, churches, political parties, pressure groups) with informal sanctions.

Nonetheless, Wilson carried the day, and we are stuck with the dichotomy. As Norton Long observed, the verbiage runs the risk of being "a fastidious piece of ivory-tower escapism."[12] The significance of the dichotomy lies not in its enduring intellectual properties but in its potential for academic abstraction. It allows serious scholars to talk about the process of administration as if that process is actually and inherently different from the process of "policy-making." Presumably, this means that the tools of administrative decisions will be qualitatively and substantively different from the techniques of policy decisions. Theoretically, this means a staff person on the Budget Committee of the Congress think differently about problems than his legally elected political boss. Even sillier—or perhaps more dangerous, depending on one's capacity for humor—is the notion that somewhere along the line in the policy-making–administrative application process, value-free administrators check the misuses and excesses of the political policymaker. We must keep this conceptual history in the forefront as we seek to understand the legitimacy of the political model of decision making. And we must return to the original authors to understand the roots of today's conceptual mire.

Models and Muddles: Two Ideals

With the policy versus administration, value versus fact distinction as background, administrative theorists realized that there was a value to the process itself.[13] The "process as a value" has two components. First, there was thought to be a distinct public style, or public sector *process* of decision making (that is, a distinct step-by-step procedure, if not a formula). Second, and more important, this process itself was thought to contain normative content.

Policy, formerly thought to be a province of value allocators (like legislatures), was ideally formulated according to a rational model following the scientific method of cause and effect or means-goals analysis. Upon closer examination, however, it was realized that there was in actual operation a kind of ad hoc, incremental, nonscientific process of "muddling through," at least in the public sector. Suddenly the very process of public administration came to have a certain attractive quality. The process of muddling through, which involved suboptimizing, incrementalism, and noneconomic criteria, was thought to be suitable, if not preferable, to elitist rational decisions.

As Charles Lindblom noted in 1959 in describing the muddling process:

> It is in fact a common method of policy formulation and is for complex problems, the principal reliance of administrators as well as other policy analysts.[14]

CASE IN POINT

Political Models: Budget Data and Political Realities

The cat clearly was out of the bag. It was only a matter of time until public decision theorists would go beyond mere distinction to actual advocacy[15] of this political model. Perhaps the best example of the process-advocacy approach lies in the work of Aaron Wildavsky. A good example of the collision course between hard-data analysis and hard-core politics is found in Wildavsky's early but still pertinent work on budgeting.

THE CASE: BUDGETING AS A POLITICAL PROCESS

Budgets are predictions. They attempt to specify connections between words and numbers on the budget documents and future human behavior. Whether or not the behavior intended by the authors of the budget actually takes place is a question of empirical observation rather than one of definition. The budget of the Brazilian government, for example, has long been known as "a great lie" (Alionar Beleeiro, reported by Frank Sherwood), with little if any connection between what is spent for various purposes and what is contained in the formal document.

Budgeting is concerned with the translation of financial resources into human purposes. Since funds are limited, a budget may become a mechanism for allocating resources. If emphasis is placed on receiving the largest returns for a given sum of money, or on obtaining the desired objectives at the lowest cost, a budget may become an instrument for pursuing efficiency. A proposed budget may represent an organization's expectations; it may contain the amounts which the organization expects to spend. A budget may also reflect organizational aspirations; it may contain figures the organization hopes to receive under favorable conditions. Since the amounts requested often have an effect on the amounts received, budget proposals are often strategies. The total sum of money and its distribution among various activities may be designed to have a favorable impact in support of an organization's goals. As each participant acts on the budget he receives information on the preferences of others and communicates his own desires through the choices he makes. Here a budget emerges as a network of communications in which information is being continuously generated and fed back to the participants. Once enacted a budget becomes a precedent; the fact that something has been done before vastly increases the chances that it will be done again.

For all purposes we shall conceive of budgets as attempts to allocate financial resources through political processes. If politics is regarded as conflict over whose preferences are to prevail in the

---

"Budgeting as a Political Process" by Aaron Wildavsky, Edited and reprinted by permission of the publisher from the *International Encyclopedia of Social Sciences*, David Sills, editor. Volume 2, pages 192-199. Copyright © 1968 by Crowell and Collier and Macmillan, Inc.

determination of policy, then the budget records the outcomes of this struggle. If one asks who get what the (public or private) organization has to give, then the answers for a moment in time are recorded in the budget. If organizations are viewed as political coalitions, budgets are mechanisms through which subunits bargain over conflicting goals, make side-payments, and try to motivate one another to accomplish their objectives.

Viewed in this light, the study of budgeting offers a useful perspective from which to analyze the making of policy. The opportunities for comparison are ample, the outcomes are specific and quantifiable, and the troublesome problem of a unit of analysis with which to test hypotheses—there is no real agreement on what a decision consists of—is solved by the very nature of the transactions in budgeting. Although a major effort has been made to collect budgetary material from many different countries. levels of government, and private firms, the results have only been fragmentary at best. Very little is available in any language on how budgeting is actually carried on. From Stourm's classic work on the budget (1889) to the present day, virtually the entire literature on budgeting has been normative in tone and content. Yet the glimpses we do get of budgetary behavior in different systems suggest that there may be profound uniformities underlying the seeming diversities of form and structure.

BUDGETARY CALCULATIONS

Decisions depend upon calculation of which alternatives to consider and to choose Calculation involves determination of how problems are identified, get broken down into manageable dimensions, and are related to one another, and how choices are made as to what is relevant and who shall be taken into account. A major clue toward understanding budgeting is the extraordinary complexity of the calculations involved. In any large organization there are a huge number of items to be considered, many of which are of considerable technical difficulty. Yet there is little or no theory in most areas of policy which would enable practitioners to predict the consequences of alternative moves and the probability of their occurring. Man's ability to calculate is severely limited; time is always in short supply; and the number of matters which can be encompassed in one mind at the same time is quite small. Nor has anyone solved the imposing problem of the interpersonal comparison of utilities. Out-

utilities. Outside of the political process, there is no agreed upon way of comparing and evaluating the merits of different programs for different people whose preferences vary in kind and in intensity.

Simplification

Participants in budgeting deal with their overwhelming burdens by adopting aids to calculation. They simplify in order to get by. They make small moves, let experience accumulate, and use the feedback from their decisions to gauge the consequences. They use actions on simpler matters they understand as indices to complex concerns. They attempt to judge the capacity of the men in charge of programs even if they cannot appraise the policies directly. They may institute across-the-board ("meat-axe") cuts to reduce expenditures, relying on outcries from affected agencies and interest groups to let them know if they have gone too far.

Incremental Method

By far the most important aid to calculation is the incremental method. Budgets are almost never actively reviewed as a whole in the sense of considering at once the value of all existing programs as compared with all possible alternatives. Instead, this year's budget is based on last year's budget, with special attention given to a narrow range of increases or decreases. The greatest part of any budget is a product of previous decisions. Long-range commitments have been made. There are mandatory programs whose expenses must be met. Powerful political support makes the inclusion of other activities inevitable. Consequently, officials concerned with budgeting restrict their attention to items and programs they can do something about— a few new programs and possible cuts in old ones.

Expectations of Participants

Incremental calculations proceed from an existing base. By "base" we refer to commonly held expectations among participants in budgeting that programs will be carried out at close to the going level of expenditures. The base of a budget, therefore, refers to accepted parts of programs that will not normally be subjected to intensive scrutiny. Since many organizational units compete for funds, there is a tendency for the central authority to include all of them in the benefits or deprivations to be distributed. Participants in budgeting often refer to expectations regarding their fair share of increases and decreases. The widespread sharing of deeply held expectations concerning the organization's base and its fair share of funds provides a powerful (though informal) means of coordination and stability in budgetary systems which appear to lack comprehensive calculations proceeding from a hierarchical center.

COORDINATION AND SUPERVISION

The most powerful coordinating mechanisms in budgeting undoubtedly stem from the role orientations adopted by the major participants. Roles (the expectations of behavior attached to institutional positions) are parts of the division of labor. They are calculating mechanisms. In American national government, the administrative agencies act as advocates of increased expenditure, the Bureau of the Budget* acts as presidential servant with a cutting bias, the House Appropriations Committee functions as a guardian of the Treasury, and the Senate Appropriations Committee serves as an appeals court to which agencies carry their disagreement with House action. The roles fit in with one another and set up a stable pattern of mutual expectations, which markedly reduces the burden of calculation for the participants. The agencies need not consider in great detail how their requests will affect the president's over-all program; they know that such criteria will be introduced by the Budget Bureau. Since the agencies can be depended upon to advance all the programs for which there is prospect of support, the Budget Bureau and the appropriations committees can concentrate respectively on fitting them into the president's program or paring them down. If the agencies suddenly reversed roles and sold themselves short, the entire pattern of mutual expectations would be upset, leaving the participants without a firm anchor in a sea of complexity. For if agencies refuse to be advocates, congressmen would not only have to choose among the margins of the best programs placed before

---

*Presently titled OMB (Office of Management and Budget).

them, they would also have to discover what these good programs might be. Indeed, the Senate Appropriations Committee depends upon the agency advocacy to cut its burden of calculation; if the agencies refused to carry appeals from House cuts, the senators would have to do much more work than their busy schedules permit.

BUDGETARY GOALS

Possessing the greatest expertise and the largest numbers, working in the closest proximity to their policy problems and clientele groups, desirous of expanding their horizons, administrative agencies generate action through advocacy. But how much shall they ask for? Life would be simple if they could just estimate the costs of their ever-expanding needs and submit the total as their request. But if they ask for amounts much larger than the appropriating bodies believe are reasonable, the credibility of the agencies will suffer a drastic decline. In such circumstances, the reviewing organs are likely to apply a "measure of unrealism," with the result that the agency gets much less than it might have with a more moderate request. So the first decision rule is: Do not come in too high. Yet the agencies must also not come in too low, for the assumption is that if agency advocates do not ask for funds they do not need them. Since the budgetary situation is always tight, terribly tight, or impossibly tight, reviewing bodies are likely to accept a low request with thanks and not inquire too closely into the rationale. Given the distribution of roles, cuts must be expected and allowances made.

The agency decision rule might therefore read: Come in a little high (padding), but not too high (loss of confidence). But how high is too high? What agency heads do is to evaluate signals from the environment—last year's experience, legislative votes, executive policy statements, actions of clientele groups, reports from the field—and come up with an asking price somewhat higher than they expect to get.

The Bureau of the Budget in the United States takes on the assigned role of helping the president realize his goals when it can discover what they are supposed to be. This role is performed with a cutting bias, however, simply because the agencies normally push so hard in asking for funds. The bureau helps the president by making his preferences more widely known throughout the executive branch so that those who would like to go along have a chance to find out what is required of them. Since Congress usually cuts the president's budget, Bureau figures tend to be the most the agencies can get, especially when the items are not of such paramount importance as to justify intensive scrutiny by Congress. Yet the power of the purse remains actively with Congress. If the Budget Bureau continually recommended figures which were blatantly disregarded by Congress, the agencies would soon learn to pay less and less attention to the president's budget. As a result, the Bureau follows consistent congressional action; it can be shown empirically that the Bureau recommendations tend to follow congressional actions over a large number of cases.

In deciding how much money to recommend for specific purposes, the House Appropriations Committee breaks down into large autonomous subcommittees in which the norm of reciprocity is carefully followed. Specialization is carried further as subcommittee members develop limited areas of competence and jurisdiction. Budgeting is both incremental and fragmented as the committees deal with adjustments to the historical base of each agency. Sequential decision making is the rule as problems are first attacked in the jurisdiction in which they appear and then followed step-by-step as they manifest themselves elsewhere. The subcommittee members treat budgeting as a process of making marginal monetary adjustments to existing programs, rather than as a mechanism for reconsidering basic policy choices every year. Fragmentation and specialization are further increased through the appeals functions of the Senate Appropriations Committee, which deals with what has become (through House action) a fragment of a fragment. When the actions of subcommittees conflict, coordination may be achieved by repeated attacks on the problem or through reference to the House and Senate as a whole when the appropriations committees go beyond the informal zone of indifference set up by the more intense preferences of the membership. When one thinks of all the participants who are continually engaged in taking others into account, it is clear that a great many adjustments are made in the light of what others are likely to do.

BUDGETARY STRATEGIES

Having decided how much to ask for, agencies engage in strategic planning to secure their budgetary goals. Strategies are the links between the goals of the agencies and their perceptions of the kinds of actions which their political environment will make efficacious.

Budget officers in the U.S. national government uniformly believe that being a good politician—cultivating an active clientele, developing the confidence of other officials (particularly of the appropriations subcommittees), and using skill in following strategies that exploit opportunities—is more important in obtaining funds than demonstration of efficiency. Agencies seek to cultivate a clientele that will help them to expand and that will express satisfaction to other public officials. Top agency officials soon come to learn that the appropriations committees are very powerful; their recommendations are accepted approximately 90 per cent of the time. Since budgetary calculations are so complex, the legislators must take a good deal on faith. Hence their demand that agency budget officers demonstrate a high degree of integrity. If the appropriations committees believe that they have been misled, they can do grave damage to the career of the offending budgeting officer and to the prospects of the agency he represents. While doing a decent job may be a necessary condition for success, the importance of clientele and confidence are so great that all agencies employ these strategies.

In addition to these ubiquitous strategies there are contingent strategies which depend upon time, circumstance, and place. In defending the base, for example, cuts may be made in the most popular programs so that a public outcry results in restoration of the funds. The base may be increased within existing programs by shifting funds between categories. Substantial additions to the base may come about through proposing new programs to meet crises and through campaigns involving large doses of advertising and salesmanship. The dependence of these strategies on the incremental, increase-decrease type of budgetary calculation is evident. By helping determine the ways in which programs are perceived and evaluated, the forms of budgetary presentation may assume considerable importance.

Organizations wish to maintain themselves in their environment. For governmental agencies this can be taken to mean maintenance of political support from clientele groups and other governmental participants. We expect that policies are chosen not only because of any intrinsic merit but also because they add to, or at least do not seriously detract from, the necessary political support. The heads of agencies can expect to lose internal control, to be fired, to see their policies overturned, or even to find their organization dismembered if their recommendations are continually disapproved. They therefore seek to maintain a reasonable record of success (to guard their professional reputation, as Richard Neustadt put it) in order to maintain the confidence of the key people in and out of their agency. Thus, they are compelled to consider the probable actions of others differently situated who have a say in determining their income.

CASE REVIEW

The above case described a decisional process in which the participants operated in the context of overwhelming political, social, and fiscal calculations. Uncomplicated rational means-ends choices simply are not available. The sheer number of participants and their diverse policy and value orientations nullifies the possibility of efficient, apolitical, value-free choices. Time pressures are enormous, thus precluding the application of time-consuming, data-base methodologies.

What lessons might be drawn from this case whereby the political context precludes the application of rational methodologies? Again, there are both general and specific conclusions.[16]

General Thoughts

Complexity and Simplification

The case illustrates that although decisions are complex, they can be simplified in order to deal expeditiously with available choices. Thus aids to calculation are utilized. These aids are neither mysterious nor particularly rational. Sometimes the aid amounts to nothing more than what Thomas Schelling[17] has termed the "self-evident solution." Other examples such as rounding off, splitting differences down the middle, and making rough guesses are only examples of what people do everyday. Other aids such as basing complex choices on simpler items are well-worn rational surrogates.

Wildavsky has described the budgeting phenomenon in the context of a public choice model. The same factors operate in the private sector regarding budget and nonbudget decisions. For example, in evaluating personnel for promotions to more responsible positions, it is common practice to base promotions on past performance on less complex projects. In making space allocations there is an informal "divide the pie" kind of mentality. Budget disputes are often resolved by the time-honored, split-the-difference technique.

Incrementalism and Comprehensiveness

The pervasive phenomenon of incrementalism suggests that very little decision making occurs in the first place. This is not a facetious or a cute conclusion; it is a reality. For example, there is very little change or flexibility in the size and content of the budget from one year to the next. Mandatory expenditures, untouchable programs, fixed scales of increase, and prior commitments all are realities that reduce variation, new programs, new ideas, or decisions per se. In a sense the great bulk of decision making is completed before the process begins.

This notion of fixed or frozen methodologies is doubly disturbing when one considers the major criticism leveled at incrementalism. The criticism is that the incremental method (proceeding in bits and pieces) gives the decision maker only a small, narrow, parochial, and extremely limited view of the larger social good. That is, personal preferences, narrow constituencies, and limited programs all are considered; nowhere is the common good taken into account.

The criticism is met by the argument that there are natural checkpoints along the path of the fragmented, sequential process so that over time a natural built-in system of coordination and comprehensiveness occurs. Moreover, comprehensiveness is a rational goal that exists only in science fiction. That is, no system of decision making is perfect. But at least one approach, the incremental process, works. The question is, For whom?

Insiders, Outsiders, and the Fair Share

The case notes[18] that decisions are governed by an intangible but powerful "fair share" concept whereby each participant is awarded a proportional fair share of any increases or decreases in budget amount. Several significant points emerge.

The central intellectual assumption (or conclusion) is that budgeting is not merely a numbers game—that the process of budgeting transcends mathematical calculations and represents larger political/philosophical aspirations and factors. The fair share phenomenon represents a force that governs all products of the process—not just money matters but political hopes and dreams, raw power, and control. The rationality of the fair share means, for example, that only actual participants get a share, however fair. It also means that over time, especially with dwindling resources, a small share will proportionally become reduced, minuscule, and logically nonexistent. While this effect can be calculated in terms of mathematical factors, the effect is incalculable in terms of political realities and reactions.

Political Perspectives: Self and Others

"There's nothing wrong per se with politics," so goes the argument. "It occurs all the time, everywhere, in both the public *and* the private sector. What we need to do is understand it."[19] This essentially is the policy analysis school of thought, and it carries some merit.

The argument is that politics, particularly organizational politics, is an influential force in modern organizational life. Gary Wamsley and Mayer Zald have defined *politics*—in the economic context—as "the structure of authority and power and the dominant values, goals, and ethos institutionalized in that structure."[20] To be sure, this abstraction exists in institutional life, but it hardly provides a framework for understanding the day-to-day meaning of the word *politics*.

Another point of view is that organizational politics consists of the irrational influences on decision making in complex organizations. *Nonrational* in this sense refers to outcomes or goals sought by individual members that are different (not merely inconsistent) from those espoused by the organization as a whole.

Organizational politics may be viewed as those *processes* whereby interdependent individuals or groups exercise power in order to influence the goals, criteria, or processes of organizational decision making to advance their own interests. Note that this definition rests on a power model. This model is explained by Jeffrey Pfeffer who argues that "those interests, subunits, or individuals within the organization who possess the greatest power, will receive the greatest rewards from the interplay of organizational politics."[21] Power is thus seen not just as a variable but as the critical intervening variable between goals and outcomes. Note also that this definition does not view politics as bad or evil. Nor does this definition carry an inherently pejorative meaning. For example, an employee may engage in whistle-blowing in order simultaneously to protect the public against wasteful Pentagon expenditures and thereby protect himself in his professional career as an accountant. Nonetheless, it is clear that the political process introduces factors that are inherently different from the rational process. In part these factors or criteria are the differences between the microperspective (self-interested individuals or fragmented committees) and the larger macroperspective (commonwealth). The ethical implications, however, are broader.

Washing Up the Truth

A good deal of the literature and analysis of governmental processes in the United States is concerned with reform. This is seen in the recent emphasis on business integrity, legal reforms, and political accountability. The goals of the proposed reforms are stated in familiar normative terms: economy, efficiency, improvement, making things better, making institutions ethical.

Apologists for the present political model argue that we already have the best system; that the political process, while not utopia, is the best we can hope for. For example, Wildavsky writes:

> In appraising the budgetary process, we must deal with real men in the real world for whom the best they can get is to be preferred to the perfection they cannot achieve. Unwilling or unable to alter the basic features of the political system they seem to make it work for them. . . . rather than against them. . . . To argue that an existing order is "imperfect" in comparison with an alternative order of affairs that turns out, upon careful inspection, to be unobtainable may not be different from arguing that the existing order is "perfect."[22]

Political theorists and process apologists argue that the political system of incremental, ad hoc, experiential choices has inherent value and beauty, and that through an intricate system of carefully balanced pressures and checks the truth consistently filters up. Political detractors and natural theorists argue the opposite: that the noncomprehensive, self-interest model of decisions necessarily thwarts intelligent choices and stifles the greater good.

This poses the ethical question: Does the truth wash up, or is politics an inherently soiling process? Does self-interest result ultimately in the greater good, or does it lead to a distortion of social good? These questions cannot be answered in the abstract, and so we turn to specific criteria of analysis.

Specific Implications and Trends

Dual Realities: Public Goals — Actual Goals

The existence of political forces within rational frameworks illustrates a central tension: there are two realities. As in Middle Ages theology, there is a kind of "double truth." For example, most modern organizations (public or private) promulgate a public, formal statement that operates as the rational articulation of goals and guidelines. Whether it is called a "mission statement" or "plans for the future," most large organizations publicize highly rationalized sets of objectives. These represent the public face of the institution. For example, a public university may have as its mission statement the primary goal of providing general liberal arts education to urban youth. At the same time, this institution will have an actual agenda, perhaps focusing on activities that are very different from its formal public mission statement. In the actual agenda we may see a great and disproportionate percentage of operating budget costs directed to programs such as doctoral programs or big-time athletics.

In short there are dual realities. To the extent that the actual political agenda matches the public formal agenda, politics enhances or is consistent with rationality. To the extent there is conflict between the formal and the actual, other behavioral questions must be raised.

Careerism and Organizationalism

As the budgeting case stresses, a participant's perception of his role often *is* the decision. Perception is conditioned upon what crassly might be called *careerism*, that is, the impulse to move up the hierarchical ladder.

This raises an obvious but fundamental reality: decision making in an institution is affected by goals and preferences not held in common by all parts of the organization. Individual members behave in response to their immediate tasks and to organizational norms; but they also respond to personal career goals and personal preferences.

Individuals who seek to make "the best case" for their segment of the budget, and who are motivated to make the best case for their own career ambitions, arguably are not making the best case for the budget per se. If the budget process, or any other decisional process, is as complex as described, then there are many points of conflict, change, and pressure along the path to the best case. With such multiple opportunities, in a pressured situation at any moment, one's career motivation case may conflict with the organization's best case. Is there any doubt, given primary security motivations, which will be discarded?

Subunit Differentiation and Comprehensiveness

The genius of the modern organization is its ability to departmentalize and to specialize within a clearly defined hierarchical order of subordinates and superordinates.

Subunit differentiation refers to the organization's division of work into lower units or separate groups whose activities and objectives are centrally coordinated. Sometimes the coordination is formal (rational), sometimes informal (political). Because of the segmented nature of their tasks and because of specialist power bases, these subunits often differ and perhaps conflict on a number of important dimensions such as orientation toward time, adherence to organizational norms, use of language and other symbols, socialization, and commitment. These differences obviously can be a barrier to overall organizational goal accomplishment.

In the public sector this procedural problem of segmented units transforms into a substantive issue of the public interest. In the case of budgeting, for example, the conflict is between a partial view of the public interest versus a total view of the public interest. In short, in the public arena the issue of comprehensiveness is a substantive, normative, and perhaps ethical concern. The standard justifications for procedural differentiation are: man's inability to calculate the preferences of the whole; subunit specialization as being more efficient for resolving problems; and ultimate goal achievement based on firm political alliances as opposed to shaky formalistic arrangements. These arguments evaporate against the backdrop of the transcendent public interest. Procedural genius does not match substantive need. The gimmick is not equal to the goal.

Fragmentation and Coordination

Systematic, or procedural, fragmentation of task (for example, segmentation of activity into temporal and spatial factors) is, of course, a logical necessity. Very few tasks can be accomplished at one spot, in one moment. But as Wildavsky notes, the causal circumstances underlying fragmentation of effort are not necessarily or primarily procedural. The lack of coordination, he observes, is the result of conflicting values and viewpoints. This surely is accurate. The causal factors are political and derive from substantive conflicts—not neutral, value-free techniques. This is Wildavsky's important insight, and this is the nub of the problem.

Conflicting viewpoints mean, for example, that the budget will not be considered as a whole; it will be considered in bits and pieces; its component parts will not be formally related to one another; the process will operate in fits and starts. On the other hand, there are multiple viewpoints that can be expressed at multiple points of access; informal coordination through political logrolling does take place; and finally, vesting overall central power in a solo dictatorial-type decision maker is unwise.

But, again, the problem is deeper. The insight that fragmentation is the result of different political viewpoints suggests that over time these viewpoints will become encrusted, entrenched, and institutionalized. Ultimately the process (the subunit, the committee, the specialization, the aids) become *the* end. For example, in the U.S. Congress, the fragmented committee system is an end; it is a value in itself. Even if there were a substantive issue capable of comprehensive coordinated treatment, the institutionalized process would factor and fragment it.

Merits and Demerits

And so the question arises: should not strategies or decisions be based on merits rather than special interests? One response is that asking the participants to ignore their personal career needs is politically ridiculous. Moreover, it is argued these participants do believe, firmly and morally, that their subunit/career interest is deserving and is based on merit. Self-interest coincides with social interest, they argue.

Another response is that self-interest/careerism/subunit calculation disregards merits and aims instead at building coalitions and clientele. The long-run effect, it is argued, is corrosive. Literature, and life, is replete with examples of failed programs and inverted policies where the regulated become the regulators and the program administrator becomes the program recipient.

In short, it is petty, short-term, and marginal to suggest that presenting the best case is an aid to calculation for the other participants. To be sure, other participants in the process know they do not have to dig further to spot issues. And to be sure, other participants realize that calculation is not based on merits alone. But over time the process corrodes and cheapens. It violates the principle of principled decisions.

Secrecy and Bargaining

Wildavsky notes that the list of essentially deceitful practices that envelop the political process is seemingly endless. More generally bothersome is the notion that the strategies of budgeting (threats to cut the favorite program; withholding of key data) suggest a certain amount of trickery or duplicity.

As any marketing specialist might observe, these strategies are based on techniques of salesmanship, and they are evaluated (good or bad) on the basis of whether or not they are effective. Good programs in business or in government, the argument goes, cannot sell themselves. And so strategies and techniques of salesmanship are employed.

But there is another issue apart from the fact that salesmanship occurs and aside from the fact that it is unreasonable to expect program directors not to engage in strategies. The larger issue concerns secrecy, which is the context in which bargaining, logrolling, and compromise occur, especially in the public sector. As Pfeffer observes: if there is a very centralized, powerful authority, secrecy is not as necessary. "It is when there is dissensus and power is more dispersed that secrecy is required for the influentials to be able to make decisions they desire without arousing powerful opposition."[23] Based on the budgeting case, it is precisely because of the pluralistic, fragmented power system that bargaining and logrolling do occur. Secrecy thus emerges as a dynamic of its own; and the chemical reactions are significant.

Legitimacy and Covert Behavior

Secrecy is viewed as a dual process of submerging certain information and, at the same time, surfacing other information. It is a two-part process because government, while operating partly in secrecy, must at least give the *appearance* of doing something, and that something must be public, legitimate, and authoritative. This is the "goldfish" bowl problem referred to in administrative theory. The public sector lives under intense public scrutiny.[24] Herein lies the dualism: the pressures of secrecy complicated by the need to be open and public. This makes the important point that covert behavior alone is not sufficient. It must be balanced by overt legitimating devices. How does it work? That is, what is the "political" process of submerging certain information or values while simultaneously surfacing safe issues? Two examples are offered, each representing a different aspect of the two-part process.

Selectivity: The Use of Objective Criteria

Because modern organizations are departmentalized and because activities are specialized, different criteria are used to evaluate different programs. Hence subunits (and individuals and groups within subunits) will promote those criteria that are favorable to their interests. For example,

> [I]n universities, teaching faculty will emphasize the quality of teaching in decisions regarding the hiring of new members or the retention or promotion of existing members, whereas faculty primarily engaged in research will tend to push for the quality of publications and

research grants of a member in these decisions. Arguments around the criteria to be employed are likely to be particularly pronounced in decisions regarding the allocation of scarce resources. Therefore, persons, as individuals or members of subunits, are likely to determine first what criteria are likely to be most favorable to their position and then to use their influence to get others in the organization to accept them as legitimate in the decision process.[25]

As Robert H. Miles notes, this process is unobtrusive because there are a wide array of objective criteria that can be surfaced through legitimating techniques and public view processes. But this is only part of the explanation. The rest is that the actors are not proud of covert behaviors. Particularly in governmental agencies, obfuscation, secrecy, and "back-room politics" carry a pejorative connotation. This, in fact, may be the source of the negative view of politics. Consider in this context the importance of techniques that give the appearance of legitimacy.

Legitimation: Mobilizing Respectability and Acceptance

Opposition in a fragmented, politicized environment will not be overcome or neutralized unless dominant policies are perceived as legitimate. In fact, policies need not actually be legitimate. They may be based on selective use of objective data. Policies need only be *perceived* as legitimate. Thus, in the political process there is available a wide range of norms, attitudes, procedures, and resources that buttress the perception of legitimacy.[26]

One classic example is the pervasive use, in the business and government, of committees. As Miles notes, committees are frequently employed for the legitimating purpose,

> especially when the dominant coalition in the organization is strong enough to influence the decision outcome, because it is generally believed that participation of representatives of a variety of interest groups in decision making ensures that influence will be shared.[27]

The key characteristic of these ritualistic legitimating devices is that they are instruments of the dominant faction.

These are hardly profound insights. The inversion of means and ends is known to theorists as well as to practitioners.[28] The enduring, troublesome issue is, Does the process make sense and in what terms?

Some would argue that the political process, while violative of certain norms, is nonetheless highly rational, and therefore the process should be nurtured and expanded, not criticized.

Congruence of Goals: Political Is Rational

To the extent that political decision making is consistent with rational decision making, politics is eufunctional. For example, if one's self-interest career goals are in perfect congruence with the organization's rational goals, politics is recognized as good, as positive, and as valuable.

In this context politics is viewed as not necessarily evil. The process is said to have both eufunctional and dysfunctional results. If the survival of an organization depends on the wheeler-dealer abilities of its sales staff, politics is viewed as a positive force. Likewise, if the successful implementation of a government program depends on the coalition-building skills of a self-interested career employee, politics in the limited sense is not bad.[29]

CONCLUSION

A major thesis of this work is that politics is a decisional process to be evaluated in the context of a variety of factors. The elements of the political process have been outlined and considered above. The process must now be reconsidered in its nonpure, applied form. The inquiry in Chapter Four was concerned with the functions and consequences of the political process model in its actual operation and the focus was on a case of decision making in a political environment. Most theoreticians conclude that this "political" approach generally is eufunctional and practicable. Is it?

The next chapter explores the counterpoint: the notion that in actual operation the political model is more accurately an administrative model of feasibility. As such the administrative models assume a less desirable set of characteristics and results in decisions which are not only disjointed but sometimes disastrous.

NOTES

1. One of the central assumptions of this work is that the terms *private sector* and *public sector* are artificial constructs, figments of the imagination, that do little to explain or help understand the important

interactions between and within institutions, corporations, and agencies, which comprise a mix of government and nongovernment activities and resources.

2. The term *organization* refers to a structure (it may be public or private) wherein there is a planned activity of two or more people in order to achieve common and explicit goal(s) through division of labor and according to hierarchical authority systems of superordinate and subordinate relationships.

3. Fredric H. Genck, "Public Management in America," *AACSB Bulletin* (April 1973): 6. This is a generally accepted, although not inclusive, set of activities.

4. Michael A. Murray, "Comparing Public and Private Management," in *Public Management: Public and Private Perspectives*, ed. James L. Perry and Kenneth L. Kramer (Palo Alto, Calif.: Mayfield, 1983). In this work the writer has discredited the assumption that there is a clear or meaningful difference between the public and private sectors.

5. Note the word *pure* refers not to a value-free or perfect or ideal form but to a theoretically sound approach. The *applied*, or *impure*, forms refers to the pure model in its distorted or modified form.

6. Murray, "Comparing Public and Private Management."

7. John Dewey, *The Public and Its Problems* (New York: Holt and Co. 1927), p. 15–16.

8. Ibid., p. 15.

9. Sociobiology (studying behavior from a biological basis) in primate research attempts to measure mathematically the number of interactions between members of primate groupings and the spatial distances between age group and sex group in order to determine leadership, authority, affection, and other qualities.

10. Woodrow Wilson, "The Study of Administration," *Political Science Quarterly*, June 1887, pp. 197–222.

11. W. Jethro Brown, *The Austinian Theory of Law*, (London: John Murray, 1920). Analytical positivism, the conceptual framework for positive law, was developed by John Austin, a nineteenth century Englishman. Positivism in administrative law consists of (1) a rule (2) from a political authority (3) with official sanctions.

12. Norton E. Long, "Public Policy and Administration: The Goals of Rationality and Responsibility," *Public Administration Review* 14, no. 1 (Winter 1954): 22.

13. Charles Lindblom, "The Science of Muddling Through," *Public Administration Review*, 19, no.2 (Spring 1959): 79–80. (No doubt the point was expressed before 1959, but until this article the point was expressly not articulated.

14. Ibid., p. 88. Note that Lindblom's analysis devastates Wilson's original legalistic distinctions between policy and administration (or value and fact). Writing in *Public Administration Review* in November-December 1979, pp. 517−26, "Still Muddling, Not Yet Through," Lindblom observed that it is difficult for many political leaders, and for ordinary citizens as well, to open their minds to the possibility that the American Constitution, with its many curbs on the popular will, including the Fourteenth Amendment's guarantees to corporations, is not an adequate set of rules for coping with our current problems.

15. Not all or even most nonquantitative theorists present their work from an advocacy position. As Charles Lindblom wrote in 1958 in "Policy Analysis," *American Economic Review* 48 (June 1958): 299−312: "In seeking to formalize some of our methods of policy analysis, this paper is one of *a growing family of ventures into clarification of nonquantitative and largely nontheoretical methods*. One noteworthy characteristic of these studies is that they are not argumentative: they do not urge this or that method upon social scientists; they merely make explicit and formalize the methods already in use" (p. 299, emphasis added).

16. This portion of the analysis is based partly on Aaron Wildavsky's expanded work: *The Politics of the Budgetary Process*, 2d ed. (Boston: Little, Brown, 1964).

17. Thomas C. Schelling, *Arms and Influence* (New Haven, Conn.: Yale University Press, 1966). The example of two stranded boaters separated on an ocean island is offered as one common example. Assuming a low hill in the middle of the island, the self-evident choice is for each searcher to move independently toward the top of the hill or rise, in order to meet up with the other.

18. Richard J. Stillman II, *Public Administration: Concepts and Cases* (Boston: Houghton-Mifflin, 1974), chap. 11, pp. 245−46.

19. This refrain is heard especially in business management classes, which attempt to introduce the realities of political variables into organizational theory.

20. Gary L. Wamsley and Mayer N. Zald, *The Political Economy of Public Organizations* (Lexington, Mass.: Lexington Books, 1973).

21. Jeffrey Pfeffer, *Power in Organizations* (Boston: Pitman, 1981), p. 28.

22. Wildavsky, *Politics of the Budgetary Process*, p. 128.

23. Jeffrey Pfeffer, "Power and Resource Allocation in Organizations," *New Directions in Organizational Behavior*, ed. Barry M. Staw and Gerald R. Salanzik (Chicago: St. Clair Press, 1977), pp. 235−66.

24. Scrutiny is becoming more intense as evidenced by statutory trends. Note the Freedom of Information Act (1966) US Code 1976 Title 5

sec. 552; PL 89−554, 80 Stat. 378, sec. 1. and the Government in the Sunshine Act (1976). US Code 1976 Title 5 sec. 552 b; Sept. 13, 1976, P.L. 94−409, 90 Stat. 1241.

25. Robert H. Miles, *Macro Organizational Behavior* (Santa Monica: Goodyear, 1980) Again these sections draw heavily from Pfeffer, *Power in Organizations* and from the earlier seminal work by Peter Bachrach and Morton S. Baratz, "Two Faces of Power," *American Political Science Review*, (December 1962), pp. 948−50.

26. Bachrach and Baratz, ("Two Faces of Power") identified a number of "biases" that can be mobilized to give the appearance of legitimate decision making. These include safe "technical" issues, legalistic rituals, incremental adjustments, fiscal propriety as a norm, and so on.

27. Robert H. Miles, *Macro Organizational Behavior*, p. 163.

28. In the context of this case the term "means" refers to: law, ritual and committees; and the term "ends" refers to: legitimacy, authority and values.

29. George Stigler, *The Citizen and the State* (Chicago: University of Chicago Press, 1982).

'What is that noise?'
   The wind under the door.
'What is that noise now? What is the wind doing?'
   Nothing again nothing.

                                              'Do
'You know nothing? Do you see nothing? Do you remember Nothing?'

                                            T. S. Eliot
                                      "The Wasteland"

CHAPTER FIVE

ADMINISTRATIVE MODELS

DEFINITIONS AND CONCEPTS

Policy analysts argue that the encroachment of economic theory (and financial values and data) into such inherently political processes as budget making is the consequence of a vacuum in political theory into which economic notions of expediency and efficiency have moved.[1] That is, no matter how rational political choice judgements are, they resist legitimacy and acceptability because of the lack of theory.[2]

The Screening Model

One way to understand political environments, institutions, and factors is to view politics not only as a process but as a result.[3] That is, politics or political decisions are the product of a clearly definable screening process that is only partly political in makeup. This screening process, which is common to decision making in business, as well as in government, might be referred to as the *administrative model*. This terminology flows from the basic assumption that the transcendant activity in modern organized life is administrative and that politics represents only another important administrative force to consider.

For example, whether broadly social or narrowly organizational, policy formation has been viewed in one of two ways: (1) as a rational decisional model of problem solving whereby programs are derived from an analysis of causation and change processes or (2) as a political process model whereby the authoritative institutions of a society (or an organization) identify problems, select preferred problem-solving approaches from among several available alternatives, formulate a problem definition to rationalize these programs and then administer resources for the implementation of these preferred program modes.

The key difference between the rational model and the political model is in the sequence of steps. Rational approaches derive solutions from underlying problems. Prior causal analysis defines the problem to be addressed. Political models first select preferred problem-solving approaches. Subsequently, the problem solver crystalizes a "problem definition" to justify the programs.

It is in this procedurally characteristic sequence that political models and rational models differ. As noted, in content or in substance, political *is* rational and vice versa. For example, it is highly rational behavior to consider political realities and to calculate optimum choices based on political variables. Likewise, using rational (read *hard*) data to justify political goals is intelligent behavior.

Nevertheless, despite apparent consistent rationality there is an inherent lack of logical integrity in the political model.[4] As a problem-solving approach becomes adopted as the basis for policy (whether governmental or corporate or other), the model undergoes a screening process whereby it is adapted to the various financial, social, racial, psychological, and administrative interests on which it impinges. That is to say, just as the rational model is not purely rational (that is, it involves necessarily political factors), so, too, the political model is not purely political.[5] It is more properly an administrative model or a profile of feasibility. In the process of adjusting to these administrative factors, the political model tends to lose its initial character as an internally rational, logically consistent framework. In reality the political model assumes the features of a disjointed, pragmatic profile of feasibility.[6]

Administrative Factors Defined

How specifically does a political model, with its elements of rationality, differ from an administrative model and its framework of feasibility? Is not

Definitions and Concepts 131

workability the same as rationality? Is it not rational to be practical? In one sense the answer is yes: paying heed to, and taking into consideration, administrative factors that infringe on a policy choice is smart, intelligent, necessary, and therefore rational.

In another sense, however, practicality allows no choice, no deliberation, and no calculation. In the context of feasibility, factors and forces exist that themselves determine choice. It is like a runaway train whose fate is governed no longer by the rational mind of the engineer and his manipulations of the internal machinery. Suddenly the train is controlled or affected by forces in place and in a sense beyond calculation: the grade of the track, the force of quality, the size of the engine, the direction of the wind.

Consequently, in looking at the political model it is not particularly useful to look at individual preference factors (careerism, calculation, coalition building, personal ideology). These are factors, but they are not the only or even the most important factors. Inherently, of course, they are rational factors, however irrationally applied.

More importantly, there are forces beyond logic—administrative factors compelled by practicality to reach an end result. Since what is practical may not be that which is desired, the results may be disastrous. But first the elements.

History as an Administrative Factor

Political pundits quip that the presence of a historian should be an absolute prerequisite for any federally funded program. That is, no matter the field (health, engineering, space, military) a historian should be an essential element in the workup of the program proposal and in the implementation of the project. While the idea may sound tongue-in-check, it is not entirely facetious. Very few programs lack histories. Very few disciplines do not have antecedents. Very few ideas lack precedents.

History and historical data and realities are present forces. When one seeks to implement a project or a program, one encounters historical realities, forces, and combinations presently in place. The past is the present, and thus these historical forces bear on present realities as much as commonly considered administrative factors such as financing, management, institutional structure, and span of control.

The important question is, What is History? That is, what should one look to, to discover significant historical forces that may impinge on a project or on a problem-solving activity?

In seeking to answer the question What is History? a noted historian wrote:

> Our answer, consciously or unconsciously, reflects our own position in time, and forms part of our answer to the broader question, what view we take of the society in which we live.[7]

In a word, history is an organic (that is, living) phenomenon. Its organic features are what make history different from other phenomena (for example, economic, political, legal) that are impacted by history. In this regard it should be noted that history is different from precedent. The latter, so important to legal, analytical processes, is not history but fact. Edward Hallett Carr answered the question What is History? by noting: "It is a continuing process of interaction between the historian and his facts, an unending dialogue between the present and past."[8] Thus the legalist or jurist may interact with history via legal precedents. But note that it is the substance of history and not the fact of precedent that guides.[9] Precedence becomes an analytical device for revealing the historical impulse.

Likewise, rational decisions are founded to some extent in historical forces. Rationality is derivative; the goal is produced by a prior reality. The rational objective departs from a given base. Rationality does not exist in the abstract.

Ideology as a Guiding Hand

In addition to historical forces, there may be a psychic necessity for taking action for doing something or for deciding a matter a certain way. To a degree this compulsion is rooted in the deep recesses of norm, character, culture, and personality. At another level, however, decision making is simply the product of ideology, that is, the outcome of political ideas in a society. Ideology or political ideas are not to be confused with the political process that is governed by small-case *politics*: careerism, incrementalism, self-interest, factionalism, coalition building, and elections. Ideology is political ideas writ large; ideology transcends one's self. Daniel Bell would argue that ideology is dead. By this he presumably means that social theories about America are inadequate in today's world.[10] In one sense Bell may be correct: because of profound civic illiteracy political theory may be unachievable. Political theory may be exhausted and diluted. But ideology as common sense—not as intellectual idealism nor as deterministic

tic theory—is not dead. That is, people naturally will make decisions, especially about important matters, by going back to the basics: love, beauty, truth, equity. One's adherence to, or deviation from, these basics is a standard intellectual reference point. Ideology, or the application of common sense maxims of right and wrong, thus becomes a serious consideration in analyzing anyone's decision—and especially in analyzing administrative/political decisions.

Race and Class: Particular Status Considerations

In the United States, particularly with regard to public policy decisions, the dual elements of race and class provide a self-generating force for decisions. Race and class may be merging (or blurring) in social life; but, nonetheless, a status factor exists whereby political power and therefore choice is correlated with race/class positions.

For example, decisions that cut against a society's norm (imprisonment, the death penalty) are apparently acceptable (and even defined) in the context of social (race/class) status.[11] This is not accidental. Race and class in America define social and political position. For instance, those characteristics define one's place in policy decisions. Thus coal miners will be treated one way by administrations; state legislators will be treated another way.

Sometimes the administrative model may lead to incompetence or to the lack of coordination or to unethical choices. It is important to note, however, that the shortcomings are not primarily or solely due to politics or simply to procedures. Failures and breakdowns are due to administrative choices that in turn are derived from the larger forces of historical determinism, ideological framework, and race/class status.[12]

CASE IN POINT

Administrative Models: The Politics of Getting Something Done

The following case describes in overwhelming necessary detail the bureaucratic obstacles to achieving simple policy goals. The administrative world is a complicated place. The following case study provides a blow-by-blow description of the administrative realities of history, ideology, and status factors.

THE CASE: THE BLAST IN CENTRALIA NO. 5: A MINE DISASTER NO ONE STOPPED

Already the crowd had gathered. Cars clogged the short, black rock road from the highway to the mine, cars bearing curious spectators and relative and friends of the men entombed. State troopers and deputy sheriffs and the prosecuting attorney came, and officials from the company, the Federal Bureau of Mines, the Illinois Department of Mines and Minerals. Ambulances arrived, and doctors and nurses and Red Cross workers and soldiers with stretchers from Scott Field. Mine rescue teams came, and a federal rescue unit, experts burdened with masks and oxygen tanks and other awkward paraphernalia of disaster.

One hundred and eleven men were killed in that explosion. Killed needlessly, for almost everybody concerned had known for months, even years, that the mine was dangerous. Yet nobody had done anything effective about it. Why not? Let us examine the background of the explosion. Let us study the mine and the miners . . . and also the numerous people who might have saved the miners' lives but did not. The miners had appealed in various directions for help but got none, not from their state government not their federal government nor their employer nor their own union. (In threading the maze of officialdom we must bear in mind four agencies in authority: The State of Illinois, the United States Government, the Centralia Coal Company, and the United Mine Workers of America, that is, the UMWA of John L. Lewis.) Let us seek to fix responsibility for the disaster. . . .

The Centralia Mine No. 5 was opened two miles south of Centralia in 1907. Because of its age, its maze of underground workings is extensive, covering perhaps six square miles, but it is regarded as a medium-small mine since it employs but 250 men and produces but 2,000 tons of coal daily. It was owned by the Centralia Coal Company, an appendage of the Bell & Zoller empire, one of the Big Six among Illinois coal operators . . . The Bell & Zoller home office was in Chicago (most of the big coal operators' home offices

---

John Bartlow Martin, "The Blast in Centralia No. 5: A Mine Disaster No One Stopped," *Harper's Magazine*, March 1948, pp. 193–220. Copyright © by John Bartlow Martin. Copyright renewed 1975 by John Bartlow Martin.

are in Chicago or St. Louis); no Bell & Zoller officers or directors lived at Centralia.

There are in coal mines two main explosion hazards—coal dust and gas. Coal dust is unhealthy to breathe and highly explosive. Some of the dust raised by machines in cutting and loading coal stays in suspension in the air. Some subsides to the floor and walls of the tunnels, and a local explosion will kick it back into the air where it will explode and, in turn, throw more dust into the air, which will explode; and as this chain reaction continues the explosion will propagate throughout the mine or until it reaches something that will stop it.

The best method of stopping it, a method in use for some twenty-five years, is rock dusting. Rock dusting is simply applying pulverized stone to the walls and roof of the passageways; when a local explosion occurs it will throw a cloud of rock dust into the air along with the coal dust, and since rock dust is incombustible the explosion will die. Rock dusting will not prevent an explosion but it will localize one. Illinois law requires rock dusting in a dangerously dusty mine. Authorities disagreed as to whether the Centralia mine was gassy but everyone agreed it was exceedingly dry and dusty. The men who worked in it had been complaining about the dust for a long time—one recalls "the dust was over your shoe tops," another that "I used to cough up chunks of coal dust like walnuts after work"—and indeed by 1944, more than two years before the disaster, so widespread had dissatisfaction become that William Rowekamp, as recording secretary of Local Union 52, prepared an official complaint. But even earlier, both state and federal inspectors had recognized the danger.

Let us trace the history of these warnings of disaster to come. For in the end it was this dust which did explode and kill one hundred and eleven men, and seldom has a major catastrophe of any kind been blueprinted so accurately so far in advance.

Driscoll O. Scanlan was appointed one of 16 Illinois state mine inspectors by Governor Green upon recommendation of the state representative from Scanlan's district. Speaking broadly, the job of a state inspector is to police the mine operators—to see that they comply with the state mining law, including its numerous safety provisions. But an inspector's job is a political partronage job. Coal has always been deeply enmeshed in Illinois politics.

Dwight H. Green, running for Governor the preceding fall, had promised the miners that he would enforce the mining laws "to the letter of the law," and however far below this lofty aim his administration fell (as we shall see), Scanlan apparently took the promise literally. Scanlan is a stubborn, righteous, zealous man of fierce integrity. Other inspectors, arriving to inspect a mine, would go into the office and chat with the company officials. Not Scanlan; he waited outside, and down in the mine he talked with the miners, not the bosses. Other inspectors, emerging, would write their reports in the company office at the company typewriter. Not Scanlan, he wrote on a portable in his car. Widespread rumor had it that some inspectors spent most of their inspection visits drinking amiably with company officials in the hotel in town. Not Scanlan. Other inspectors wrote the briefest reports possible, making few recommendations and enumerating only major violations of the mining law. Scanlan's reports were longer than any others (owing in part to a prolix prose style), he listed every violation however minor and he made numerous recommendations for improvements even though they were not explicitly required by law.

Scanlan came to consider the Centralia No. 5 mine the worst in his district. In his first report on it he made numerous recommendations, including these: "That haulage roads be cleaned and sprinkled. . . . That tamping of shots with coal dust be discontinued and that clay be used." Remember those criticisms, for they were made February 7, 1942, more than five years before the mine blew up as a result (at least in part) of those very malpractices.

Every three months throughout 1942, 1943, and 1944 Scanlan inspected the mine and repeated his recommendations, adding new ones: "That the mine be sufficiently rock dusted." And what became of his reports? He mailed them to the Department of Mines and Minerals at Springfield, the agency which supervises coal mines and miners. In theory, the Mining Board makes policy to implement the mining law, the Director executes its dictates; in practice, the Director possesses considerable discretionary power of his own.

In 1941 Governor Green appointed as Director Robert M. Medill, a genial, paunchy, red-faced man of about sixty-five. Medill had gone to work in a mine at sixteen; he rose rapidly in management. He had a talent for making money and he enjoyed spending it. He entered Republican politics in 1920, served a few years as director of the Department of Mines and Minerals, then returned to business (mostly managing mines); and then, after working for Green's election in 1940, was rewarded once more with the directorship. Green reappointed him in 1944 with, says Medill, the approval of "a multitude of bankers and business men all over the state. And miners. I had the endorsement of all four factions." By this he means the United Mine Workers and its smaller rival, the Progressive Mine Workers, and the two associations of big and little operators; to obtain the endorsement of all four of these jealous, power-seeking groups is no small feat.

To Medill's department, then, came Driscoll Scanlan's inspection reports on Centralia Mine No. 5. Medill, however, did not see the first thirteen reports (1942–1944); they were handled as "routine" by Robert Weir, an unimaginative, harassed little man who had come up through the ranks of the miners' union and on recommendation of the union had been appointed Assistant Director of the Department by Green (at $4,000 a year, now $5,200). When the mail brought an inspector's report, it went first to Medill's secretary who shared the office next to Medill's with Weir. She stamped the report (with date of receipt) . . . and put it on Weir's desk. Sometimes, but by no means always, Weir read the report. He gave it to one of half-dozen girl typists in the large outer office. She edited the inspector's recommendations for errors in grammar and spelling, and incorporated them into a form letter to the owner of the mine, closing:

> The Department endorses the recommendations made by Inspector Scanlan and requests that you comply with same.
> Will you please advise the Department upon the completion of the recommendations set forth above?
> Thanking you . . .

When the typist placed this letter upon his desk, Weir signed it and it was mailed to the mine operator.

But the Centralia company did not comply with the major recommendations Scanlan made. In fact, it did not even both to answer Weir's thirteen letters based on Scanlan's reports. And Weir did nothing about this. Once, early in the game, Weir considered the dusty condition of the mine so serious that he requested the company [inspect] it within ten days; but there is no evidence that the company even replied.

This continued for nearly three years. And during the same period the federal government entered the picture. In 1941 Congress authorized the U.S. Bureau of Mines to make periodic inspections of coal mines. But the federal government had no enforcement power whatever, the inspections served only research. The first federal inspection of Centralia Mine No. 5 was made in September of 1942. In general, the federal recommendations duplicated Scanlan's—rock dusting, improving ventilation, wetting the coal to reduce dust—and the federal inspectors noted that "coal dust . . . at this mine is highly explosive, and would readily propagate an explosion." In all, they made 106 recommendations, including 33 "major" ones (a government official has defined a "major" hazard as one that "could . . . result in a disaster"). Four months passed before a copy of this report filtered through the administrative machinery at Washington and reached the Illinois Department at Springfield, but this mattered little: the Department did nothing anyway. Subsequent federal reports in 1943 and 1944 showed that the "major" recommendations had not been complied with. The federal bureau lacked the power to force compliance; the Illinois Department possessed the power but failed to act.

What of the men working in the mine during these three years? On November 4, 1944, on instructions from Local 52 at Centralia, William Rowekamp, the recording secretary, composed a letter to Medill: "At the present the condition of those roadways are very dirty and dusty . . . they are getting dangerous. . . . But the Coal Co. has ignored [Scanlan's recommendations]. And we beg your prompt action on this matter."

The Department received this letter November 6, and four days later Weir sent Inspector Scanlan to investigate. Scanlan reported immediately:

> The haulage roads in this mine are awful dusty, and much dust is kept in suspension all day. . . . The miners have complained to me . . . and I have wrote it up pretty strong on my inspection reports. . . . But to date they have not done any adequate sprinkling. . . . Today . . . [Superintendent Norman] Prudent said he would fix the water tank and sprinkle the roads within a week, said that he would have had this work done sooner, but that they have 20 to 30 men absent each day.

At any rate, Rowekamp's complaint got results. On December 2, 1944, he wrote Scanlan: "Well I am proud to tell you that they have sprinkled the 18th North Entry & 21st So. Entry and the main

The Case: The Blast in Centralia No. 5

haulage road. . . . Myself and the Members of Local Union appreciate it very much what you have done for us." It is apparent from this first direct move by Local 52 that Scanlan was working pretty closely with the Local to get something done.

But by the end of that month, December 1944, the mine once more had become so dirty that Scanlan ended his regular inspection report, "[i]f necessary the mine should discontinue hoisting coal for a few days until the [cleanup] work can be done." But all Weir said to the company was the routine "The Department endorses . . . "

Early in 1945 it appeared that something might be accomplished. Scanlan, emerging from his regular inspection, took the unusual step of telephoning Medill at Springfield. Medill told him to write him a letter so Scanlan did:

> The haulage roads in this mine are in a terrible condition. If a person did not see it he would not believe. . . . Two months ago . . . the local officers [of Local Union 52] told me that . . . if [the mine manager] did not clean the mine up they were going to prefer charges against him before the mining board and have his certificate canceled. I talked them out of it and told them I thought we could get them to clean up the mine. But on this inspection I find that practically nothing has been done. . . . The mine should discontinue hoisting coal . . . until the mine is placed in a safe condition. . . . The coal dust in this mine is highly explosive. . . .

This stiff letter was duly stamped "Received" at Springfield on February 23, 1945. A few days earlier a bad report had come in from Federal Inspector Perz. And now at last Medill himself entered the picture. What did he do? The Superintendent at Centralia had told Scanlan that, in order to clean up the mine, he would have to stop producing coal, a step he was not empowered to take. So Medill bypassed him, forwarding Scanlan's letter and report to William P. Young, Bell & Zoller's operating vice-president at Chicago: "Dear Bill . . . Please let me have any comments you wish to make. . . . Very kindest personal regards." From his quiet, well-furnished office near the top of the Bell Building overlooking Michigan Avenue, Young replied immediately to "Dear Bob" (Medill): "As you know we have been working under a very severe handicap for the past months. The war demand for coal . . . we are short of men. . . . I am hopeful that the urgent demand of coal will ease up in another month so that we may have available both the time and labor to give proper attention to the recommendations of Inspector Scanlan. With kindest personal regards. . . . "

A week later, on March 7, 1945, Medill forwarded copies of this correspondence to Scanlan, adding: "I also talked with Mr. Young on the phone, and I feel quite sure that he is ready and willing. . . . I would suggest that you ask the mine committee [of Local 52] to be patient a little longer, inasmuch as the coal is badly needed at this time."

On the first of April the president of Local Union 52 asked Scanlan to attend the Local's meeting on April 4. The miners complained that the company had not cleaned up the mine and, further, that one of the face bosses, or foreman, had fired explosive charges while the entire shift of men was in the mine. There can be little doubt that to fire explosives on-shift in a mine so dusty was to invite trouble—in fact, this turned out to be what later caused the disaster—and now in April 1945 the union filed charges against Mine Manager Brown, asking the State Mining Board to revoke his certificate of competency (this would cost him his job and prevent his getting another in Illinois as a mine manager). Rowekamp wrote up the charges: "And being the Mine is so dry and dusty it could of caused an explosion . . . "

Weir went to Centralia on April 17, 1945, but only to investigate the charges against Brown, not to inquire into the condition of the mine. He told the miners they should have taken their charges to the state's attorney. Nearly a month passed before, on May 11, Weir wrote a memorandum to the Mining Board saying that the company's superintendent had admitted the shots had been fired on-shift but that this was done "in an emergency" and it wouldn't happen again; and the Board refused to revoke Manager Brown's certificate.

Meanwhile, on April 12 and 13, Scanlan had made his regular inspection and found conditions worse than in February. He told the Superintendent: "Now, Norman, you claim Chicago won't give you the time to shut your mine down and clean it up. Now, I am going to get you some time," and he gave him the choice of shutting the mine down completely or spending three days a week cleaning up. The Superintendent, he said, replied that he didn't know, he'd have to "contact Chicago," but Scanlan replied: "I can't possibly wait for you to contact Chicago. It is about time that you fellows who operate the mines get big enough to operate your mines without contacting Chicago." So on Scanlan's recommendation the mine produced coal only four days a week and spent the remaining days cleaning up. For a time Scanlan was well satisfied with the results, but by June 25 he was again reporting excessive dust and Federal Inspector Perz was concurring: "No means are used to allay the dust." Following his October inspection Scanlan once more was moved to write a letter to Medill; but the only result was another routine letter from Weir to the company, unanswered.

Now, one must understand that, to be effective, both rock dusting and cleanup work must be maintained continuously. They were not at Centralia No. 5. By December of 1945 matters again came to a head. Scanlan wrote to Medill, saying that Local 52 wanted a sprinkling system installed to wet the coal, that Mine Manager Brown had said he could not order so "unusual" an expenditure, and that Brown's superior, Superintendent Prudent, "would not talk to me about it, walked away and left me standing." And Local 52 again attempted to take matters into its own hands. At a special meeting on December 12 the membership voted to prefer charges against both Mine Manager Brown and Superintendent Prudent. Rowekamp's official charge, typed on stationary of the Local, was followed next day by a letter, written in longhand on two sheets of dime-store notepaper, and signed by 28 miners. . . . At Springfield this communication too was duly stamped "Received." And another Scanlan report arrived.

Confronted with so many documents, Medill called a meeting of the Mining Board on December 21. Moreover, he called Scanlan to Springfield and told him to go early to the Leland Hotel, the gathering place of Republican politicians, and see Ben H. Schull, a coal operator and one of the operators' two men on the Mining Board. But when the Mining Board met in Medill's inner office, Scanlan was not called before it though he waited all day, and after the meeting he was told that the Board was appointing a special commission to go to Centralia and investigate.

On this commission were Weir, two state inspectors, and two members of the Mining Board itself, Schull and Murrell Reak. Reak, a miner himself, represented the United Mine Workers of America on the Mining Board.

The commission had before it a letter from Superintendent Prudent and Manager Brown setting forth in detail the company's "absentee experience" and concluding with a veiled suggestion that the mine might be forced to close for good (once before, according to an inspector, the same company had abandoned a mine rather than go to the expense entailed in an inspector's safety recommendation).

Weir wrote to Prudent, notifying him that the commission would visit Centralia on December 28 to investigate the charges against him and Brown; Medill wrote to the company's vice-president, Young, at Chicago ("You are being notified of this date so that you will have an opportunity to be present or designate some member of your staff to be present"); but Medill only told Rowekamp, "The committee has been appointed and after the investigation you will be advised of their findings and the action of the board"—he did not tell the Local when the commission would visit Centralia nor offer it opportunity to prove its charges.

Prudent—remember, the commission was investigating charges against Prudent—led the commission through the mine. Rowekamp says, "They didn't see nothing. They didn't get back in the buggy runs where the dust was the worst; they stayed on the mainline." Even there they rode, they did not walk through the dust. Riding in a mine car, one must keep one's head down. On January 22, 1946, Medill replied: the Mining Board, adopting the views of the special commission, had found "insufficient evidence" to revoke the certificates of Prudent and Brown.

He did not elaborate. Next day, however, he sent to Scanlan a copy of the commission's report. It listed several important violations of the mining law.

The miners at Centralia were not satisfied. "It come up at the meeting," Rowekamp recalls. They wanted to do something. But what? The state had rebuffed them. Well, why did they not go now to the higher officials of their own union, the UMWA? Why not to John L. Lewis himself?

One of them has said, "You have to go through the real procedure to get to the right man, you got to start at the bottom and start climbing up, you see? If we write to Lewis, he'll refer us right back to Spud White." Spud White is Hugh White, the thick-necked president of the UMWA in Illinois (District 12), appointed by Lewis.

Evidently the perplexed miners at Centralia already had appealed to District 12 for help, that is to White. Jack Ripon, the bulky vice-president of District 12 and White's right-hand man, said recently, "We heard there'd been complaints but we couldn't do a thing about it; it was up to the Mining Department to take care of it."

And yet in the past the UMWA has stepped in when the state failed to act. One unionist has said, "White could have closed that mine in twenty-four hours. All he'd have to do was call up Medill and tell him he was going to pull every miner in the state if they didn't clean it up. It's the union's basic responsibility—if you don't protect

The Case: The Blast in Centralia No. 5

your own wife and daughter, your neighbor down the street's not going to do it."

Perhaps the miners of Local 52 knew they must go it alone. They continued to address their official complaints to the State of Illinois. No answer. And so the members of Local 52 instructed Rowekamp to write to higher authority, to their Governor, Dwight H. Green.

It was a two-page letter saying, in part:

Dear Governor Green:

We, the officers of Local Union No. 52, U.M.W.A., have been instructed by the members . . . to write to you in protest against the negligence and unfair practices of your department of mines and minerals. . . . we want you to know that this is not a protest against Mr. Driscoll Scanlan . . . the best inspector that ever came to our mine. . . . But your mining board will not let him enforce the law or take the necessary action to protect our lives and health. This protest is against the men above Mr. Scanlan in your department of mines and minerals. In fact, Governor Green, this a plea to you, to please save our lives, to please make the department of mines and minerals enforce the laws at the No. 5 mine of the Centralia Coal Co. . . . before we have a dust explosion at this mine like just happened in Kentucky and West Virginia. For the last couple of years the policy of the department of mines and minerals toward us has been one of ignoring us. [The letter then recited the story of the useless special commission.] We are writing you, Governor Green, because we believed you want to give the people an honest administration and that you do not know how unfair your mining department is toward the men in this mine. Several years ago after a disaster at Gillespie we seen your pictures in the papers going down in the mine to make a personal investigation of the accident. We are giving you a chance to correct the conditions at this time that may cause a much worse disaster. . . . We will appreciate an early personal reply from you, stating your position in regard to the above and the enforcement of the state mining laws.

The letter closed "Very respectfully yours" and was signed by Jake Schmidt, president; Rowekamp, recording secretary; and Thomas Bush and Elmer Moss, mine committee. Today, of these, only Rowekamp is alive; all the others were killed in the disaster they foretold.

And now let us trace the remarkable course of this letter at Springfield. It was stamped in the red ink "Received March 9, 1946, Governor's Office." In his ornate thick-carpeted offices, Governor Green has three male secretaries (each of whom in turn has a secretary) and it was one of these, John William Chapman, that the "save our lives" letter, as it came to be called was routed. Two days later Chapman dictated a memorandum to Medill:"[i]t is my opinion that the Governor may be subjected to very severe criticism in the event that the facts complained of are true and that as a result of this condition some serious accident occurs at the mine. Will you kindly have this complaint carefully investigated so I can call the report of the investigation to the Governor's attention at the same time I show him this letter?" Chapman fastened this small yellow memo to the miners' letter and sent both to Medill. Although Medill's office is only about sixty yards from the Governor's, the message consumed two days in traversing the distance.

The messenger arrived at the Department of Mines and Minerals at 9:00 a.m. on March 13 and handed the "save our lives" letter and Chapman's memorandum to Medill's secretary. She duly stamped both "Received" and handed them to Medill. He and Weir discussed the matter, then Medill sent the original letter back to the Governor's office and dictated his reply to Chapman, blaming the war, recounting the activities of the special commission, saying: "The complaint sounds a good deal worse than it really is. The present condition of the mine is not any different than it has been during the past ten or fifteen years. . . . I would suggest the Governor advise Local Union No. 52, U.M.W. of A., that he is calling the matter to the attention of the State Mining Board with instructions that it be given full and complete consideration at their next meeting."

This apparently satisfied Chapman for, in the Governor's name, he dictated a letter to Rowekamp and Schmidt: "I [i.e., Governor Green] am calling your letter to the attention of the Director of the Department of Mines and Minerals with the request that he see that your complaint is taken up at the next meeting of the State

The Case: The Blast in Centralia No. 5 145

Mining Board . . . " This was signed with Governor Green's name but it is probable that Green himself never saw the "save our lives" letter until after the disaster more than a year later. Nor is there any evidence that the Mining Board ever considered the letter. In fact, nothing further came of it.

One of the most remarkable aspects of the whole affair was this: An aggrieved party (the miners) accused a second party (Medill's department) of acting wrongfully, and the higher authority to which it addressed its grievance simply, in effect, asked the accused if he were guilty and, when he replied he was not, dropped the matter. A logic, the logic of the administrative mind, attaches to Chapman's sending the complaint to the Department—the administrative mind has a pigeonhole for everything, matters which relate to law go to the Attorney General, matters which relate to mines go to the Department of Mines and Minerals, and that is that—but it is scarcely a useful logic when one of the agencies is itself accused of malfunction. Apparently it did not occur to Chapman to consult Inspector Scanlan or to make any other independent investigation.

As for Medill, on the day he received the letter he called Scanlan to Springfield and, says Scanlan, "severely reprimanded him." According to Scanlan, Medill "ordered me to cut down the size of my inspection report," because Medill though that such long reports might alarm the miners, "those damn hunks" who couldn't read English (Medill denied the phrase); but Scanlan took this order to mean that Medill wanted him to "go easy" on the operators—"it is the same thing as ordering you to pass up certain things." And one day during this long controversy, Medill buttonholed Scanlan's political sponsor in a corridor of the Statehouse and said he intended to fire Scanlan; Scanlan's sponsor refused to sanction it and but for this, Scanlan was convinced, he would surely have lost his job.

But now hundreds of miles away larger events were occurring which were to affect the fate of the miners at Centralia. In Washington, D.C., John L. Lewis and the nation's bituminous coal operators failed to reach an agreement and the miners struck, and on May 21, 1946, President Truman ordered the mines seized for government operation. Eight days later Lewis and Julius A. Krug, Secretary of the Interior, signed the famous Krug-Lewis Agreement. Despite strenuous protests by the operators, this agreement included a federal safety code. It was drawn up by the Bureau of Mines (a part of the U.S. Department of the Interior). And now for the first time in history the federal government could exercise police power over coal mine safety.

Thus far the efforts of the miners of Local 52 to thread the administrative maze in their own state had produced nothing but a snowfall of memoranda, reports, letters, and special findings. Let us now observe this new federal machinery in action. We shall learn nothing about how to prevent a disaster but we may learn a good deal about the administrative process.

Not until November 4 did Federal Inspector Perz reach Centralia to make his first enforceable inspection of Centralia No. 5. Observe, now, the results.

After three days at the mine, Perz went home and wrote out a "preliminary report" on a mimeographed form, listing 13 "major violations" of the safety code. He mailed this to the regional office of the Bureau of Mines at Vincennes, Indiana. There it was corrected for grammar, spelling, etc., and typed; copies then were mailed out to the Superintendent of the mine (to be posted on the bulletin board), the CMA in Washington, the CMA's regional office at Chicago, the District 12 office of the UMWA at Springfield, the UMWA international headquarters at Washington, the Bureau of Mines in Washington, and the Illinois Department at Springfield. While all this was going on, Perz was at home, preparing his final report, a lengthy document listing 57 violations of the safety code, 21 of them major and 36 minor. This handwritten final report likewise went to the Bureau at Vincennes where it was corrected, typed, and forwarded to the Bureau's office in College Park, Maryland. Here the report was "reviewed," then sent to the Director of the Bureau at Washington. He made any changes he deemed necessary, approved it, and ordered it processed. Copies were then distributed to the same seven places that had received the preliminary report, except that the UMWA at Springfield received two copies so that it could forward one to Local 52. (All this was so complicated that the Bureau devised a "flow sheet" to keep track of the report's passage from hand to hand.)

We must not lose sight of the fact that in the end everybody involved was appraised of Perz's finding: that the Centralia Company was violating the safety code and that hazards resulted. The company, the state, and the union had known this all along and done nothing, but what action now did the new enforcing agency take, the CMA?

The CMA in Washington received Perz's preliminary report November 14. Eleven days later it wrote to the company ordering it to correct one of the 13 major violations Perz found (why it said nothing about the others is not clear). On November 26 the CMA

The Case: The Blast in Centralia No. 5 147

received Perz's final report and on November 29 it again wrote to the company, ordering it to correct promptly all violations and sending copies of the directive to the Bureau of Mines and the UMWA. Almost simultaneously it received from Superintendent Niermann a reply to its first order (Niermann had replaced Prudent, who had left the company's employ): "Dear Sir: In answer to your CMA8-gz of November 25, 1946, work has been started to correct the violation of article 5, section 3c, of the Federal Mine Safety Code, but has been discontinued, due to . . . a strike . . . " This of course did not answer the CMA's second letter ordering correction of all 57 violations, nor was any answer forthcoming, but not until two months later, on January 29, 1947, did the CMA repeat its order and tell the company to report its progress by February 14.

This brought a reply from the company official who had been designated "operating manager" during the period of government operation, H. F. McDonald. Now he reported to CMA that "a substantial number of reported violations have been corrected and others are receiving our attention and should be corrected as materials and manpower become available." For obvious reasons, CMA considered this reply inadequate and on February 21 told McDonald to supply detailed information. Three days later McDonald replied ("Re file CMA81-swr"): He submitted a detailed report—he got it from Vice-President Young, who got it from the new General Superintendent, Walter J. Johnson—but McDonald told the CMA that this report was a couple of weeks old and he promised to furnish further details as soon as he could get them. The CMA on March 7 acknowledged this promise but before any other correspondence arrived to enrich file CMA81-swr, the mine blew up.

Now, the Krug-Lewis Agreement set up two methods of circumventing this cumbersome adminstrative machinery. If Inspector Perz had found what the legalese of the Agreement called "imminent danger," he could have ordered the men removed from the mine immediately (this power was weakened since it was also vested in the Coal Mines Administrator, the same division of authority that hobbled the state enforcers). But Perz did not report "imminent danger." And indeed how could he? The same hazardous conditions had obtained for perhaps twenty years and the mine hadn't blown up. The phrase is stultifying.

In addition, the Krug-Lewis Agreement provided for a safety committee of miners, selected by each local union and empowered to inspect the mine, to make safety recommendations to the management, and, again in case of "an immediate danger," to order the men out of the mine (subject to CMA review). But at Centralia No. 5 several months elapsed before Local 52 so much as appointed a safety committee, and even after the disaster the only surviving member of the committee didn't know what his powers were. The UMWA District officers at Springfield had failed to instruct their Locals in the rights which had been won for them. And confusion was compounded because two separate sets of safety rules were in use—the federal and the state—and in some instances one was the more stringent, in other instances, the other.

There was yet time for the miners to make one more try. On February 24, 1947, the safety committee, composed of three miners, wrote a short letter to the Chicago area office of the Coal Mines Administration: "The biggest grievance is dust . . . " It was written in longhand by Paul Compers (or so it is believed: Compers and one of the two other committee members were killed in the disaster a month later) and Compers handed it to Mine Manager Brown on February 27. But Brown did not forward it to the CMA; in fact he did nothing at all about it.

And now almost at the last moment, only six days before the mine blew up, some wholly new facts transpired. Throughout this whole history one thing has seemed inexplicable: the weakness of the pressure put on the company by Medill's Department of Mines and Minerals. On March 19, 1947, the *St. Louis Post-Dispatch* broke a story that seemed to throw some light upon it. An Illinois coal operator had been told by the state inspector who inspected his mine that Medill had instructed him to solicit money for the Republican Chicago mayoralty campaign. And soon more facts became known about this political shakedown.

Since no Illinois law forbids a company or an individual to contribute secretly to a political campaign we are dealing with a question of political morality, not legality. The Department of Mines and Minerals long has been a political agency. An inspector is a political appointee and during campaigns he is expected to contribute personally, tack up candidates' posters, and haul voters to the polls. Should he refuse, his local political boss would have him fired.

What bearing, now, did this have on the Centralia disaster? Nobody, probably, collected from the Centralia Coal Company. But the shakedown is one more proof—stronger than most—that Governor Green's department had reason to stay on friendly terms with the coal operators when, as their policemen, it should have been aloof. As a miner at Centralia said recently: "If a coal company gives you a thousand dollars, they're gonna expect something in return."

Here lies Green's responsibility—not that, through a secretary's fumble, he failed to act on a miners' appeal to "save our lives" but rather that, while the king makers were shunting him around the nation making speeches, back home his loyal followers were busier building a rich political machine for him than in administering the state for him.

As the Chicago campaign ground to a close, down at Centralia on March 18 Federal Inspector Perz was making another routine inspection. General Superintendent Johnson told him the company had ordered pipe for a sprinkler system months earlier but it hadn't arrived, "that there would be a large expenditure involved there . . . they had no definite arrangements just yet . . . but he would take it up with the higher officials of the company" in Chicago. Scanlan and Superintendent Niermann were there too. No rock dusting had been done for nearly a year but now the company had a carload of rock dust underground and Scanlan got the impression it would be applied over the next weekend. (It wasn't.) Perz, too, thought Johnson "very conscientious . . . very competent." Scanlan typed out his report—he had resorted wearily to listing a few major recommendations and adding that previous recommendations "should be complied with"—and mailed it to Springfield. Perz went home and wrote out his own report, acknowledging that 17 hazards had been corrected but making 52 recommendations most of which he had made in November (the company and the CMA were still corresponding over that November report). Perz finished writing on Saturday morning and mailed the report to the Vincennes office, which presumably began processing it Monday.

The wheels had been turning at Springfield, too, and on Tuesday, March 25, Weir signed a form letter to Brown setting forth Scanlan's latest recommendations: "The Department endorses . . ." But that day, at 3:26 P.M., before the outgoing-mail box in the Department was emptied, Centralia Mine No. 5 blew up . . .

Six separate investigations began, two to determine what had happened, and four to find out why. Federal and state experts agreed, in general, that the ignition probably had occurred at the extreme end, or face, of the First West Entry, that it was strictly a coal-dust explosion, that the dust probably was ignited by an explosive charge which had been tamped and fired in a dangerous manner—fired by an open-flame fuse, tamped with coal dust—and that the resulting local explosion was propagated by coal dust throughout four working sections of the mine, subsiding when it reached rock-dusted areas . . .

And what resulted from all the investigations into the Centralia disaster? The Washington County Grand Jury returned no-bills—that is, refused to indict Inspector Scanlan and five company officials ranging upward in authority through Brown, Niermann, Johnson, Young, and McDonald. The Grand Jury did indict the Centralia Coal Company, as a corporation, on two counts of "willful neglect" to comply with the mining law—failing to rock dust and working more than 100 men on a single split of air—and it also indicted Medill and Weir for "palpable omission of duty." The company pleaded nolo contendere—it did not wish to dispute the charge—and was fined the maximum: $300 on each count, a total of $1,000 (or less than $10 per miner's life lost). The law also provides a jail sentence of up to six months but of course you can't put a corporation in jail.

Why did nobody close the Centralia mine before it exploded? A difficult question. Medill's position (and some investigator's) was that Inspector Scanlan could have closed it. And, legally, this is true: The mining law expressly provided that an inspector could close a mine which persisted in violating the law. But inspectors have done so very rarely, only in exceptional circumstances, and almost always in consultation with the Department. Scanlan felt that had he closed the Centralia mine Medill simply would have fired him and appointed a more tractable inspector. Moreover, the power to close was not his exclusively: it also belonged to the Mining Board. (And is not this divided authority one of the chief factors that produced the disaster?) Robert Weir has said, "We honestly didn't think the mine was dangerous enough to close." This seems fantastic, yet one must credit it. For if Scanlan really had thought so, surely he would have closed it, even though a more pliable inspector reopened it. So would the federal authorities, Medill, or the company itself. And surely the miners would not have gone to work in it.

Governor Green's own fact-finding committee laid blame for the disaster upon the Department, Scanlan, and the company. The Democrats in the Illinois joint legislative committee submitted a minority report blaming the company, Medill, Weir, and Green's administration for "the industrial and political crime"; the Republican majority confessed itself unable to fix blame. After a tremendous pulling and hauling by every special interest, some new state legislation was passed as a result of the accident, but nothing to put teeth into the laws: violations still are misdemeanors (except campaign solicitation by inspectors, a felony); it is scarcely a serious blow to a million-dollar corporation to be fined $1,000. Nor does the law yet charge specific officers of the companies—rather than the abstract corporations—with legal responsibility, so it is still easy for a company official to hide behind a nebulous chain of command reaching up to the stratosphere of corporate finance in Chicago or St. Louis. It is hard to believe that compliance with any law can be enforced unless violators can be jailed.

As for the Congress of the United States, it did next to nothing. The Senate subcommittee recommended that Congress raise safety standards and give the federal government power to enforce that standard—"Immediate and affirmative action is imperative." But Congress only ordered the Bureau of Mines to report next session on whether mine operators were complying voluntarily with federal inspectors' recommendations . . .

After the Centralia disaster each man responsible had his private hell, and to escape it each found his private scapegoat—the war-time manpower shortage, the material shortage, another official, the miners, or, in the most pitiful cases, "human fraility." But actually responsibility here transcends individuals. The miners at Centralia, seeking somebody who would heed their conviction that their lives were in danger, found themselves confronted with officialdom, a huge organism scarcely mortal. The State Inspector, the Federal Inspector, the State Board, the Federal CMA, the company officials—all these forever invoked "higher authority," they forever passed from hand to hand a stream of memoranda and letters, decisions and laws and rulings, and they lost their own identities. As one strives to fix responsibility for the disaster, again and again one is confronted, as were the miners, not with any individuals fused into a vast, unapproachable, insensate organism. Perhaps this immovable juggernaut is the true villain in the piece. Certainly all those in authority were too remote from the persons whose lives they controlled. And this is only to confess once more that in making our society complex we have made it unmanageable.

CASE REVIEW

Since the blast in "No. 5," there have been notable changes in mine safety and mine policy administration. OSHA is but one example. Such departmentalized changes, are perhaps only pudding proof of the political model of fragmentation and incrementalism. But this is not the issue. Rather, the case as presented provides significant insights into policy analysis and public administration theory.

General Thoughts

Fact versus Value

The relatively dated Woodrow Wilson/Herbert Simon debate regarding fact and value in administrative decisions is now seen to be much less significant than early theorists thought. Wilson posited the theory that legislators set policy (determine values) and administrators simply implement (in a neutral, objective fashion). Simon, not the last but perhaps the most prolific writer to deal with this dichotomy, carried the assumption of bifurcation to its psychological source: the premise. Simon reconstructed the Wilsonian policy-administration bifurcation and argued a related dualism: namely, that the fact (the verifiable phenomenon) is the ideal premise (assumption upon which conclusions are reached).[13] At least in modern organizations, the value-free factual premise provides greater control for the administrator who seeks to minimize value-laden nonneutral choices.

Despite the theoretical contributions of these bifurcated models, they essentially ignored the nonquantifiable, nonobjectifiable presence of the administrative factors of history, ideology, and status. This is not to confuse history, ideology, and status with values.[14] Values themselves, ultimately, are verifiable and exist as facts within the psychic infrastructure of each decision maker. History (the tradition of mine negligence), ideology (the norm of ignoring miners as opposed to deferring to mine corporations), and low-status (the lack of power) exist apart from the individual administrator and his role. Consequently, administrative decisions and cases cannot be analyzed in the simplistic context of the old fact/value framework. Administrative factors are forces in and of themselves. They transcend values.

Accountability and Avoidance

A central maxim of organizational behavior is that the primary function of the organization is to ensure responsibility. This has two aspects. The first is to make certain that responsible individuals within the organization are accountable (read *answerable*) for decisions. The second is to enforce the conformity (read *competence*) of the subordinate to norms established by the authoritative structure.

It is the accountability notion that compels our attention with regard to the mine disaster case. Since accountability is so central to organizational life and so powerful a concept (that is, it presupposes that someone will be held answerable), it assumes that lines of accountability are predetermined. At least in formalized organizations one might suspect a countereffect to the accountability force. The countereffect is avoidance or the mechanics of non–decision making.

Avoidance has two dynamics. First, it involves the process of actually submerging or ignoring issues (for example, costly mine hazards) that are unsafe, risky, or conflict laden. Second, it involves the process of substituting safe issues, or engaging in safe activities (paperwork), in place of those issues that are to be avoided. For example, it would be irresponsible for safety officials to ignore their formal charge (checking on mines) completely; at the same time, there were incentives to avoid actually doing this. The effect of this set of conflicting forces was to create a countereffect of substituting other marginally relevant activities such as processing memos, instituting delaying procedures, or meeting formal, ritualized commitments such as policy statements or public expressions of concern. The effect of the avoidance strategy was to give the impression that something tangible was being done (the flurry of paperwork) but actually to deflect meaningful responses to the problem of impending disaster.[15]

Bias and the Weight of History

As a two-step process (involving, first, the submergence of an unsafe topic and, second, the substitution of safe activities or "safe" issues), the phenomenon of avoidance is the administrator's answer to the pressures of accountability. As such, *avoidance theory* explains a rather traditional and commonplace reality to describe how avoidance actually operates is, however, a more significant and more complicated matter. Avoidance involves the subtle interplay of biases that are first mobilized against unsafe issues and later mobilized in favor of safe administrative concerns. For example, non–decision making (not visiting a mine) helps to explain one half of the avoidance process; that is, it suggests how certain duties and issues are submerged. It does not explain how the appearance of decision making is simultaneously projected—that is, how the illusion of responsible administration is projected.

To understand this phenomenon completely one must consider the term *bias* as referring to those factors that "singly or in combination effectively prevent certain grievances from developing into full-fledged issues which call for decisions."[16] Biases are mobilized (set into action) both to submerge and to surface certain issues. This involves "mobilization of values," not in the Wilsonian sense but in the empirical sense, as the avoidance process of mobilization is observable. That is, one can observe the use of committee structures, administrative resources, procedural rules, bureaucratic paperwork, organizational tasks, and the like, to delay or to impede discussion of an issue. It happens all the time. What is significant is that this process involves more than the individual and more than organizational norms, attitudes, procedures, and resources. It involves historical momentum. The fact is that larger forces determine what is to be decided and what is to be avoided. Like the grade of the track, often these forces are in place long before the administrator perceives a problem or before a problem condition emerges.

Bias as Ideology

History is not deadweight. It carries normative content. In retrospect it is viewed as almost immoral (certainly shocking) that mine safety at "No. 5" was avoided for so long. At the time, however, it was deemed acceptable for administrators to behave as they did.

Ideology, then, is viewed as the preferential choice (the right or wrong choice) that the administrator makes on an individual level. It, too, should be viewed as a bias to be mobilized in favor of some concerns and against others.

The mobilization of one's gut feeling (or common sense) attitudes toward or against a policy is the threshold concern for policy decisions. One's ideology, then, is central to the process of decisions. It is like the force of gravity.

Status as Bias

Race and class are factors taken into consideration in many public decisional areas.[17] The color of one's skin and one's socioeconomic position are critical indicators of one's power position in American society. Increasingly it is recognized that gender and life-style are also key factors in establishing one's power position. For example, poor black females in public housing are generally considered to be near the bottom of the power pole. Consequently, that population will be relatively disadvantaged in securing favors by administrators who respond (as the political model tells us) to pressure and to power resources.

Status as a critical choice factor has not been studied as extensively as status as a position factor within an organization. Nonetheless, it is clear that status is a key administrative factor, subtly but powerfully influencing bias.[18]

Specific Implications and Trends

Deliberate or Accidental

If such a latticework (administrative screening) model exists as an overlay on the already latticed political model, is it important whether the screen is deliberately or only accidentally placed before the administrator? Remember that in terms of the political model there is said to be an inherent (and arguably positive) normative content: it works. Thus, secondary ethical concerns are only that: secondary.

In terms of the administrative screen, however, the question is even less relevant. History, ideology, and status concepts are not neutral, however, they exist as givens. They operate apart from any conspiracies or accidents. It is perhaps unusual to discuss the administrative process in this context using these words, but it can hardly be doubted that these forces operate. Why not include them in our analytical framework, and why not deal with their normative impact?

Tangibles and Intangibles

The history of mine disasters is an intangible concept. Mine explosions are not. Ambulances, fire trucks, and screaming sirens trigger immediate reactions. Administrators respond to the tangible more readily than they respond to the intangible. In order to factor history into the calculus of decision making, it seems necessary to reduce the factor to a tangible, loud concrete force. Numbers, words, and ritual ceremonies are all objectified symbols; yet we are not able to translate historical reality into conscious policy-making.

Perhaps administrators should be schooled in the history of a subject matter rather than in the procedures of administration. Certainly a sense of the history of a problem is relevant.

Triage and Mitigating Disasters

Some very competent public administrators argue (and hold as high principle) the notion that the objective of good administration is to mitigate disasters.[19] This, they say, is the best that can be done. And perhaps they feel noble in the effort. Yet, there is a disturbing contradiction in this position. Administrators cannot have it both ways. They cannot argue (contra to the Wilsonian ethic) that they are central to the process of decision making and at the same time apologize for their limited role in affecting events.

Administrators and managers are increasingly assuming critical roles in society. Like the physician, they must assume the duties of prevention. Triage programs and mitigating disasters are not adequate if one assumes the role of active player.

Redefining the Ethic

It is ridiculous to espouse the ethic that the administrator's role is neutral and objective. Neither the political model nor the administrative model tolerates the simplicity of the Wilsonian deal. A more intelligent ethic would dismiss the rationale that because "it exists" or because "it works" the administrative process is acceptable and even preferable. The issue is whether we can transcend procedural measures and to create an administrative ethic in terms of substantive factors. For example, legislator-administrator dichotomies are concepts flowing from a ficticious procedural model. Harmony, truth, and justice are substantive concepts linked closely to actual community concerns. It should be recognized that the starting point for effective/ethical administration is a substantive theory linked to a particular society's norms and values.[20]

Mores and Morals

This is not to be read as a treatise on morality. Given the dominant influence of history, ideology, and status, it is, nonetheless, essential for administrators to have a clear sense of the mores of a society. William Graham Sumner defined *mores* as "the ways of doing things which are current in a society to satisfy human needs and desires, together with the faiths, notions, codes, and standards of well living, which inhere in those ways."[21]

In this context it is not to be inferred that administrative reform is hopeless. With regard to administrative models, however, there are distinct problems:

> Inasmuch as the mores are a phenomenon of the society and not of the state, and inasmuch as the machinery of administration belongs to the state and not to the society, the administration of the mores presents peculiar difficulties.[22]

Administrators fail if they try to deal with questions that are beyond their scope of authority (for example, divorce, abortion, prayer). Administrators also fail if they do not respond to the guidance of societal mores (the blast in Mine No. 5).

What's Wrong with Administration?

Nothing. Despite the horror stories presented by such disasters as the Centralia mine blast, there is nothing inherently evil about administrative practice as known in the United States. The political model guarantees that with some shortcomings the system of public administration is responsive to values and preferences. The administrative model, with attention to subjective procedures, can be fine-tuned. Mistakes will occur. Human nature is not perfect.

If there is anything amiss, it is the absurd notion that administration is neutral, that it operates in the laboratory conditions of the Wilsonian era or in the value-free world of the budgetary process.

Foci of Change

Introduction of nontangible criteria (history, ideology, status) might occur at two particularly desirable points: planning and review. Planning (prior to implementation of a program) permits the initial control and thus ensures that the impact of historical insight will not be lost. Review, a feedback or evaluative process, reintegrates these nontangible factors into the overall program model. Obviously, the planning and review sequences themselves are subject to political variables and to individual adaptation. But if the administrative process works as theorists believe, these steps can be preplanned and adjustments can be made in advance to screen out certain disruptive factors.

Public Worlds—Private Worlds

Public administration and business administration are still largely presented as separate and discrete worlds. The Centralia case reveals that these areas are intricately related. This does not deny that there are significant distinctions in terms of institutional forces and consequences of decisions. But it is delusion to follow the dualism of public and private authority. More and more, government specialists interact with business specialists, and vice versa. It is interaction at the level of instrumental specialization, not at the level of hierarchical formalism, that sets the tone of today's administrative practice. It is no longer critical whether the setting is OSHA or Peabody Coal Co.

Administration, Tools, and Sorting

Do administrators administer? The word *administration* implies a process of systemmatically matching goals with means, that is, implementing resources to attain objectives. The process is thought by some to be rational, by others to be political, and by a few to be a mix of the two. This chapter argues that administration meets none of the criteria suggested by these traditional models. Administration is, at the same time, less and more than the rational and political models imply. It is less in the sense that administration is not based on cause-effect analysis, and thus it is not inherently rational. Nor is it governed strictly by personal preference models, and thus it is not purely political.

In brief, administration transcends individual choice and rationality and embraces historical forces, ideological norms, and power concepts.

What, then, do administrators do? They sort. They sort out responses to problems. Merely traffic cops? Hardly. Akin to judges? Yes, but without the strict rules of the courtroom to guide or to impose sanctions. Even the tools (systems analysis, linear programming, computer methodology, operations research) are designed to help sort, whether along a temporal or a spatial model.

Ultimate Decision Makers

It is this sorting process—what to put in, what to leave out, what to respond to, what to ignore—that puts the administrator in the driver's seat. In fact, today's administrator (or manager in the business world) acts and behaves very much in the traditional judge role: sorting and brokering between contesting parties or resources. Indeed the role of the judge today is becoming more and more the administration of the legal system It is the same process—just a different setting.[23]

CONCLUSION

These thoughts will be examined in detail in the concluding chapter. The issue remaining is whether there are alternatives to the shortcomings of the rational and political models. In this context the legal model (Chapter Six) with its counterpart the discretionary model (Chapter Seven) is introduced. It should be noted that the legal/justice model or approach is not viewed in Western tradition as merely an alternative approach but as a method of the highest order. That is to say: the legal model carries normative content. The rule of law is a goal of the highest order.

Hence it becomes doubly necessary to analyze this remaining approach. Not only does the legal approach represent a third major institutional reality and method, but the legal model represents an end in itself. The following two chapters will examine this powerful interplay of means and ends—how it works and what it does.

NOTES

1. Ida R. Hoos, *Systems Analysis in Public Policy* (Berkeley: University of California Press, 1972), pp. 74–75.

2. John Kenneth Galbraith, *The Anatomy of Power* (Boston: Houghton-Mifflin, 1983); and George Stigler, *The Citizen and the State* (Chicago: University of Chicago Press, 1982). It is interesting that the reverse may be occurring. That is, economists are beginning, after decades of avoidance, to deal with political theory concepts.

3. This section is based largely on an unpublished report on the Willow Village Community Action Program by Alan Haber prepared for the Office of Economic Opportunity, Washington, D.C., 1967. Copies are available from the Institute for Policy Studies, Washington, D.C.

4. And in the rational model, they are one and the same—that is, the political model is merely a subset of rationality. Thus it can be argued that being "political" is being "rational" if the objective is to get things done.

5. This is the case unless one defines *politics* so broadly as to include all social, racial, financial, and psychological factors—hardly a helpful definition.

6. Haber, *Report on the Willow Village Community Action Program*, p. 1–2.

7. Edward Hallett Carr, *What is History?* (New York: Alfred A. Knopf, 1963), p. 5.

8. Ibid., p. 35.

9. This will become clearer in Chapters Six and Seven, which explore the legal model.

10. Daniel Bell, *The End of Ideology* (New York: Free Press, 1962).

11. The overwhelming majority of prison inmates are lower class and racial minorities, disproportionately related to their actual numbers in

society. For example: blacks make up 11 percent of the U.S. adult population, but 47 percent of state prisoners. See "The Prevalence of Imprisonment" a Justice Department study as reported in *The Arizona Daily Star*, July 29, 1985, p. 5. "Any statistical overview of capital punishment inevitably leads to race.": 43 of 47 individuals executed since the reinstatement of the death penalty in 1977 were convicted of killing whites, as were 77 percent of those remaining on death row. Linda Greenhouse, "Charting the Course of Capital Punishment," *New York Times*, July 24, 1985, p. 10.

12. In a penetrating and dated but still pertinent study, Gilbert Y. Steiner described the realities (race, money, politics) that render areawide metropolitan government schemes administratively impossible. The ideas in this section trace back to that 1966 study entitled: *Metropolitan Government and the Real World: The Case of Chicago* (Chicago: Loyola University, 1966).

13. Herbert Simon, *Administration Behavior*, 2d ed. (New York: Free Press, 1965).

14. Simon, of course, considered value in great detail (as a nonverifiable phenomenon) but did not consider history, ideology, or race/class. Note that "facts" are sometimes nothing more than other people's "values," thus clarifying the substantive similarity in both Wilson's and Simon's dualism.

15. The process of avoidance as a deliberate strategy (substituting safe activities for risky activities or issues) was explored in detail in Michael A. Murray, "The House Education—Labor Committee and the 1967 Poverty Controversy: A Study of Congressional Avoidance" (Ph.D. diss., Urbana, University of Illinois, 1967).

16. Peter Bachrach and Morton S. Baratz, "Decisions and Non-Decisions: An Analytical Framework," *American Political Science Review*, September 1963, p. 641.

17. A recent study on death penalty inmates has caused the U.S. Supreme Court to reexamine the impact of race on capital punishment decisions. The study, done by a team of researchers from the University of Iowa led by David Baldus, concludes that if a person is indicted for murder, the odds are that the person is four times more likely to receive the death penalty if the victim is white rather than black. Fay S. Joyce, "One Slayer Executed with Another to Die Today," *New York Times*, December 15, 1983, p. 2. See also footnote 11 above.

18. "Status" as a choice-determining factor cuts both ways. Just as some administrators may be biased in favor of rich white males, some may be biased in favor of poor black females. The point is that the status element is a part of the administrative model.

19. As an example see *Toward a New Public Administration*, ed. Frank Marini (Scranton, Pa., Chandler, 1971), for a collection of essays decrying threats to society and noting the central but limited role of the public administrator.

20. The writer refers not to a personal ethic but to a societal ethic. Peter Drucker declares that it is not "genius" but "character" that the manager must possess. See Peter Drucker, *The Practice of Management* (New York: Harper and Brothers, 1954). Such an individualistic orientation is pointless in the face of the overwhelming procedural and substantive forces of the political and administrative models.

21. William G. Sumner, *Folkways* (Boston: Ginn, 1906), p.59.

22. Ibid., p. 117.

23. Note that administrative feasibility is becoming more and more a criterion of decision in legal rulings. See *Union Electric Co.* v. *Environmental Protection Agency* et al. 427 U.S. 246, 96 S.Ct. 2598 (1976).

While you and I have lips and voices
*   which are for kissing*
*   and to sing with*
Who cares if some one-eyed
*   son of a bitch*
*   invents an instrument*
*   to measure spring with.*

e. e. cummings
"Voices to Voices, Lip to Lip"

CHAPTER 6

LEGAL MODELS

DEFINITIONS AND CONCEPTS

Power may well be the essential ingredient of both the rational model and the political model. But is power essential to the legal model? Is power the driving force of legal ethics? Plato recognized this possibility when he argued, "Justice is the will of the stronger."[1] The disturbing corollary is that might makes right.[2]

Despite this reality, there is an intellectual counterweight to the rational and political models that are driven by power factors. The intellectual counterweight, at least in its pure form, is the so-called legal model. This approach, based on positive law (or analytical positivism), consists of the development of nonarbitrary rules by a political sovereign (or governmental authority), enforced by sanctions. Chapters Six and Seven explore the legal approach and its derivative the discretionary model.

Positivism and Legalism

When most people use the word *law*, or refer to the *legal process*, they have in mind positive law (or analytical positivism) as described by John Austin.[3] In this context *law* (or *positive law*) refers to an almost physical or tangible object—e.g., a government institution, a court house, an objectified set of legal procedures. Thus, for instance, when we talk of a *rule,* we mean a rule (an order, a statute) issued by a government (or its legal subdivision, a court); generally, we leave out nongovernmental actions. When we refer to *legal superiors* or *legal authority*, we limit the concept to legitimate, official, political sovereigns; thus we leave out informal, behind-the-scenes actors and participants. When we speak of *sanctions*, we refer to authoritatively issued rewards and penalties; we do not include private incentives or disincentives. The positivistic view, by this definition, is narrow and akin to Easton's notion (Chapter One) of a political system where the focus is on the authoritative institutions that determine the legitimate or final values for a society.[4]

Nonetheless, political scientists and other behavioralists have begun to look beyond the concept of the *state* as the conceptual framework for political study.[5] For example, political scientists formerly studied government (qua government) as the focus of analysis.[6] Accordingly, one examined the visible, tangible, objectifiable elements of government: the institutions that issued the authoritative values for a society or the processes that objectified those values. Left out of the calculus of decision making were those myriad actors and participants (private sector firms, lobbyists, pressure groups, pacs, community activists) with all of their institutions. For example, one formerly studied urban affairs by focusing on the institution of urban government: the executive branch, (the mayor or the city manager's office); the legislative branch (the city council); the legal branch (the courts). Today one studies an array of urban abstractions, such as racism, metropolitanization, power structures, and decentralization. The focus is no longer exclusively on the visible, institutional aspects of government or politics. Likewise with the law. The focus is no longer exclusively on the positivistic aspects of the courts or on legal procedure. Abstractions are important to the legal model.

Justice as an Abstraction

Consider the phenomenon in legal reasoning that deduces "the law" from general abstractions. For example, the phrase "all men are created equal" is a general "preamble" that finds specific embodiment in the Fourteenth Amendment to the United States Constitution: no government shall deny any person "the equal protection of the laws."

Equal protection, due process (procedural and substantive), civil liberty, freedom of speech, right to privacy—these likewise are judicial abstractions that find expression in specific actual cases and statutes. The function of the judicial process (and of legal reasoning) is to apply the

Definitions and Concepts 165

principle to the case in question. In this sense the method is deductive.

At the same time, the courts and the legal system must deal with the specifics of the case and with the circumstances before it. Thus the fact-finding process (by judge or by jury) is a critical prerequisite to the application of a decision. In this sense the method goes from the particular to the general and is inductive in form. The inductive process, however, aims at reconciling the specific case with the general precedent and in this sense is also governed by the overriding abstraction.

To argue that justice is an abstraction (an intellectual goal or concept) is not to deny or preclude positivistic content. Very often the judicial abstraction (separation of power, checks and balances, corporate responsibility, fiduciary relationship) is embodied in specific laws and in constitutional references. Nonetheless, the positivistic content—the rigid, unalterable, black and white law—exists more in the abstract than it does in reality.

This is to point out that the legal model is not a clear, unalterable set of positive rights and wrongs. Rather, it is an organic process that is an admixture of positive abstraction and of both inductive and deductive logic applied to actual facts. The legal model, then, is a mix of general principle and specific case. In this sense it is distinct from the rational model (based on hard discrete data) and the political model (flowing from personal preference).

The Legal Model: Maxims and Modifiers

As a distinct and separate method for making decisions,[7] the legal model has several unique characteristics.

The Justice Ethic

In Western, civilized, law-based societies the free development of expression and individuality is one of the leading essentials of "well-being."[8] And yet liberty of thought, discussion, and action is not absolute; it is constrained. One of the strongest restraining forces on utility or happiness is the idea of justice. Justice, in legalized societies, operates as a criterion of right and wrong and thus is viewed as a check on unrestrained behavior.[9]

If this is so, and if justice is the heart of the legal society, then what is justice? Contrary to the outmoded positivists, it is not simply an amalgamation of institutionalized, statutory law. Nor is power the key element; justice does not exist as the by-product of judicial or administrative agencies, no matter how influential these may be.[10] The connection between justice and law is not direct, and in fact there is no clear, unambiguous connection between the legal model and the justice ethic.

The Balance Test

Some judges have suggested that the notion of modern justice lies in Plato's philosophy of good as harmony—or as balance between forces and circumstances. True justice is true harmony is true balance. This concept is sometimes reflected in Supreme Court decisions that suggest that the answer to pressing social claims can somehow be reconciled by balancing conflicting facts or demands.[11] In a well-known housing discrimination case the Court applied an informal and vaguely defined test that "balanced" competing, conflicting rights.[12] But as one noted observer wrote:

> . . . [I]t is dangerous to let any constitutional guarantee rest on an ad hoc balancing test . . . [I]t is extremely difficult to weigh liberty against equality; the outcome depends entirely on the views of the particular judges.[13]

Earlier cases promoted a vaguely defined balancing approach. In the 1945 Case of *Southern Pacific Co.* v. *Arizona ex rel. Sullivan, Attorney General* 325 U.S. 761, 65 S. Ct. 1515, the U.S. Supreme Court suggested that the danger of large trains to human safety could be weighed against the need for uniform and unhindered flow of interstate commerce. The state of Arizona had objected to trains of more than 14 passenger cars and of more than 70 freight cars. In disallowing the state regulation, the Supreme Court relied on a kind of weighing process. The fallacy in the Court's logic, however, is that one cannot weigh a life (whether it be 1 human life or 6 million) against a commercial need or force. There is no parity or equality of factors (life versus money) to be measured. The logic is inherently misleading. In short, the balance test is seen as nothing more than mere rhetoric or disguise for the underlying power ethic that rests on the accumulation of force and weight, with resultant decisions favoring the side with the most force or weight.

Ambiguity as an Element

In all cases and doctrines reviewed it is apparent that the legal model is not fixed, clear, or necessarily logical. The legal model in theory rests on the bedrock of ambiguity. This has both positive and negative connotations.

If legal reasoning and the justice ethic are linked to the power concept, then the legal model does not follow clear bright lines of principled logical reasoning. Reliance on the fiction of positivism does not solve this difficulty, nor do the abstractions of due process or checks and balances resolve the contradiction in a pluralistic, multidimensional society such as contemporary America. It is in fact absurd to assume, or even to desire, that there should be clear, fixed, immutable laws, rules, and standards that apply to all citizens, for all time, under all conditions. Ours is a dynamic society (it changes), and our system of laws is accordingly organic (it also changes and develops). This seems to be the fact of the matter, and there are rationalizations that justify the reality.

First, positive law, to the extent it does exist, does represent the basic social ethic regarding a social issue. In other words positive law is society's ethical floor[14]— not the ceiling or the highest standard but at least a minimum of expectations. Second, the justice abstraction with its bedrock concepts of fairness, equality, equal protection, due process, and fundamental liberties does provide a principled framework for legalistic theory. For example, if procedural due process means nothing more, it means the right to "some kind of a hearing"[15] before one is deprived of a right. Conceptually, it is not critical that the hearing be formal (as opposed to informal) or that it be in court (as opposed to extrajudicial). The right exists as a concept of justice. Third, the balance test and other forms of legal reasoning do not represent alternatives to the positive law/justice mix as much as a legal rationale or an argument for a particular decision. The legal concepts of balance, utility, administrative costs, burden on government, custom, and usage are only reasons why a decision goes one way as opposed to another. They are not principles or ethical standards in themselves.

On the other hand the purpose of positive law, as it is expressed in written constitutions, codified laws, and published regulations, is to provide notice and predictability for societies' members. Thus, if one parks in front of a fire hydrant, one violates positive law, and one knows this in advance. Consequently, laws that are vague, or inherently ambiguous, are suspect and fail for lack of due process. Additionally, where competing claims need to be resolved (the sociological school of law as propounded by Roscoe Pound), there must be clear, fixed standards for fairly arbitrating such contests. A body of laws or a legal methodology that fails to accomplish this task is of questionable value. The legal process may exacerbate the problem by giving the appearance that fairness is achieved when in fact there is inconsistency and illogic in decision making.

Ambiguity as the Model (Goal)

In the late 1700s the written Constitution of the United States specifically provided for the enslavement of blacks. In the 1800s women were not allowed to vote. In many jurisdictions in the 1900s homosexuality was considered a crime and homosexuals were treated as repugnant criminals. None of this would have changed if the law were not a flexible, mutable, organic process of reasoning. The beauty of the law, it can be argued, lies in its ability to adapt, grow, evolve, and change. Change occurs partly because the law is inherently ambiguous. That is, the law does not seek to provide final solutions or ultimate answers. The logic of the law is to grope, to restrain itself, to deal with ambiguous situations as they exist. Rarely does the law, in its wisdom, attempt to define complex social questions by establishing hard, clear, bright lines.

A Non Optimizing Strategy

Recall the elements of the heretofore discussed rational model and political model. While each model was distinguished by certain procedural and conceptual characteristics (social constraints, size of organization, degree of external review), these two models shared one vital characteristic: optimization. That is, the purpose of rational decisions or of political decisions was to maximize output or to maximize control over other goals.

In this regard the legal model is somewhat distinct. While a decision may be written so as to secure maximum compliance by the public,[16] or even to enhance or increase a judge's standing among his or her peers,[17] the thrust of a decision is to deal with a specific legal question and to resolve it by relying on established principles and precedents. In reaching decisions the process requires that the participating parties (the lawyers) narrow the legal positions, refine the issues, and limit the impact of the decision. The process requires a narrowing of facts, a shrinking of the net, a limitation of impact. Exceptions and qualifications are part of any decision, so there is room later for change or modification. Absolutes are disdained. Rationality is refused. Hard data are rejected. Scientific processes are questioned. Where possible, a back door is left open and broad, far-reaching implications are conditional. In this regard ambiguity rather than clarity is the goal. This is not to argue that a strategy of suboptimization (with inherently discordant, illogical consequences) is the result. Note that the legal model is not to be compared with the rational or political model—at least on this point.

In short, although there is no discernible attempt to optimize (by data gathering, or by resource manipulation), there is no attempt to suboptimize (that is, minimize payoff). Legal reasoning is unlike rational modeling and political modeling in that (1) it does not seek to determine *all* potentially favorable and unfavorable consequences, and (2) it does not deliberately seek to arrange power resources to effect its policies. Accordingly, there is no set goal to suboptimize, that is, to reach the less-than-desirable or principled goal. Rather, the decisional objectives seem to be:

1. To set no final, immutable course;
2. To provide limits on policies where feasible;
3. To allow for later, principled change;
4. To stick to the particular facts; and
5. To qualify by conditions and examples.

In this way the courts leave the door open for future evolutionary processes to work their natural course.

CASE IN POINT

Legal Models: The Balance Test and Cost-Benefit Analysis

Few areas of the law are more important than the recent developments in administrative law[18] and government regulation. In this area one would find the "hard case," that is, the case that would illustrate the reasoning process whereby the judicial system (judges, juries, lawyers, agencies) makes or does not make choices regarding critical issues. The term *hard case* is used in the sense that in the area of administrative law one would find the greatest pressures or forces on the judicial system to make choices and decisions. It is against the sheer weight and force of these extrajudicial pressures that one finds the most revealing judicial responses. Such a case is found in the recently developed Supreme Court decision *American Textile Manufactuers Institute Inc.* v. *Donovan, Secretary of Labor, et al.*, 452 U.S. 490, 101 S. Ct. 2491 (1981).

  Most readers are familiar with the issues surrounding the controversy of government regulation. Some, primarily conservative businesspersons, charge that there is too much government interference via costly regulatory activity. Others, citing the need for checks on rapacious private sector activities, cry for even more regulation of externalities and an end to the myth that the courts will balance the value of a life against industrial costs.

  Recent criticism of perceived government intrusion (overregulation) led Congress to consider and the president[19] to require agencies to perform cost-benefit analyses prior to actually promulgating[20] regulations.

In 1981 the U.S. Supreme Court was presented a central methodological and legal question: whether the Occupational Safety and Health Act requires that a cost-benefit study be done before OSHA promulgates regulations controlling toxic materials or harmful agents, that cause "brown lung," a serious industrial disease. The Supreme Court's answer provides a rare insight into legal reasoning specifically as it relates to decision-making methodologies.

THE CASE: AMERICAN TEXTILE MANUFACTURERS INSTITUTE, INC., ET AL. V. DONOVAN, SECRETARY OF LABOR, ET AL.[*]

Representatives of the cotton industry brought a suit challenging the validity of the cotton dust standard promulgated by the Secretary of Labor, acting through the Occupational Safety and Health Administration [OSHA]. The Court of Appeals upheld the standard in all major respects. On appeal the Supreme Court, through Justice Brennan, held that: (1) the Secretary, in promulgating standards dealing with toxic materials or harmful physical agents under provision of the Occupational Safety and Health Act which requires the Secretary to set the standard "which most adequately assures, to the extent feasible, on the basis of the best available evidence" that no employee will suffer material impairment of health, is not required to determine the costs of the standard bear a reasonable relationship to its benefits; cost-benefit analysis by OSHA is not required by the statute because feasibility analysis is; and (2) the Court of Appeals, on the basis of the whole record, did not misapprehend or grossly misapply the substantial evidence test when it upheld OSHA's findings; and (3) whether or not OSHA had the underlying authority to promulgate a wage guarantee requirement with respect to employees transferred to another position when they are unable to wear a respirator, OSHA failed to make the necessary determination or statement of reasons that such requirement was related to achievement of health and safety goals. Therefore the Court:

affirmed in part, vacated in part, and remanded. The Court's reasoning is fascinating.

---

[*]Author's note: Citations and internal footnoting are omitted.

The Case: American Textile Manufacturers Institute, Inc. 171

I

[Following a review of the procedural facts of the case the Court (Justice Brennan) moved into a decision of the central issues.]

II

The principal question presented in these cases is whether the Occupational Safety and Health Act requires the Secretary, in promulgating a standard pursuant to S. 6(b)(5) of the Act, to determine that the costs of the standard bear a reasonable relationship to its benefits. Relying on S. 6(b)(5) Act . . . petitioners urge not only that OSHA must show that a standard addresses a significant risk of material health impairment, but also that OSHA must demonstrate that the reduction in risk of material health impairment is significant in light of the costs of attaining that reduction. Respondents on the other hand contend that the Act requires OSHA to promulgate standards that eliminate or reduce such risks "to the extent such protection is technologically and economically feasible." To resolve this debate, we must turn to the language, structure, and legislative history of the Act.

IIA

The starting point of our analysis is the language of the statute itself.

> The Secretary, in promulgating standards dealing with toxic materials or harmful physical agents under this subsection, shall set the standard which most adequately assures, *to the extent feasible*, on the basis of the best available evidence, that no employee will suffer material impairment of health or functional capacity even if such employee has regular exposure to the hazard dealt with by such standard for the period of his working life.

Although their interpretations differ, all parties agree that the phrase "to the extent feasible" contains the critical language in S. 6(b)(5) for purposes of these cases.

The plain meaning of the word "feasible" supports respondents' interpretation of the statute. According to Webster's Third New International Dictionary of the English Language 831 (1976), "feasible" means "capable of being done, executed, or effected." . . . Thus, S. 6(b)(5) directs the Secretary to issue the standard that "most adequately assures . . . that no employee will suffer material impairment of health," limited only by the extent to which this is "capable of being done." In effect then, as the Court of Appeals held, Congress itself defined the basic relationship between costs and benefits, by placing the "benefit" of worker health above all other considerations save those making attainment of this "benefit" unachievable. Any standard based on a balancing of costs and benefits by the Secretary that strikes a different balance than that struck by Congress would be inconsistent with the command set forth in S. 6(b)(5). Thus, cost-benefit analysis by OSHA is not required by the statute because feasibility analysis is.

When Congress has intended that an agency engage in cost-benefit analysis, it has clearly indicated such intent on the face of the statute.

[Prior statutes] demonstrate that Congress uses specific language when intending that an agency engage in cost-benefit analysis. Certainly in light of its ordinary meaning, the word "feasible" cannot be construed to articulate such congressional intent. We therefore reject the argument that Congress required cost-benefit analysis in S. 6(b)(5).

IIB

Even though the plain language of S. 6(b)(5) supports this construction, we must still decide whether S. 3(8), the general definition of an occupational safety and health standard, either alone or in tandem with S. 6(b)(5), incorporates a cost-benefit requirement for standards dealing with toxic materials or harmful physical agents. Section 3(8) (emphasis added) of the Act provides:

> "The term 'occupational safety and health standard' means a standard which requires conditions, or the adoption or use of one or more practices, means, methods, operations, or processes, *reasonably necessary or appropriate* to provide safe or healthful employment and places of employment."

Taken alone, the phrase, "reasonably necessary or appropriate" might be construed to contemplate some balancing of the costs and benefits of a standard. We need not decide whether S. 3(8), standing alone, would contemplate some form of cost-benefit analysis. For even if it does, Congress specifically chose in S. 6(b)(5) to impose separate and additional requirements for issuance of a subcategory of occupational safety and health standards dealing with toxic materials and harmful physical agents: it required that those standards be issued to prevent material impairment of health *to the extent feasible*. . . .

Agreement with petitioners' argument that S. 3(8) imposes an additional and overriding requirement of cost-benefit analysis on the issuance of S. 6(b)(5) standards would eviscerate the "to the extent feasible" requirement. Standards would inevitably be set at the level indicated by cost-benefit analysis, and not at the level specified by S. 6(b)(5). We cannot believe that Congress intended the general terms of S. 3(8) to countermand the specific feasibility requirement of S. 6(b)(5). Adoption of petitioners' interpretation would effectively write S. 6(b)(5) out of the Act. We decline to render Congress' decision to include a feasibility requirement nugatory, thereby offending the well-settled rule that all parts of a statute, if possible, are to be given effect . . .

IIC

The legislative history of the Act, while concededly not crystal clear, provides general support for respondents' interpretation of the Act. The Congressional reports and debates certainly confirm that Congress meant "feasible" and nothing else in using that term. Congress was concerned that the Act might be thought to require achievement of absolute safety, an impossible standard, and therefore insisted that health and safety goals be capable of economic and technological accomplishment. Perhaps most telling is the absence of any indication whatsoever that Congress intended OSHA to conduct its own cost-benefit analysis before promulgating a toxic material or harmful physical agent standard . . .

Not only does the legislative history confirm that Congress meant "feasible" rather than "cost-benefit" when it used the former term, but it also shows that Congress understood that the Act would create substantial costs for employers, yet intended to impose such costs when necessary to create a safe and healthful working environment . . .

IIIA

Therefore, whether or not in the first instance we would find the Secretary's Conclusions supported by substantial evidence, we cannnot say that the Court of Appeals in this case "misapprehended or grossly misapplied" the substantial evidence test when it found that OSHA reasonably evaluated the cost estimates before it, considered criticisms of each, and selected suitable estimates of compliance costs."

IIIB

After estimating the cost of compliance with the Cotton Dust Standard, OSHA analyzed whether it was "economically feasible" for the cotton industry to bear this cost. OSHA concluded that it was, finding that "although some marginal employers may shut down rather than comply, the industry as a whole will not be threatened by the capital requirements of the regulation." In reaching this conclusion on the Standard's economic impact, OSHA made specific findings with respect to employment, energy consumption, capital financing availability, and profitability.

IV

The final Cotton Dust Standard places heavy reliance on the use of respirators to protect employees from exposure to cotton dust, particularly during the 4-year interim period necessary to install and implement feasible engineering controls. One part of the respirator provision requires the employer to give employees unable to wear a respirator the opportunity to transfer to another position, if available, where the dust level meets the Standard. When such a transfer occurs, the employer must guarantee that the employee suffers no loss of earnings or other employment rights or benefits. Petitioners do not object to the transfer provision, but challenge OSHA's authority under the Act to require employers to guarantee employees' wage and employment benefits following the transfer. The Court of Appeals held that OSHA has such authority. We hold that, whether or not OSHA has this underlying authority, the agency has failed to make the necessary determination or statement of reasons that its wage guarantee requirement is related to the achievement of a safe and healthful work environment.

Congress gave OSHA the responsibility to protect worker health and safety, and to explain its reasons for its actions. Because the Act in no way authorizes OSHA to repair general unfairness to employees that is unrelated to achievement of health and safety goals, we conclude that OSHA acted beyond the statutory authority when it issued the wage guarantee regulation.

V

When Congress passed the Occupational Safety and Health Act in 1970, it chose to place pre-eminent value on assuring employees a safe and healthful working environment, limited only by the feasibility of achieving such an environment. We must measure the validity of the Secretary's actions against the requirements of that Act. For "[t]he judicial function does not extend to substantive revision of regulatory policy. That function lies elsewhere—in Congressional and Executive oversight or amendatory legislation."

Accordingly, the judgment of the Court of Appeals is affirmed in all respects except to the extent of its approval of the Secretary's application of the wage guarantee provision of the Cotton Dust Standard. . . . To that extent, the judgment of the Court of Appeals is

Case Review   *175*

vacated and the case remanded with directions to remand to the Secretary for further proceedings consistent with this opinion.

It is so ordered.

Justice POWELL took no part in the decision of these cases.[21]

CASE REVIEW

Certainly it is possible to "overread" a Supreme Court decision. After all, each case rests on its own unique set of facts, and each case is decided on its own merits, with the narrow "holding" applied only to the immediate factual presentation. Nonetheless, the rationale behind the holding is important and the reasoning in *American Textile* is as significant as the narrow ruling. What is the important rationale that *American Textile* reveals? Again there are both general and specific points.

General Thoughts

The Psychological Foundations of Judicial Behavior

Behavioral scientists like to talk about the socialization process,[22] that is, the process whereby one learns the ropes—learns to adopt those values and norms that are essential to full-fledged membership in an organization.

Organizational behaviorists see the socialization process largely in terms of individual-organizational interactions.[23] Additionally, however, the process view incorporates an acknowledgment that the individual comes to the organization with preexisting sets of values, attitudes, and expectations. To the extent that the preexisting mind set conforms to the organization's needs, socialization is smooth; to the degree that incompatibilities exist, socialization is disruptive. The point is that these individual "prearrival" psychological foundations exist; and they are either destroyed or reinforced during the process of interaction with the organization.[24]

One element of the prearrival foundation concerns how newcomers think. Once they arrive as judges or jurists, lawyers think according to legally prescribed, time-honored, acceptable patterns. As law students, lawyers are taught to think in a certain way; simply reading and preparing thousands of cases in law school anchors this mind set.[25] Conferences, briefs, oral arguments, and trial preparation reinforce this psychological foundation. Acceptance to the bench means one has arrived, with the psychological foundation intact.

What are the elements of this psychological foundation? How do these prearranged values, attitudes, and norms affect how legalists think?

Groupthink and Consensus

Groupthink has been defined as the psychological phenomenon that occurs when group members, in making group decisions, become so enamored with concurrence that the norm for consensus overrides full appraisal of more realistic options. Critics suggest that groupthink is a desperate drive for consensus at any cost that suppresses dissent. Usually the groupthink phenomenon is applied to "Bay of Pigs" kinds of disastrous decisions and usually in the context of powerful, governmental, military or business organizations. The judiciary, in our overly polite (and unrealistic) way, has been excluded from analysis.

This is curious because the driving force behind judicial reasoning (particularly U.S. Supreme Court decisions) is to reach a consensus that will be acceptable to, and implemented by, more powerful administrative agencies and legislative institutions. And so consensus emerges as a goal in itself. To a greater or lesser degree, dissent, disagreement, and disfavor are unwelcome ingredients in decisions. This is not to say that distinctions and dissent are not allowed. They are; but they are categorically rejected as majority thinking and thus are valueless as precedent.

A Distinction, Not a Difference

The quest for consensus is dramatically narrated in court studies and in legal anecdotes surrounding the historic decision in *Brown et al.* v. *Board of Education of Topeka et al.* 347 U.S. 483, 74 S.Ct. 686 (1954).[26] The famous 9−0 majority consensus is a classic illustration of the Court's ability to fashion agreement even on the most sensitive and socially explosive issues. Moreover, this consensus was achieved against the force of precedent [*Plessy* v. *Ferguson*, 163 U.S. 537, 163 S.Ct. 1138 (1896)], which weighed against the *Brown* decision.

The interesting point is not the realization that consensus building is a goal and that it occurs. The interesting question is how consensus is built, how it operates in a detailed, practical way. One way that legal consensus occurs is through the device of distinctions. This device allows the Court to circumvent precedent. As Justice Felix Frankfurter wrote: "[A]lthough *stare decisis* means 'respect for decisions' it did not prohibit re-examination of the reasoning and principles on which they were based."[27]

What is the justification for the reasoning that what was equal in

1896 (racial segregation at the time of *Plessy*) is not equal in 1954 (at the time of *Brown*)? How does the Court justify reversing older cases and lines of reasoning? Noting that times have changed, and that psychological inferiority is the damage, the Court was able to distinguish the facts in *Brown* from the facts in *Plessy*. Thus the fiction is constructed that *Brown* and *Plessy* are not different rulings on similar facts and issues. Rather, they are presented as principled decisions flowing from distinct facts and unique concerns.

The Basic Values Approach

Counterbalanced against a methodology that seeks distinctions, gradations, and qualifications is a reliance on, or at least an appeal to, "basic values." For example, basic values might include such maxims (in *American Textile*) as:

- Refusal to impute to Congress contradictory purposes: for example, paralyzing OSHA (burden of data) while seeking to promote societal goals (toxic controls).
- Insistence on the "plain language" approach in examining the meanings of words.
- Reliance on the assumption that the words "to the extent feasible" are so commonly understood that operational parameters, or implementation strategies, are self-evident (that is, the thing can be done).
- *Expressio unius, exclusio alterius*: ("what is expressed implies exclusion of other matters"),[28] or the notion that Congress does not require cost-benefit analysis where it is not specifically indicated on the face of the statute.

Note also that these examples of legalistic methodology range from common sense axioms to ancient legal maxims. The point is that the law and legal reasoning rely heavily on basic value assumptions.

Induction, Deduction, and Intuition

The inductive (or scientific) method proceeds from the particular to the general. Just as science builds upon experience in reaching postulated generalizations, so, too, the law uses actual specific cases in arriving at broad conclusions.[29] In relying upon experience, history, tradition, and custom the law is, however, more organic than scientific.

    The deductive method employs general reason and logic as premises for new deductions. Likewise, the law, utilizing general principles (all men are created equal), deduces specific conclusions (no state shall deprive "any person" of equal protection of the laws).[30] Once the deductive process begins, further deductions are then possible. For example, the word *persons* is held to mean citizens and noncitizens; therefore, each should be treated equally.[31]

Comparing Figures 6.1 and 6.2, one sees that the two methodologies appear contradictory.

Figure 6.1
The Inductive Method

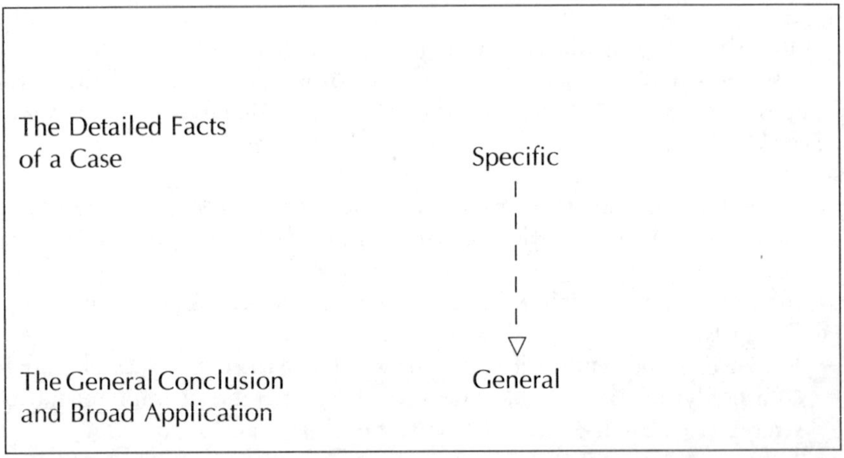

The Detailed Facts of a Case	Specific
	∣
	∣
	∣
	∣
	∇
The General Conclusion and Broad Application	General

Figure 6.2
The Deductive Method

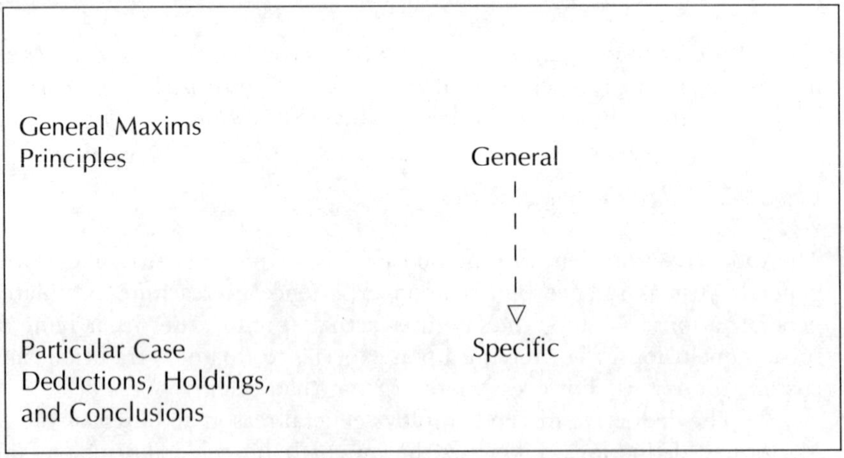

General Maxims Principles	General
	∣
	∣
	∣
	∇
Particular Case Deductions, Holdings, and Conclusions	Specific

It is clear that legal reasoning uses both, or parts of both, approaches. It is the interaction of the two processes, and the tension between their respective logics, that produces reliance on a third approach, the intuitive method.

The intuitive approach may merely be polite language for ambiguous, arbitrary reasoning processes, for which judges are criticized. Or the intuitive approach may represent a quite legitimate form of mental artistry—a way of reasoning that is, in some intangible way, distinct from induction or deduction. At any rate it is clear that neither induction nor deduction alone describes or explains the legal method. Together induction and deduction create a tension that leads to a third method: intuition. What is intuition? And more important, how does it work? (This will be explained in detail in Chapter 8.) For the moment consider that intuition uses such creative devices as common sense (everyday experience), self-evident solutions (split the difference), moral maxims, justice as fairness, and social welfare considerations.

As Judge Jerome Frank is quoted: "Judges, like musical performers, are to some extent creative artists."[32]

Specific Implications and Trends

Deference

As far back as *Marbury* v. *Madison*[33] the courts, pursuant to a philosophy of judicial intervention, recognized that they possess very little enforcement power. In short, there is no way, other than relying on voluntary compliance, that the courts can force implementation or acceptance of judicial decisions. Thus, for example, the courts are much less inclined to issue *positive injunctions* (in effect, an order that requires doing something and thus requires enforcement or implementation) than they are inclined to issue *negative injunctions* (an order that restrains an act, thus not requiring legal oversight). In *American Textile*, accordingly, the Court deferred to Congress. In effect the Court said that Congress already defined the basic relationship between costs and benefits in the Occupational Safety and Health Act of 1970[34] and since the "plain meaning" of the word *feasible* is to be read as "capable of being done," there was no reason for judicial interference.

Ricorsi *and the Case Method*

Machiavelli saw in the history nothing but ups and downs—cyclical reruns, or as he said, *ricorsi*. More significantly (in a negative way),

Machiavelli saw in human history a fixed oscillation between the bad and the good. In a chapter titled "The World as a Whole Is Always the Same," Machiavelli reportedly wrote:

> When I meditate on how these things move, I judge that the world has always gone on in the same way, and that there has been as much good as bad, but that this bad and this good have varied from land to land, as anyone understands who knows about these ancient kingdoms which differed from one another because of the difference in their customs, but the world remained the same.[35]

It is a disturbing thought that the much vaunted case method approach of stare decisis is not a progressive accumulation of "good" decisions but rather a constant bouncing back and forth on the walls of good and bad. In Western civilization the hope of continuous progress is powerful. But as the *American Textile* case shows the legal approach leaves winners and losers and not final answers. There is no final resolution of absolute good or of ultimate evil. Such concepts are not resolved or offered in the law.

Definitions and Deflection

The legal approach to "words" and the Court's ability to define and use words is curious. On the one hand, there are important words that the law resists clarifying. For example, in the law of commercial transactions the word *unconscionable* has taken on new and important meaning.[36] While the principle of unconscionable contracts is not novel, the use of the word in a statute dealing with commercial transactions is profound. And yet the Uniform Commercial Code provides little by way of explication. On the other hand, the law will define in laborious language certain other words. For example, the word *merchant* in the Uniform Commercial Code is defined in great detail.[37] In addition, 16 sections of the code contain special rules that apply to transactions between merchants and nonmerchants or to transactions in which a merchant is a party. These rules do not apply to nonmerchants, and thus by definitional constraint the law and the courts have placed a higher standard of conduct and greater responsibility on merchants as a class.

In *American Textile* the Court offers little operational meaning to the word *feasible* except to say that it means "capable of being done." The ultimate effect of such vagueness or intended ambiguity is to deflect responsibility for defining the term. The Court thereby insulates itself from involvement in the ongoing controversy regarding the phrase. The issue here is not whether it is wise or unwise (or desirable or undesirable) to offer vague definitional content. Not only that the effect is to deflect responsibility. Yet in other circumstances (the definition of *merchants*) the Court will offer detailed content and place exacting standards and responsibilities on defined parties, classes, or actions. Is the effect the same? Probably. Deflecting responsibility by embroidering a word in such detail that accountability is impossible is only another way of deflecting involvement for definitions. (This contradiction in the Court's approach is itself interesting and will be analyzed in Chapter 7.)

What Balancing Test *Means*

In deciding cases it is clear that the courts weigh competing or conflicting claims. Aside from reasoning process based on principle, the courts balance the choices; that is, judges look at pros and cons, advantages and disadvantages, and benefits and costs. The question is, What do the courts balance? What do they factor in and factor out? This has been a misinterpreted area of judicial reasoning. Nonetheless, it is clear from a perusal of even the earliest cases that the courts have never explicitly balanced life (as a benefit) against inefficiency (as a cost). For example, in *Southern Pacific Co. v. Arizona ex el. Sullivan, Attorney General* 325 U.S. 761, 65 S.Ct. 1515 (1945) a state regulation of the length of railroad trains was invalidated as an unconstitutional burden on interstate commerce. The Court noted:

> The contrast between the present regulation and the full train crew laws in point of their effects on the commerce, and the like contrast with the highway safety regulations, in point of the nature of the subject of regulation and the state's interest in it, illustrate and emphasize the considerations which enter into a determination of the *relative weights* of state and national interests where state regulation affecting interstate commerce is attempted. Here examination of all the relevant factors makes it plain that the state interest is outweighed by the interest of the nation in an adequate, economical and efficient railway transportation service which must prevail. [Emphasis Added][38]

Perhaps because of the murky rhetoric, this and other cases [39] were read as if the courts add up and balance the number of lost human lives against a cold efficiency/economy standard. But the Court in *Southern Pacific* clearly stated that more frequent but shorter trains would result in *more* accidents than less frequent but longer trains with the dangerous slack-action effect of multi-couplings.[40] There was no balance of life versus cost. The Court realized that the Arizona law had no reasonable relation to safety and so struck down the law.

Likewise, in *American Textile* the Court held that "cost-benefit" analysis is not required by the OSHA [act] because feasibility analysis is required. The word "feasible" directs the Secretary of Labor to assure *"to the extent feasible*, on the basis of the best available evidence, that no employee will suffer material impairment of health . . . limited only by the extent to which this is 'capable of being done'."[41] While some may read this as a refinement of the nonexisting balancing test, it surely is not a balance of life versus cost, which in human cases is the only factor to balance. As yet, courts have not gone quite that far, that is, to add and weigh the number of lives to be discarded in the balancing process.

Rational Relationships

Legal scholars would be quick to note that the court in *South Carolina State Highway Department et al. v. Barnwell Brothers, Inc. et al.*[42] and in *Southern Pacific*[43] relied on a standard of reasonableness to secure the safe and economical use of highways (*Barnwell*) and to secure a reasonable relationship to the health, safety, and well-being of the people of Arizona (*Southern Pacific*). In this context these standards rely on the traditional, rational basis test. This is the "equal protection" standard applied generally to economic and social regulation. The test requires that governmental classifications have a reasonable or rational[44] relationship with a valid governmental objective in order to be constitutional. However, the term *rational relationship* does not mean a scientific relationship based on neutral, objective, quantified data or correlations. It means that any differential treatment given to one class over another must be justified by a "rational connection" within a permissible public purpose or governmental goal.[45]

Note that the word *rational* in its legal context (reasonable, permissible) is different than the word *rational* in the business sense (objective, purposive).

Judicial Strategies

It is no accident that the Court selected Justice Brennan, a longtime advocate and spokesman for organized labor, to draft the decision in *American Textile*. The decision thereby becomes, presumably, more acceptable to labor interests. Likewise, it was no coincidence that in *City of Burbank et al. v. Lockheed Air Terminal, Inc., et al.* the Court selected Justice

Douglas, a noted environmentalist and an active outdoors enthusiast, to draft what might be viewed as an antienvironmental decision.[46]

The recent revelations of the Frankfurter-Brandeis "political connection" shocked some legal observers because of the revealed blatant and heretofore unacknowledged political reasoning as opposed to legal or principled reasoning.[47] A book titled *Inside the Warren Court* has dramatically illustrated behind-the-scenes "politicking" regarding significant judicial decisions.[48] The point is that strategies are used.

Power, Selectivity, and the Application of Principle

Although judicial or legal power is often a function of position in the governmental structure or a product of legal resources, there are "still some strategies and tactics that could enhance the power of the actor within those constraints."[49] One key tactic has been referred to as "the selective use of objective criteria"—that is, the use of criteria, even though "hard" and "objective," that favor one's position. The courts and jurists utilize this technique when they select one principle (or one precedent) as opposed to another. Thus a principled decision is made, but it is hardly a nondiscretionary or value-free decision.

Problems and Definitions

In Chapter 7 the discretionary aspect of case law (the judicial process) will be described in detail. At this point analysis focuses on the prerequisite of legal reasoning and the circumstances that account for ambiguous, arbitrary choices. Selective use of established precedents (or principles) is only one such tactic. Definitions of problems is another; that is, judges by selecting certain issues as problematic, and discarding other issues as nonproblematic, become key and central participants in the reciprocal relationship between individual thought and the moral consciousness of a society. In a word the definition of a problem—as an emergency or a crisis, as a systematic failure or an individual shortcoming, or as an evidentiary or non-evidentiary issue—becomes the critical intervening variable between a social condition and a judicial response to it.[50]

The Nature of Questions and the Logic of Case Law: Why Do Human Beings Have Lungs?

The distinctive aim of the legal method is to provide society with legitimate and responsibly supported answers to questions: in short, to justify why A wins and B loses. The chief methodological tool in this enterprise is the case method with its accumulation of binding precedents. In this context of case law development, there are four primary patterns of reasoning:

1. The *deductive model*, in which the explicandum is a logical consequence of explanatory premises;
2. The *law of probability*, in which explanations are contained in a statistical assumption about some class of elements;
3. The *inductive model*, in which experimentation leads to generalization; and
4. The *functional* (or *teleological*) *explanation*, in which explanations take the form of indicating one or more functions that a unit performs in maintaining or realizing certain traits to which the unit belongs.[51]

To illustrate this fourth "functional" method, one might analyze the question, Why do human beings have lungs? The typical answer: "The occurrence of lungs in the human body is explained by showing that they operate in a stated manner in order to maintain a chemical process and thereby to assure a continuance of life for the body into the future."[52] In short, a functional explanation is not an answer or an explanation but a description. There is no logic involved.

Likewise, consider the "legal" question presented in the brown lung case, namely: Why not utilize cost-benefit analysis to deal with the problem of lung disease? The Court's answer is descriptive in nature and not logical. The answer is: Because Congress did not require it for the health of the larger social system. In short, cost-benefit analysis would be dysfunctional and, in this case, not desirable. That is not logic. That is power.[53]

Power, Progress, and the Case Methods

This chapter began and ended with reference to the concept of power. Assuming that power (or authority, or force, or a mix of these elements) underlies legal reasoning, the larger question is, Where does this phenomenon take us, and where does the case method lead in terms of Western ideas of intellectual and societal progress?

Some advocates of the Anglo-American case method might argue that if historical patterns of case decision were plotted on some massive computerized printout, they would fall, as tiny dots, along a clear trend line indicating upward progress, and thereby affirming social advancement and social good. Such a chart might look like Figure 6.3.

Conclusion 185

Figure 6.3
Legal-Social Progress: Trend Line

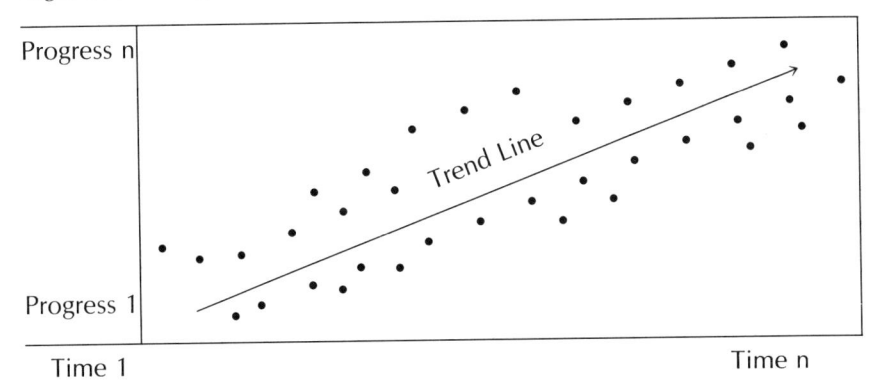

Others, more skeptical, might observe that the accumulated weight of case law represents not a clear, consistent trend but a rather haphazard and arbitrary "fallout" with no discernible logic underlying the pattern. To such observers the same chart might look like Figure 6.4.

Figure 6.4
Legal-Social Progress: No Trend Line

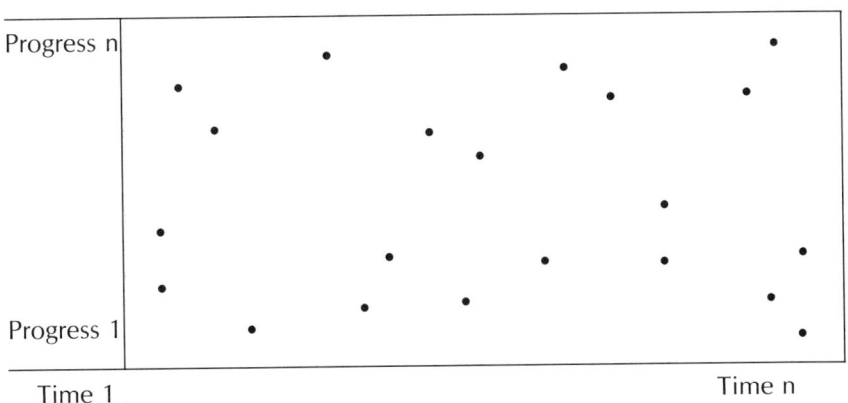

CONCLUSION

The possibility that the minority, less optimistic point of view might be valid is the subject of Chapter Seven. Therein the question is reconsidered: whether the legal model is logical and progressive or whether it is unprincipled and discretionary? Again, Chapter Seven utilizes the case method drawing analysis and evaluation from a classic Supreme Court controversy. The analysis in Chapter Seven, regarding the methodology of discretion and the case and conclusions, should be viewed as counterpoint to the analysis in Chapter Six. That is: Discretion is not necessarily an illogical, or even socially regressive, approach. The argument is, simply, that discretionary methods exist and that these methods merit serious study. Chapter Seven represents only a first analysis of this complicated phenomenon.

NOTES

1. Plato, *The Republic*. See Ernest Baker, *The Political Thought of Plato and Aristotle* (New York: Dover, 1959), pp. 116−18, wherein Plato's distaste for law is explained.

2. Some may argue that the law is ready and able to take on the "mighty." See *Brown et al.* v. *Board of Education of Topeka et al.*, 347 U.S. 483, 74 S.Ct. 686, (1954), issued on May 17, 1954. But because of anticipated resistance to the *Brown* decision, the Court moved reargument on the implementation question and in the following case *Brown et al.* v. *Board of Education of Topeka et al.* 349 U.S. 294, 75 S.Ct. 753, (1955), limited relief or "full implementation" to local conditions guided by "equitable principles" such as "all deliberate speed." See the fascinating narrative in *Inside the Warren Court 1953−1969* by Bernard Schwartz and Stephan Lesher (New York: Doubleday, 1983), pp 79−89.

3. Austin, a nineteenth century English philosopher, developed the idea of positive law as we know it today. Austin argued that positive law consists of three essential and distinctive elements: (1) a *rule* (2) derived from a political *superior*, (3) which imposes *sanctions* if violated. See the summary in the *Legal Environment of Business* by Bruce D. Fisher and Michael J. Phillips (St. Paul: West, 1983), chap. 1, pp. 2−3.

4. David Easton, *The Political System* (New York: Alfred Knopf, 1953), pp. 96−101, and Chapter One of this book.

5. Easton, *The Political System*, p. 115.

6. Interestingly, most departments of political science were formerly called departments of government, reflecting the positivistic orientation. Today only a relative few departments of government are found in major universities.

7. More directly, the legal model or jurisprudential process operates as a "truth-seeking" mechanism, allowing society to predict behavioral outcomes on the basis of a clearly defined set of principles.

8. John Stuart Mill, *Utilitarianism, Liberty and Representative Government* (New York: E.P. Dutton, 1910, p. 111−14).

9. Mill, *Utilitarianism, Liberty and Representative Government*, p. 38.

10. The institutions are themselves subject to the justice concept. Thus the office of the president of the United States is subject to Judicial Review. See *United States* v. *Nixon, President of the United States, et al.*, 418 U.S. 683, 94 S.Ct. 3090 (1974).

11. *Southern Pacific Co.* v. *Arizona ex rel. Sullivan, Attorney General*, 325 U.S. 761, 783, 65 S.Ct. 1515, 1527 (1945) used the phrase "relative weights" in examining the impact of a state (safety) law as a burden on interstate commerce (train length). This phrase, perhaps, is the origin of the misplaced notion that the courts will balance the value of life against administrative costs.

12. *Shelley et ux.* v. *Kraemer et ux.* 334 U.S.1, 68 S.Ct. 836, (1948). The case involved state action as a form of racial discrimination. One question was whether rights of liberty and property might be balanced against the right not to have the state enforce discrimination against the victims.

13. David Haber, "Notes on the Limits of *Shelley* v. *Kramer*," 18 Rutgers L.Rev. 811, 813, 824−25 (1964).

14. Bruce D. Fisher and Michael J. Phillips, *The Legal Environment of Business* (St. Paul: West, 1983), p. 17.

15. Judge Henry J. Friendly, "Some Kind of a Hearing" (Owen J. Roberts Memorial Lecture at University of Pennsylvania Law School, April 3, 1975).

16. *William Marbury* v. *James Madison, Secretary of State of the United States*, 5 U.S. (1 Cranch) 137, 2. L.Ed. 60, (1803) in which Chief Justice Marshall declared portions of the Judiciary Act of 1789 unconstitutional, thereby invalidating a judicial appointment that the Supreme Court could not have enforced at any rate. In the process of course the Court established the significant principle of judicial review.

17. See the discussion regarding the role of Chief Justice Earl Warren and the racially explosive decision regarding *Brown et al.* v. *Board of Education of Topeka et al.*, 347 U.S. 483, 74 S.Ct. 686, (1954), in *Inside the Warren Court: 1953−1969*, pp. 77−90. Warren played a moderating broker role so as to minimize internal dissent.

18. *Administrative law* is a phrase with more than one meaning. It is used in the broad sense to refer to all laws and judicial activities pertaining to administrative agencies (including statutes, rules, regulations, and court and agency review of the above). An administrative agency is a nonlegislative, nonjudicial governmental body that formulates and enforces rules and regulations that impact virtually every aspect of contempo-

rary life. Administrative law covers such diverse topics as constitutional law, securities regulation, antitrust, labor law, employment discrimination, environmental law, occupational law, and other areas.

19. *Executive Order 1229 Sec. 2(b)* signed by President Ronald Reagan, required that federal executive agencies perform cost/benefit analysis before implementing any major regulation (one imposing costs of $100 million or more). Code of Federal Regulations, Title III, 1982, p. 128.

20. Promulgating regulations is the final official step in the lengthy rule-making process which includes: drafting legislation, conduct-ing agency investigation, and drafting regulations.

21. Justice Stewart filed a separate dissenting opinion, and Justice Rehnquist, with whom Chief Justice Burger joined, filed a separate dissenting opinion.

22. Stephen P. Robbins, *Organizational Behavior* (Englewood Cliffs, N.J.: Prentice-Hall, 1984), p. 455. Robbins defines *socialization* as the process of adaptation. "It is the process by which employees come to understand the values, norms, and customs essential for assuming an organizational role and for becoming an accepted member of an organization."

23. Edgar Schein in Alvar O. Elbing, "Perception, Motivation and Business Behavior," *Behavioral Decisions in Organizations* (Glenview, Ill: Scott Foresman 1970).

24. John Van Maanen and Edgar Schein have conceptualized socialization as a process made up of three stages: prearrival, encounter, and metamorphosis. See "Career Development," in *Improving Life at Work*, ed. by V. Richard Hackman and J. Lloyd Suttle (Santa Monica, Calif. Goodyear, 1977), pp. 58−62.

25. One cynical law professor quipped: "As law students you are as intellectually free as a bird in a cage. You can fly anywhere you want . . . within the cage."

26. Schwartz and Lesher, *Inside the Warrern Court: 1953−1969*, pp. 80−102.

27. Ibid., p. 81.

28. *American Textile Manufacturers Institute, Inc. et al.* v. *Donovan, Secretary of Labor, et al.*, 452 U.S. 490, 101 S.Ct. 2491.

29. The cases became precedent for future cases, thus expanding the specifics. This is known as stare decisis ("the decision stands").

30. *U.S. Constitution*, Fourteenth Amendment.

31. *Yick Wo* v. *Hopkins, Sheriff.*, 118 U.S. 356, 6 S.Ct. 1064, (1886), where a Chinese laundry sued the city of San Francisco, alleging discriminatory (unequal) treatment in zoning regulations.

32. Quoted in Len Young Smith and George Gale Roberson, *Business Law*, 5th ed. (West, 1983), p. 5. The authors also provide the

thoughts for the distinction between induction, deduction, and intuition.

33. *William Marbury* v. *James Madison, Secretary of State of the United States,* 5 U.S. *(1 Cranch)* 137, 2 L.Ed. 60 (1803). Justice Marshall realized that finding a law (Judiciary Act 1789) unconstitutional was a much wiser course than trying to force the appointment of Magistrate Marbury against the wishes of a newly elected president, Thomas Jefferson.

34. Occupational Health and Safety Act, 29 U.S.C.A. 655, Sec. 6(b)(5), 1970.

35. Robert Nisbet, *History of the Idea of Progress* (New York: Basic Books, 1980), p. 106. Some say Machiavelli saw bad as the dominant feature.

36. The *Uniform Commercial Code*, Sec. 2−302 states that the courts may refuse to enforce contracts that are "unconscionable." *Ill. Rev. Stat.* 1977, Ch. 26. See also other state codes.

37. The *Uniform Commerical Code,* Sec. 2−104 defines a merchant as a person (1) who is a dealer in the goods or (2) who by his occupation holds himself out as having knowledge or skill peculiar to the goods or practices involved or (3) who employs an agent or broker whom he holds out as having such knowledge or skill. *Ill. Rev. Stat.* 1977, Ch. 26. See also other state codes.

38. *Southern Pacific Co.* v. *Arizona ex rel. Sullivan, Attorney General* 325 U.S. 783−784, 65 S.Ct. 1527 (1945).

39. *South Carolina State Highway Department et al.* v. *Barnwell Brothers, Inc., et al.*, 303 U.S. 177, 58 S.Ct. 510, (1938).

40. *Southern Pacific Co.* v. *Arizona ex rel. Sullivan, Attorney General*, 325 U.S. 776−778, 65 S.Ct. 1524−1525 (1945).

41. *American Textile Manufacturers Institute, Inc. et al.* v. *Donovan, Secretary of Labor, et al.*, 452 U.S. 508−509, 101 S.Ct. 2490 (1981).

42. 303 U.S. 177, 58 S.Ct. 510, (1938).

43. *Southern Pacific Co.* v. *Arizona ex rel. Sullivan, Attorney General*, 325 U.S. 761, 65 S.Ct. 1515 (1945).

44. For example, if state X legislates and subjects Brown Corp. to a disadvantage (or advantage) but does not give Black Corp. the same treatment, then there must be a reason for the distinction or discrimination. Fisher and Phillips, *The Legal Environment of Business*, pp. 186−87.

45. Ibid., p. 188.

46. *City of Burbank et al* v. *Lockheed Air Terminal, Inc., et al.*, 411 U.S. 624, 93 S.Ct. 1854 (1973): The decision, written by Douglas, struck down a local ordinance that attempted to regulate air traffic noise pollution in Burbank, California.

47. Bruce Allen Murphy, *The Brandeis-Frankfurter, Connection: The Secret Political Activities of Two Supreme Court Justices* (New York: Oxford University Press, 1982).

48. Schwartz and Lesher, *Inside the Warren Court*.

49. See Jeffrey Pfeffer, *Power in Organizations* (Boston: Pitman Press, 1981), p. 137. Although Pfeffer was referring to "political" strategies and tactics, the point applies to judicial tactics as well.

50. Albert K. Merton and Robert A. Nisbet, *Contemporary Social Problems* (New York: Harcourt Brace, 1964), p. 5.

51. Ernest Nagel, *The Structure of Science* (New York: Harcourt Brace, 1961), p. 24. Also see pp. 15−26. Nagel includlues genetic explanation as a major fourth category. I have substituted the more generic concept of induction.

52. Ibid., p. 24.

53. And the case and precedent may be reversed by a "power" method. Note the recent attempt by the OMB to require EPA (Environmental Protection Agency) to weigh the dollar value of human life when considering how to regulate asbestos. See "U.S. Budget Office Disputed on Cost Basis for Asbestos," *New York Times*, April 17, 1985, p. 12.

It is an established rule in the exposition of statutes, that the intention of the lawgiver is to be deduced from a view of the whole and of every part of the statute, taken and compared together. The real intention, when accurately ascertained, will always prevail over the literal sense of terms. . . . {A}nd the reason and intention of the lawgiver will control the strict letter of the law, when the latter would lead to palpable injustice, contradiction and absurdity.

Chancellor Kent
Commentaries on American Law

CHAPTER SEVEN

DISCRETIONARY MODELS

DEFINITIONS AND CONCEPTS

Discretion, and its interaction with the law, is no more dramatically or grotesquely illustrated than in a recent article that reported:

> NO EXECUTIONS PLANNED, GUINEA STRONGMAN SAYS
>
> Conakry, Guinea, April 8—The Guinean Army colonel who took power here in a military coup last week said today that none of the officials of the ousted Government had been harmed and that none would be executed. He indicated that some of them would face trial.
>
> "These will not be political trials," Col. Lansana Conté said at a news conference. "People will no longer be punished for their politics. Now it is administrative offenses, economic errors that we are going to punish."[1]

The distinction between political errors and administrative or economic errors is blatantly discretionary. The distinction is discretionary in that it is vague and derives from a subjective or non-explicit meaning and interpretation of critical words. Equally significant, the distinction is discretionary, as it involves a subtle but sophisticated choice of one term over another. The effect of subjective choice of words is to allow for, or to legitimize, a course of action without giving meaningful content to the words used or to the principle applied.

The purpose of this chapter is to address several questions: What is meant by the term *discretion*? How does discretion operate in organized, institutionalized life? And specifically, what is the interaction between discretion and law (or the justice model)?

Discretion as an Abstraction: A Continuum or a Phenomenon?

In a penetrating study entitled *Discretionary Justice*[2] Kenneth Culp Davis queried:

> If all decisions involving justice to individual parties were lined up on a scale, with those governed by precise rules at the extreme left, those involving unfiltered discretion at the extreme right, and those based on various mixtures of rules, principles, standards and discretion in the middle, where on the scale might be the most serious and the most infrequent injustice?[3]

Davis answered this question by stating flatly that the greatest and most frequent injustice occurs at the discretion end of the scale,

> where rules and principles provide little or no guidance, where emotions of deciding officers may affect what they do, where political or other favoritism may influence decisions, and where the imperfections of human nature are often reflected in the choice made.[4]

Such observations regarding an ignored area of research are provocative and important; yet they miss a significant point of inquiry, a critical prerequisite issue. Davis and others observe that discretion is simply an extreme on a fixed range of a continuum— that it is the same thing as justice, just a different form. That is to say that discretion exits at the other end of the justice scale. By this view discretion is simply a variation on a methodology.

This inquiry begins with a different question. The prerequisite issue here is not whether discretion is good or bad (the justice/injustice

Definitions and Concepts

continuum); rather, the question is, What is it? That is, what are the intellectual and behavioral components of discretion as an abstraction, as a phenomenon, and as a pervasive methodology with its own distinct components?[5]

The Generic Approach

One view of discretion is that it exists as an intellectual approach in a variety of institutional settings. Discretion is usually studied in the context of the legal environment, or as a part of administrative law or public administration. Yet it is possible that as a decision-making tool discretion operates in both the public and the private sectors, in several institutional contexts, and at all levels of organized activity. This is to suggest that while discretion is perceived as an illegitimate and therefore informal activity or process, it may actually be characterized by legitimizing processes and by formal elements.[6]

It should be noted that discretion as a separate and distinct decision-making process is rarely treated in the literature on decision making. Values, personality, motivation, leadership, power, and conflict are all given detailed attention. Discretion, perhaps the most prevalent phenomenon, is generally ignored or, when treated, is dealt with in the same context as justice.

Justice and Discretion

Is discretion properly to be viewed as the antithesis of justice? That is to ask, Is discretion necessarily an undesirable mental process or a dysfunctional behavioral result? If justice is akin to a clear and predictable set of legitimate laws and legitimating procedures (for example, due process), then is discretion simply the breakdown or the extreme opposite of that end state and thus necessarily undesirable?

There are at least two responses to this issue, both of which cut at the issue of progress and the hopes of Western civilization. One notion is that justice (and its concomitant, progress) is achieved by articulation of and respect for clearly defined and democratically achieved laws. While these laws need not be positivistic in form (that is, they may result from mere promulgation in the *Federal Register*), they are positive in content in that they are perceived as legitimate.[7] In this context positive law is derived from several sources: constitutional law, statutory law, judge-made law, and administrative law.[8]

Arbitrary or Nonarbitrary. Discretion, as a phenomenon of logical reasoning, has several connotations and meanings. One meaning, akin to the use of the word *politics*, defines discretion as a nonlegitimate and perhaps nonbinding problem-solving method. By this view discretion as a concept and as a goal is discredited. Consider, for example, that discretionary policies are often linked to regulations or rules that are vague and therefore arbitrary. Especially in certain legal areas, judgments are considered harsh or unfair because the judgment was reached via an arbitrary process. This was the case with early death penalty issues and particularly with challenges to imposition of the death penalty as violative of due process.

In *Furman* v. *Georgia* the U.S. Supreme Court considered a petitioner's challenge to a jury's absolute discretion to impose the death penalty. In sustaining petitioner's challenge (and denying imposition of the death penalty on grounds of cruel and unusual punishment), the Court emphasized that due process compels the States to make explicit the fundamental policy choices upon which any exertion of state power is based. That is: a death penalty is "unusual" if it is imposed "under a procedure that gives room for the play" of inappropriate and unconstitutional social, religious, racial or other prejudices.[9] In this and other cases, the Court's concern with arbitrary state action is not that the state legislatures had established clearly violative capital punishment procedures. On the contrary, the concern was that the state legislatures had left the process open to discretionary judgments.[10] In its concern however, the Court made the semantic (or perhaps logical) misstep of commingling discretion with arbitrariness. This is a confusion that exists in other fields as well.

It is important to understand that arbitrariness is not discretion; in fact, *arbitrariness* may be the exact opposite of *discretion*. Discretion requires a methodology or reasoning process whereby (1) a problem is defined as requiring solution or action, (2) a clear-cut path or goal is selected based not on fixed procedures but on non-explicit or preferential factors, and (3) the subjective solution reached is applied to the problem at hand.

Arbitrary actions are just the opposite. Arbitrary decisions lack foundation; they are without prejudice or prejudgment. Ironically, arbitrary judgments lack the attributes of unfairness, vagueness, unreasonableness, or discretion. For example, the least discretionary death penalty process would be one that is totally arbitrary. All convicted murderers die within 30 days after sentencing. Period. Or, as another example, convicted murderers shall be given the death sentence by random selection from a lotto-type system. Done. In either case the procedure used is purely arbitrary. It is, however, not discretionary. It does not allow for the free and unbridled application of reasoning processes or for the use of selective judgment or the application of critical faculties.

Chadi Justice and Codified Justice. Other writers[11] have described a system of justice that differs markedly from Western assumptions and procedures. Referred to as "Chadi" justice,[12] and once manifested in primitive nomadic populations in the Middle East, this form of conflict resolution is characterized by a very informal system of decisions. For example, when a problem or conflict arises, the dispute is taken to the Chadi, who periodically visits the village or oasis. A crowd gathers; each side presents its story. The Chadi, on the spot and in a seemingly arbitrary manner, dispenses judgment—without reference to codified rules and regulations and without reliance on constitutional references.[13] It is reported that the British, in their role as colonizers, were appalled at the seemingly arbitrary, disorderly, and irrational system of Chadi justice that they encountered.[14] And so the colonizers dismantled the informal indigenous system, and replaced it with a highly sophisticated, codified, rational system of rules and regulations.[15] It should be noted that those who have studied such legal cultures find in them a great deal of rationality and effectiveness. For example, Max Gluckman found among the Bartose people of Northern Rhodesia, that Bartose courts were conciliatory and compromise-minded. This was due to the fact that most relationships among the people he studied were

> multiplex, enduring through the lives of individuals, even generations. Each . . . is a part of an intricate network of similar relationships.[16]

Disputes, unlike in Anglo-American cultures, do not arise as ephemeral issues involving single interests but in relationships that embrace many interests. Hence there is no tendency or proclivity to reduce disputes to a single "legal" question or to preclude evidence by use of formal restrictive evidentiary rules. Again, discretion is not an arbitrary, groundless approach to problem solving.

Discretion in Operation

Discretion has both procedural and substantive impacts. Procedurally, for example, this intellectual device may limit the examination of issues by a kind of evidentiary rank ordering or by lining up preferred choices. Substantively, a focus on single issues has the effect not only of narrowing complexities to a select few topics, but also of serving to prevent articulation of other issues. The effect of discretion is significant, at least in the abstract.

But other questions remain. Does discretion exist and what are its methodological elements? And how specifically does discretion operate in actual cases?

Methodological Elements

Strategy of Formalism. It may appear contradictory to say that the key methodological element of discretion is formalism, but this is precisely the case. It is seemingly contradictory because discretion is often associated with vagueness, laxity, arbitrary (that is, nonrational) decisions, and with other elements of nonaccountability. Yet is is important to remember that discretionary policies *begin* at some point in time. And the critical triggering event is the selection, by deliberate choice, of a strategy of reasoning that will govern later discussion. It is this preselection choice that subsequently determines the course of the issue through the life of a legal case.

In this context discretion is not a free-floating, vague, aimless methodology. On the contrary it is a highly sophisticated choice and a means of conflict resolution that has the effect of predetermining the outcome of controversial, complex matters.

Focus on Technicalities. A key element in the choice sequence is an early focus on highly technical matters. For example, procedurally if forms are defective or if pleadings are technically inadequate, this technical issue becomes the focus of legal activity at even the trial level.[17] It is no accident that both sides in a legal contest seize on the technicality as the access point for substantive argument.

Procedural Matters over Substantive Matters. In highly contested, complex, substantive legal situations that involve a great deal of discretion (that is, initial jugments that predetermine later results), much of what the courts do is procedural.[18] The courtroom drama is not unlike dramatic international disputes or peace negotiations where the initial negotiations and discussions focus on procedural matters such as the number of participants, the location of the conference, the shape of the table,[19] or the credentials of the participants. There is much precedent in the law for such an orientation. In the field of labor law early court decisions focused on procedural matter such as the environment for union elections.[20] More recently, in cases involving OSHA the court's focus is on the procedures for investigation and inspection.[21]

It is not surprising that courts focus methodologically on the elements of formalism, technicality, and procedure. Obviously, such a formulation of the problem makes it more manageable and, in a way, provides a more tangible (read *technical*) rationale for discretion. In short, the procedural approach legitimizes and perhaps disguises discretion.

Actual Operative Elements

The following case shows how the methodology operates in the complex interaction between law and society. The case concerns the Federal Register Act of 1935, which created three new publications: the *Government Manual*, the *Federal Register* (like a small newspaper containing proclamations, notices of federal agency meetings, and proposed federal regulations), and the *Code of Federal Regulations (CFR)*, which arranges all currently effective federal agency regulations by agency. (A multivolumed set of paperbound books, each book contains all of an agency's regulations updated each year.)

CASE IN POINT

Discretionary Models: Farmers versus Square Corners

Is the average citizen, who is probably unaware of a particular agency's rules, bound under a doctrine of constructive notice[22] by the promulgations issued in the *Federal Register* and the *CFR*'s? More specifically in the case below, does an Idaho farmer have the affirmative duty to read the *Federal Register* for the latest detailed information regarding federal programs? Merrill the farmer, applied for crop insurance through a county agent of the Federal Crop Insurance Agency to insure his wheat crop, part of which was being reseeded. Merrill's crop was destroyed by drought and he applied for payment. The agency refused because a regulation printed in the obscure *Federal Register* prohibited the insuring of reseeded crops.

The question before the Court was whether the insured's failure to read the government regulation excuses the government insurer from paying on the policy. The Court answered yes: an insured's lack of knowledge of a government regulation is a defense to the agency's refusal to pay out. The reasoning is a classic example of discretion in actual operation.

THE CASE: FEDERAL CROP INSURANCE CORP. V. MERRILL ET AL., DOING BUSINESS AS MERRILL BROS.*

MR. JUSTICE FRANKFURTER delivered the opinion of the Court.
We brought this case here because it involves a question of importance in the administration of the Federal Crop Insurance Act.

---

*Author's note: Citations and internal footnoting omitted. *Federal Crop Insurance Corp. v. Merrill et al. Doing Business as Merrill Bros.*, 332 U.S. 380, 68 S.Ct. 1 (1947).

The relevant facts may be briefly stated. Petitioner (hereinafter called the Corporation) is a wholly Government-owned enterprise, created by the Federal Crop Insurance Act, as an "agency of and within the Department of Agriculture." To carry out the purposes of the Act, the Corporation, "Commencing with the wheat . . . crops planted for harvest in 1945" is empowered "to insure, upon such terms and conditions not inconsistent with the provisions of this title as it may determine, producers of wheat . . . against loss in yields due to unavoidable causes, including drought. . . ." In pursuance of its authority, the Corporation on February 5, 1945, promulgated its Wheat Crop Insurance Regulations, which were duly published in the Federal Register on February 7, 1945.

On March 26, 1945, respondents applied locally for insurance under the Federal Crop Insurance Act to cover wheat farming operations in Bonneville County, Idaho. Respondents informed the Bonneville County Agricultural Conservation Committee, acting as agent for the Corporation, that they were planting 460 acres of spring wheat and that on 400 of these acres they were reseeding on winter wheat acreage. The Committee advised respondents that the entire crop was insurable, and recommended to the Corporation's Denver Branch Office acceptance of the application. (The formal application itself did not disclose that any part of the insured crop was reseeded.) On May 28, 1945, the Corporation accepted the application.

In July, 1945, most of the respondents' crop was destroyed by drought. Upon being notified, the Corporation, after discovering that the destroyed acreage had been reseeded, refused to pay the loss, and this litigation was appropriately begun in one of the lower courts of Idaho. The trial court rejected the Corporation's contention, presented by a demurrer to the complaint, that the Wheat Crop Insurance Regulations barred recovery as a matter of law. Evidence was thereupon permitted to go to the jury to the effect that the respondents had no actual knowledge of the Regulations, insofar as they precluded insurance for reseeded wheat, and that they had in fact been misled by petitioner's agent into believing that spring wheat reseeded on winter wheat acreage was insurable by the Corporation.

The jury returned a verdict for the loss on all the 460 acres and the Supreme Court of Idaho affirmed the resulting judgment. That court in effect adopted the theory of the trial judge, that since the knowledge of the agent of a private insurance company, under the circumstances of this case, would be attributed to, and thereby bind, a private insurance company, the Corporation is equally bound.

The case no doubt presents phases of hardship. We take for granted that, on the basis of what they were told by the Corporation's local agent, the respondents reasonably believed that their entire crop was covered by petitioner's insurance. And so we assume that recovery could be had against a private insurance company. But the Corporation is not a private insurance company. It is too late in the day to urge that the Government is just another private litigant, for purposes of charging it with liability, whenever it takes over a business theretofore conducted by private enterprise or engages in competition with private ventures. Government is not partly public or partly private, depending upon the governmental pedigree of the type of a particular activity or the manner in which the Government conducts it. The Government may carry on its operations through conventional executive agencies or through corporate forms especially created for defined ends. . . . Whatever the form in which the Government functions, anyone entering into an arrangement with the Government takes the risk of having accurately ascertained that he who purports to act for the Government stays within the bounds of his authority. The scope of this authority may be explicitly defined by Congress or be limited by delegated legislation, properly exercised through the rule-making power. And this is so, even though, as here, the agent himself may have been unaware of the limitations upon his authority.

If the Federal Crop Insurance Act had by explicit language prohibited the insurance of spring wheat which is reseeded on winter wheat acreage, the ignorance of such a restriction, either by the respondents or the Corporation's agent, would be immaterial and recovery could not be had against the Corporation for loss of such reseeded wheat. Congress could hardly define the multitudinous details appropriate for the business of crop insurance when the Government entered it. Inevitably "the terms and conditions" upon which valid governmental insurance can be had must be defined by the agency acting for the Government. And so Congress has legislated in this instance, as in modern regulatory enactments it so often does, by conferring the rule-making power upon the agency created for carrying out its policy. *Just as everyone is charged with knowledge of the United States Statutes at Large, Congress has provided that the appearance of rules and regulations in the Federal Register gives legal notice of their contents.* [Emphasis added]

Accordingly, the Wheat Crop Insurance Regulations were binding on all who sought to come within the Federal Crop Insurance Act, regardless of actual knowledge of what is in the Regulations or of the hardship resulting from innocent ignorance. The oft-quoted observation in *Rock Island, Arkansas & Louisiana Railroad Co. v. United States*, 254, U.S. 141, 143, that "Men must turn square corners when they deal with the Government" does not reflect a callous outlook. It merely expresses the duty of all courts to observe the conditions defined by Congress for charging the public treasury. The "terms and conditions" defined by the Corporation, under authority of Congress, for creating liability on the part of the Government preclude recovery for the loss of the reseeded wheat no matter with what good reason the respondents thought they had obtained insurance from the Government. Indeed, not only do the Wheat Regulations limit the liability of the Government as if they had been enacted by Congress directly, but they were in fact incorporated by reference in the application, as specifically required by the Regulations.

We have thus far assumed, as did the parties here and the courts below, that the controlling regulation in fact precluded insurance coverage for spring wheat reseeded on winter wheat acreage. It explicitly states that the term "wheat crop shall not include . . . winter wheat in the 1945 crop year, and spring wheat which has been reseeded on winter wheat acreage in the 1945 crop year." The circumstances of this case tempt one to read the regulation, since it is for us to read it, with charitable laxity. But not even the temptations of a hard case can elude the clear meaning of the regulation. It precludes recovery for "spring wheat which has been reseeded on winter acreage in the 1945 crop year." Concerning the validity of the regulation, as "not inconsistent with the provisions" of the Federal Crop Insurance Act, no question has been raised.

The judgment is reversed and the cause remanded for further proceedings not inconsistent with this opinion.

Reversed.

MR. JUSTICE BLACK and MR. JUSTICE RUTLEDGE dissent.

MR. JUSTICE JACKSON, dissenting.

I would affirm the decision of the court below. If crop insurance contract made by agencies of the United States Government are to be judged by the law of the State in which they are written, I find no error in the court below. If, however, we are to hold them subject only to federal law and to declare what that law is, I can see no reason why we should not adopt a rule which recognizes the practicalities of the business.

It was early discovered that fair dealing in the insurance business required that the entire contract between the policyholder and the insurance company be embodied in the writings which passed between the parties, namely, the written application, if any, and the policy issued. It may be well enough to make some types of contracts with the Government subject to long and involved regulations published in the Federal Register. To my mind, it is an absurdity to hold that every farmer who insures his crops knows what the Federal Register contains or even knows that there is such a publication. If he were to peruse this voluminous and dull publication as it is issued from time to time in order to make sure whether anything has been promulgated that affects his rights, he would never need crop insurance, for he would never get time to plant any crops. Nor am I convinced that a reading of technically-worded regulations would enlighten him much in any event.

In this case, the Government entered a field which required the issuance of large numbers of insurance policies to people engaged in agriculture. It could not expect them to be lawyers, except in rare instances, and one should not be expected to have to employ a lawyer to see whether his own Government is issuing him a policy which in case of loss would turn out to be no policy at all. There was no fraud or concealment, and those who represented the Government in taking on the risk apparently no more suspected the existence of a hidden regulation that would render the contract void than did the policyholder. It is very well to say that those who deal with the Government should turn square corners. But there is no reason why the square corners should constitute a one-way street.

The Government asks us to lift its policies out of the control of the States and to find or fashion a federal rule to govern them. I should respond to that request by laying down a federal rule that would hold these agencies to the same fundamental principles of fair dealing that have been found essential in progressive states to prevent insurance from being an investment in disappointment.

MR. JUSTICE DOUGLAS joins in this opinion.

CASE REVIEW

One swallow does not make a summer; and one case does not support a broad legal theory. But *Merrill* offers insight into the process and content of decisions that are dramatically discretionary—and that carry implications far beyond the loss of Merrill's wheat crop. There are both general and specific points.

General Thoughts

The Importance of Administration

Justice Frankfurter opened the *Merrill* case (a significant precedent for postwar development in administrative law) with the admission:

> [W]e brought this case here because it involves a question of importance in the *administration* of the Federal Crop Insurance Act. [P. 381, emphasis added]

The focus immediately is on the administrative aspects of the issues. Other issues are ignored: justiciability, questions of equity, due process, realism regarding the reading of the *Federal Register*, financial burdens on farmers, inaccessibility of government documents, precedent for non-English-speaking farmers, complex question of principal agent liability, contract law. Ignored or avoided issues abound.

Instead, the Court focuses on an administrative question. This is understandable. Following World War II and the legacy of the New Deal, American society was blessed (or cursed) with the emergence of a myriad of federal executive and independent agencies, boards, and commissions. The machinery to operate these new entities, as in labor disputes, had to be developed. But it was the technical and mechanical aspects of development that became the focus for resolving ultimate substantive issues such as principal-agent liability, duties of care imposed on regulatory bodies, and due process as a standard of actual notice.

Indeed, the Court went far beyond the negative assertion that ignorance of the law is no excuse. The *Merrill* case, in a discretionary way, reverses burdens and imposes a standard of care on the recipient and not on the administrator. Where the focus is on the importance of administration, the methodology of discretion allows such a result.

Complexity Be Damned

In the *Merrill* case, which profoundly shaped the authorities and activities of administrative agencies (with all their emerging power), it is astonishing to read:

> Government is not partly public or partly private. [P. 383]

Knowing what we know today of the complex interaction between government agencies and nongovernment institutions, it is disconcerting to read that the policies governing such interactions are based on the absurdity that the public and private sectors exist as two distinct discrete entities with firm and fixed boundaries. Is Continental Bank, after the government bailout, a purely private entity?[23] Is Chrysler Corporation, after subsidies, a private institution? Is the Tennessee Valley Authority a public body? What does private mean? Which public? Which level of government? Which department or subunit? As most scholars and researchers note, today's institutional interactions characterize a sector that is neither public nor private but consists of a blurring and blending of each with highly detailed and complex forms of relationship emerging between government units (legislative, executive, and judicial) and nongovernment institutions (business, labor, academic, medical, et cetera).

Nonetheless, it is the premise of simplicity that allows the discretionary choice, that is, a choice linked to personal judgment as opposed to realistic assessment.

The Rhetoric of Limitation

To buttress the methodology of simplistic assumption, it is helpful to follow through with phrases and terms that are intellectually limiting. That is, once the simplistic assumption is in place (public sector/private sector), it is legitimatized by a rationale that necessarily depends on a language that limits or precludes thought.

For example, in *Merrill*, Justice Frankfurter uses such phrases as "Congress could *hardly* define the multitudinous details" for the insurance and "*Inevitably* the terms and conditions" of such activity must be defined by the agency.[24]

Actually, the issues of delegation of authority and of legislative control (enhanced by the above phrases) are much more substantive than the words "hardly" and "inevitably" suggest. It is precisely this choice of words and this rhetoric which limits the intellectual process and thus allows discretion to operate unchecked. This is, of course, the intellectual and rhetorical prerequisite of discretion.

Square Corners and the Parameters of Discretion

In dealing with the government "men must turn square corners."[25] This announcement represents a perfect conceptual example of discretionary methodology. The square corners notion provides a tight, orderly, and absolute framework for what is seen in the dissenting opinion as an "absurdity" (p. 387). The square corners concept appeals to ideas of strictness of construction; to legitimate, clear protocols; and to a fixed rule of law provides the methodological cover for the discretionary action that puts the loss on Farmer Merrill.

There are countless other decisions in administrative law and other areas of the law where the burden is on government to turn square corners[26] or where seemingly square corners have been delineated but are held to be irrational and arbitrary.[27] Thus, in some cases the existence of clear, absolute programs (death penalty decisions) is held to be unconstitutional and illegal. In another case (crop insurance) the square corner must be turned. Discretion is the method that allows the choice.

The Absurdity of Technicality

As Justice Jackson noted in dissent: "It is very well to say that those who deal with the Government should turn square corners. But there is no reason why the square corners should constitute a one-way street" (p. 387–388). In short it is an "absurdity" (to quote Chancellor Kent)[28] to hold "that every farmer who insures his crops knows what the *Federal Register* contains or even knows that there is such a publication" (p. 387). The *Merrill* majority reflects the language and the direction of discretion. The opinion begins with fixation on a legitimately existing technicality. But it proceeds in the face of glaring contradictions and despite common sense realities. Discretion is always forced.

Specific Implications and Trends

Discretionary Processes—Conditions

The conditions (or preconditions) of the discretionary process exist in the form of fact, law, and influence. More specifically, discretion operates as a complex interplay between these three elements, with the selection of fact being the critical element.

For example, "A decision as to what is desirable may include not only weighing desirability but also guessing about unknown facts and making a judgment about doubtful law."[29] The mind that makes the decision does not necessarily separate facts, law, and other influences; but fact selection is one of the critical first steps in the sequence of discretion methodology.

> For instance, the policeman finds facts that the boy has committed a misdemeanor, but his determination whether to lecture and release the boy or whether to arrest him may depend on his finding facts about the comparative effect on such a boy of either discretionary choice.[30]

Evaluating this second set of "facts," or guessing about them, is part of the exercise of discretion. But finding these facts is the critical first step. Influences other than legalisms guide the application of law; and the application of law depends in part on such limiting factors as what law is available.

But is is the selection and reselection of fact that is most significant. For example, the second set of facts is most easily usable when it is grounded in legitimate, and "neutral," technical matters.

Discretionary Processes—Issues

Not all issues lend themselves substantively to discretionary processes. There are two obvious boundaries:

1. The issue must be controversial or complex enough that it cannot be handled strictly as a matter of course or as nonconsequential routine. That is, the issue must carry enough human consequence content as to lift it out of the routinization of decisions.
2. The issue must not be so controversial that its resolution will attract a great deal of unwanted public attention and scrutiny. That is, an issue handled by the discretionary process must not be of such import that it is too hot for the cool disguise of discretion.

Issues that are defined factually as administrative, technical, or mechanical lend themselves most readily to discretionary methodologies. Issues of war and peace (national security cases) and ultimate authority (presidential powers, conflicts between branches) are not readily given to discretionary models.

Discretionary Processes—Consequences

Administrative processes (detailed in Chapter Five) may be the "window of the future" as far as decision-making models are concerned. It is no coincidence that discretion as an intellectual methodology first emerged in studies on administrative law and public administration. It is administrative content and methods that emerge as penultimate concerns. Contests over significant social questions are dealt with in administrative settings and in administrative forums. Administrative skills are tools highly prized.

As the administrative context becomes more and more important, the ability to make decisions linked to administrative discretion becomes an extraordinarily important methodology. Thus, discretionary decisions stand not only as a policy or precedent for other substantive decisions but as a model for decision making itself, thus reinforcing the centrality of the administrative issue. The method reaffirms itself.

Discretionary Processes—Biases

The reader may ask, What is an administrative issue or procedural concern, and how are decisional biases (values, attitudes, and facts) mobilized in favor of such biases?

Biases are viewed as those factors collectively or individually that effectively prevent procedural concerns from developing into substantive issues.[31] In terms of judicial or legal reasoning, biases include, but are not limited to, dominant judicial norms (caution, restraint, precedent) which serve to narrow the scope of decision making; the case method, which encourages a focus on detail and unique facts; judicial procedures such as the appellate process, which continually limits the definition of the issue for review as the case progresses; and informal protocols, which limit the courts' pronouncements to almost voluntary compliance techniques. This constellation of biases narrows the scope of decisional context.

Discretionary Processes—Mobilizing the Bias

The notion of mobilizing a bias is key to understanding discretionary processes. First it is important to make a distinction between administrative and nonadministrative issues. The former are safe and legitimate; the latter are controversial and risky. Biases within the legal process are focused to cause the safe administrative issue to emerge and the nonsafe controversial issue to submerge. That is, mobilization of the biases involves a two-part process whereby biases are mobilized in favor of some issues and concurrently mobilized against other issues. It is the essential presence of the administrative or technical issue in the process of discretion that is subtle and complex. It is not suggested that discretion is used in all cases; but where it is used, it is effective because it rests on a legitimizing (procedural) foundation.

Due Process—The Classic Example

The use of an example might clarify the meaning of the words *procedural* and *administrative*. There are fewer phrases in Anglo-American law more significant, if not sacred, than "due process." Yet even this central and basic concept contains both procedural and substantive meanings.

As a substantive concept *due process* embraces certain fundamental freedoms and rights. At the substantive level these due process rights exist almost as abstractions of basic privileges such as speech, liberty, equality, fair trial, association, and privacy.

As a procedural matter, *due process* has a more specific and practical meaning. In *Goss, et al.* v. *Lopez et al.*, the Court began an analysis of *due process* with the concession that interpretation of *due process* is an "intensely practical" matter and that universal inflexible concepts are inapplicable.[32] This "intensely practical" focus allowed the Court to define the issues in procedural terms and to view *due process* as meaning the right to "some kind of hearing." The right to the hearing means also that one has the right to be notified, as well as the concomitant rights to be appraised of charges, to offer a defense or answer, and to enjoy these rights in a manner appropriate to a fair hearing. It is significant that with regard to this most substantive of legal phrases, the courts are able to look at the words primarily in procedural, almost sequential, terms.

Delegalization and Discretion

Assume for the moment the validity of the premise that the judicial system is limited by its formal structure (formal procedures, evidentiary restrictions) and by its formal function (finding guilt or innocence on the basis of legally relevant facts and narrow legal issues).[33] An important question is whether recent reliance by the courts on informal procedures (mediation, arbitration, negotiated pleas, out-of-court settlements, and so on) is in fact an extension of the discretionary process.

Several points are offered. First, the courts may simply defer to the specialized technical expertise of the informal process (the administrative agency or the mediation board) and in this way focus again on the technical rationale as the basis for substantive decisions.[34] Second, the term *informal mechanisms* does not mean that informality will automatically result in the absence of rules and procedures. It only means that the informal process is extralegal; that is, outside the courtroom. By this analysis the extension of informal processes may well result in the extension of the discretionary model.

The Rule of Law and Bureaucracy

The rule of law, and not of men, has been the theoretical (and inspirational) source of justice and social progress in American society. Although our legal system, in actuality, reflects a unique admixture of "laws and men," discretionary processes are having an impact. If change is occurring, in what direction is it going? And what impact will this change have on institutionalized life as we see it in the form of modern organizations? In short, what are the major consequences of discretion?

The concern contains several elements. First, the preference for extralegal informality in the form of complaint hearings, dispute mediation, settlements negotiations, and program logrolling is likely to lead to even more examples of discretionary justice (albeit marked by technicalities and procedural protocols). This preference coupled with a deinstitutionalization in certain fields (education, mental health) and deregulation of certain economic activities (transportation, health) provides a potentially "open field" for delegalization. With delegalization comes a search for, or reliance on, extralegal or informal processes that, to be acceptable, must be grounded in technical or procedural legitimacy.

One sees the impact in large bureaucratic organizations. For example, corporate personnel are now routinely and regularly evaluated according to highly structured and quantified review processes. A phenomenon of recent times, there is no evidence that such purportedly objective, neutral, quantifiable data are used for anything other than old-fashioned subjective decisions about who is doing well (and gets rewarded) and who is not (and gets sanctioned). The effect, therefore, is not to change the results or the consequences per se but to change the impression regarding the process. That is, the process appears now to be more objective and neutral when in fact it may be more discretionary (as it rests on the fiction of procedural integrity). Large modern organizations, with their need for strict superordinate-subordinate relationships, may be the point of first impact in terms of discretionary practices.

The Ideology of Participation

Decentralization, deinstitutionalization, deregulation, and delegalization all may be manifestations of a deeper, more profound force, namely the ideology of participative democracy. To the extent that discretion reflects this impulse of "maximum feasible participation," then it may result in almost unforseeable forms of "Chadi justice." On the other hand, if discretion is simply a mask and tool for authoritarian and rigid forms of problem resolution, then the ideal of justice as a balance or harmony of interests is even further distorted.

Discretion and Death of the Body Politic

The demise of the Chadis meant the end of nomadic civilization—with all of its faults and all of its beauties. The end of justice, and the emergence of discretion, will introduce changes and consequences as well. "If Sparta and Rome fell, what civilization can hope to endure forever?"[35] Asking why so much respect is paid to "old laws," Jean Jacques Rousseau responded that "the precedent of antiquity makes [the laws] daily, more venerable."[36]

CONCLUSION

Rousseau's thesis is that when law, and respect for law, dies, then the state will perish. Discretion as a new form of legal reasoning carries this threat.

Discretion as a nonlegitimate, intellectual technique may well generate the forces of its own destruction. This, of course, is only a possibility. Perhaps it is only a remote possibility considering the vigorous life of the "Rule of Law" in the United States. At the same time this and other possibilities must be contemplated and this will be the focus of Chapter Eight: to restate the issues of Chapters Two through Seven and to take a brief look into the future.

NOTES

1. Clifford May, "Guinean Chief Says No Former Officials Have Been Harmed," *New York Times*, April 9, 1984. p. A−4.
2. Kenneth Culp Davis, *Discretionary Justice: A Preliminary Inquire* (Urbana:University of Illinois Press, 1976).
3. Ibid., Preface, p. v.
4. Ibid.
5. The focus of the Davis study was on law. There was no attempt to explore discretion in its wider applications, although Davis suggested such a conceptualization explicitly and implicitly, throughout his study.
6. This suggests the obvious: that discretion is not necessarily bad nor evil. The prevailing view is that discretion is bad. This writer's approach is that discretion exists, that it is pervasive, and that it is characterized by certain distinctive elements. This is not unlike the present view of conflict. Traditionally, conflict was viewed as an undesirable element of organized life. Currently, revisionists see conflict as healthy and even necessary. See M. Deutsch, *The Resolution of Conflict: Constructive and Destructive Processes* (New Haven, Conn.: Yale University Press, 1973), which explores the eufunctional and dysfunctional aspects of conflict.
7. See the case in this chapter *Federal Crop Insurance Corp. v. Merrill et al. Doing Business as Merrill Bros.*, which held that perusal of the *Federal Register* was a prerequisite to suing a federal agency over agency policy.
8. Obviously, discretion exists in each of these various sources. Nonetheless, rules, orders, laws, statutes, and policies emanating from these sources are positivistic in that they exist in some clear, tangible, expressed form to be used as a basis for nonarbitrary decisions.
9. 408 U.S. 238, 242, 92 S.Ct. 2726, 2727 (1972).
10. This was the concern in *McGautha* v. *California*, 402 U.S. 183, 91 S.Ct. 1454 (1971) which upheld the imposition of the death penalty and denied petitioners' claims.
11. Murray Edelman, *Symbolic Uses of Politics*, (Urbana: University

of Illinois Press, 1964). See also, Bernard Lewis, "The Shia," *The New York Review of Books*, August 15, 1985, pp. 7−10.

12. *Chadi* is the Arabic term for headman or chief and is Anglicized in various ways including the spelling as *qadis*. See Bernard Lewis, "The Shia," *The New York Review of Books*, August 15, 1985, p. 8.

13. To be sure, there are points of reference (the Koran, precedents, and the like). They are known informal and noncodified.

14. Paul Bohannan discussed the clash of legal cultures in his study on the ethnology of law as "The Differing Realms of the Law," in *Law and the Behavioral Sciences*, ed. Lawrence M. Friedman and Steward Macaulay (New York: Bobbs-Merrill, 1965), p. 847.

15. The lessons of this intrusion have not been lost on those who question "reform" movements. For example, to an outsider the system of government in highly political communities like Chicago appears disorderly, arbitrary, and personal. It may be; and this may result in greater equity and ultimate fairness than a rigidly structured reformist system of remote rules and rational sophisticated regulations touted in certain upper-class suburban communities.

16. Max Gluckman, *The Judicial Process among the Bartose of Northern Rhodesia* (Manchester: Manchester University Press, 1955), reprinted in *Law and the Behavioral Sciences*, ed Lawrence M. Friedman and Stewart Mcaulay (New York:Bobbs-Merrill, 1965), p. 946.

17. The irony is that both legal purists and legal reformers use the "technical defect" strategy as a way of contesting the issues in a case. See Richard L. Abel, *The Politics of Informal Justice* (New York: Academic Press, 1982), pp. 128−130.

18. Perhaps the most profound phrase in Anglo-American law has to do with the notion of "due process." Early on, even *due process* was reduced to both procedural and substantive meanings, with the former becoming the contested area. See *Goss et al.* v. *Lopez et al.*, 419 U.S. 565, 95 S.CT. 729, (1975).

19. The reader might remember the famous four-sided table dispute of the Vietnam negotiations in Paris (1972−74), or the triangular table in the Israeli-Lebanese-UNIFIL negotiations in southern Lebanon (1984−85).

20. In *General Shoe Corp.*, cited as *In the Matter of General Shoe Corporation and Boot and Shoe Workers Union, A.F.L.*, 77 N.L.R.B. 124 (1948), the National Labor Relations Board set the boundaries for "laboratory conditions," to govern clean and fair elections.

21. *Whirlpool Corp.* v. *Marshall, Secretary of Labor*, 445 U.S. 1, 100 S.Ct. 863 (1980), allowed employee enforcement of OSHA regulations.

22. Constructive notice assumes that when one is given the

opportunity to know, then one actually knows, and the opportunity binds one. Thus, legally, one is *presumed* to *know* something when the government gives constructive notice, for example, by publication.

23. "The High-Stakes Scramble to Rescue Continental Bank," *New York Times*, May 21, 1984, p. 1. This is a fascinating account of the complex interaction (involving lawyers).

24. Emphasis is the writer's.

25. *Rock Island, Arkansas & Louisiana Railroad Company* v. *United States*, 254 U.S. 141, 143, 41 S.Ct. 55, 56 (1920).

26. In *Marshall, Secretary of Labor, et al.* v. *Barlow's Inc.*, 436 U.S. 307, 98 S.Ct. 1816 (1978), the Supreme Court held that in certain cases warrantless searches by OSHA officials were unreasonable and illegal unless the owner consented, although the probable cause standard justifying the warrant was considered to be not as stringent as in criminal cases.

27. An example might be the death penalty abolition case, *Furman* v. *Georgia*, 408 U.S. 238, 92 S.Ct. 2726, (1972), which held as arbitrary and as unconstitutional (cruel and unusual) randomly administered capital punishment sentences based on state laws, which made death the mandatory punishment for persons convicted of certain designated crimes.

28. Refer to quote from Chancellor Kent at beginning of Chapter Seven. See Head Quote Sources. *Appendix*

29. Davis, *Discretionary Justice*, pp. 4–5.

30. Ibid., p. 5.

31. See (for a similar definition of *bias*) Peter Bachrach and Morton S. Baratz, "Decisions and Non-decisions: An Analytical Framework," *American Politcal Science Review*, September 1963, p. 641.

32. *Goss, et al.* v. *Lopez et al.*, 419 U.S. 565, 95 S.Ct. 729, 738 (1975). The case dealt with the suspension of public high school student without notice or hearing. Some kind of due process hearing was held to be required.

33. Richard L. Abel, ed. *The Politics of Informal Justice* (New York: Academic Press, 1982), p. 63.

34. Judicial review of agency action is established by the *Administrative Procedure Act* (APA) at the federal and often at the state levels. The doctrine of "limited judicial review" of administrative action permits courts to review questions of *law* while letting agency factual decisions stand if they are supported by sufficient evidence.

35. Jean-Jacque Rousseau, *The Social Contract*, bk 3, Chap. 11, "The Death of the Body Politic" (New York: E. P. Sutton, 1954).

36. Ibid.

The chief intellectual characteristic of the present age is its despair of any constructive philosophy—not just in its technical meaning, but in the sense of any integrated outlook and attitude . . . {t}he formation of a new, coherent view of nature and man . . . is still to be had.

The result is disillusionment about all comprehensive and positive ideas. The possession of constructive ideals is taken to be an admission that one is living in a realm of fantasy.

John Dewey
"Living Philosophies"

Chapter Eight

INTEGRATED APPROACHES

The previous seven chapters have compared and critiqued three major decision-making methodologies. At this point it might be helpful to recap the premise of the study. There are two central concerns: first, that each of these methodologies operates as a distinct and discrete device; and second, that the lack of intellectual integration results in significant dysfunctions for decisions and decision makers. The purpose of this chapter is to provide an integrated framework for decision making and to point to ways of improving decision making for the future.

Accordingly, it seems appropriate to extract from the three major methodologies certain qualities that are commonly shared. (These qualities may be both positive and negative, or eufunctional and dysfunctional.) Once common qualities are identified, it will be possible to construct a framework for the future that will create one of the conditions—the theoretical prerequisite[1]—for effective decision making in the day-to-day activities of contemporary organizations.

COMMON QUALITIES

If a visitor from another planet were to review the three methodologies (in pure and in distorted form) as presented in this study, he would be struck by the commonalities that these truth-seeking devices share. The irony is that those who are close to each field or to each discipline emphasize the differences. This is not unlike the tendency of Americans to see the British as "the English," whereas residents of Great Britain are quick to note distinctions between Ulstermen, Scotsmen, Welschmen, and Englishmen. Nonetheless, no matter how close one is to the discrete method or field, one must, upon analysis, see certain mainfestly shared qualities. For example, the mere fact that each method shares qualities (the "genericness" of decision making)[2] is a noteworthy phenomenon. It is this commonality that enlightens a vision of the future, and it is this quality that will be examined below in the context of eufunctional and dysfunctional attributes.

Positive Generic Qualities

Causation, Truth, and Decisions

One's assumptions regarding cause and effect relationships are a critical element in any decision-making model. Unless a decision maker's world view rests on the tenet that problems result from specified causes, very little can be done in a systematic way to conceptualize, much less to intersect, certain difficulties. It is this underlying assumption that there is a cause, this ability to conceptualize action as based on a reason for action, that separates decision makers from individuals who are passive or who feel hopeless in certain situations.

The notion that there is a causal, or underlying, condition is central to and is shared by decision makers in the business world (the rational approach), the government world (the political approach), and the judicial world (the legal approach). Individuals in these three areas may respond to the causal condition in different ways. For example, businesspeople tend to see "cause" as a tangible, concrete factor that can be managed or controlled. Causes are factors to be manipulated. Politicians may see the cause of problems in terms of negative factors, that is, as the absence of power or authority. But they see cause. Lawyers and judges look to policy or logic for a decision and in this sense legitimize the result or holding. Thus the law as a principle is the cause for decision.

In each of these cases there is a *reason* for action, a *basis* for decision. It may be that symptom is sometimes confused with cause,[3] and it may be that a single cause[4] is seen when most complex problems are actually multicausal. Despite these and other shortcomings, the prerequisite for decision making is present: an ability to conceptualize a reason for action. Only against this assumption will action be triggered and will decision be efficacious. Each of the models shares this *raison d'etre*. This derives from a basic assumption regarding cause-effect relationships, and this assumption is absolutely essential to taking action—to deciding. The quest for solution—for truth—can flow only from a crystalization of thought processes specifying reasons for action.

Assumptions about cause and effect relationships are identified here as a special topic because they are so fundamental to managerial thinking and to the dynamics of decision making.

Behavioral or Human Problems

Although it is obvious, it must be stated expressly that each of the three decision models deals, directly or indirectly, with human problems. This underlying element, which forms the essence of the problem definition, is usually glossed over when decisional models are analyzed. And yet is is critical to consider that regardless of the nature of the question (whether technological, ideological, or legalistic) the issue ultimately concerns humans.

This fact cannot be overemphasized—partly because decision makers sometimes ignore the human need but more because the goal of decision making, regardless of model, is purposive. That is, the goal is always directed toward human behavior and usually involves changing behavior.

For this reason significant elements of each model are driven by behavioral questions: Whose behavior needs changing? How will behavioral change best be accomplished? What will be the consequences of behavioral change? Whether dealt with directly or indirectly, whether economically or inefficiently, or whether successfully or not each model attempts or seeks purposive behavioral goals. This human focus is an important positive element shared by each model. The models thereby meet at least the threshold operational prerequisite to solving problems in contemporary organizations.

The Pervasiveness of Symbols

A symbol stands for, or represents, something other than itself. For example, the ancient Semitic symbol "1" (basically a straight line) stands for much more than a line The symbol for "one" thus represents singularity, a numerical priority, monism and the absence of pluralism and a coherence or absence of deviation.

Symbols are potent because they reduce one's critical faculties. They are reductionist in that they condense into one symbolic act, artifact, sign, or expression (verbal and nonverbal) one's thought processes. Symbols reduce one's need to think and perhaps one's ability to think as well.[5] For example, upon seeing the sign "1," the observer no longer questions, considers, or thinks about its meaning. The symbol is potent; the meaning is clear; further critical analysis is unnecessary.

Murray Edelman argues that remoteness is central to the potency of a symbol. For example, a judge's robe is a powerful symbol. It is a remote material garb (inaccessible to all but a very few). Its remoteness lends an aura of mystique and awe, thus enhancing the potency of this symbol of authority. Upon seeing the robe (the symbol), the public automatically acquiesces in its nonmaterial meanings, which include vaguely: power, legitimacy, fear, authority, the state, sanctions, justice.

Edelman emphasizes that the effect of symbols is to cause the observer or recipient of the symbol to acquiesce, to become passive, "to hold one's critical faculties in abeyance." Another significant characteristic of symbols is that they lack detail; rather there is a blurring of any realistic, specific content that might question or weaken the larger meaning conveyed.

Symbols take many forms. They may be tangible, as with a judge's robe or intangible, as with an expression such as the "bottom line." They may be verbal, both written and spoken, or nonverbal, as in the display of a flag or the size of an executive's desk. They may have an objective referent, as in the symbol "1," or they may be subjective in content, as with the color code of appropriate dress in a corporation.

The point is that symbols are pervasive. In various forms and manifestations they pervade every aspect of contemporary organized activity including decision making. In fact, it is the presence of symbols in decisional processes that represents a major commonality in such distinct fields as business, government, and law.

For example, inherent in the rational model is reliance on the "objectified" intangible symbols of numbers. Numerical symbols represent hard data, which form the core of rational decisional processes. The effect of such symbols is to reduce complications in decision processes. Numerical, mathematical symbols make the job easy. In this context it should be noted that rationality itself "offers a nice political language in which to couch management activity."[6] In government circles certain political acts promote social adjustments and compliance. For example, the convening of the legislature or the routine work of a committee, while often ceremonial, have powerful legitimizing effects on the mass public. Likewise in the legal world, reference to certain codes, or to constitutional precepts, or the use of awe-inspiring magical words like *due process* or *estoppel* have a powerful effect on people's behavior.

Obviously, symbols can be manipulated to suit one's purposes. This is not the issue. The larger point is twofold: (1) that symbols exist and represent a key decisional resource, and (2) that they make the job easy, or at least possible. Accordingly, symbols in the decisional process should be viewed as money or machinery or humans: they should be viewed as another important resource to be utilized. This resource is positive in that, like other resources, it provides the technical element prerequisite for getting things done, an important part of any decisional process.

This last point becomes increasingly significant, as one of the major negative elements of each model is the presence of hurdles or obstacles to sound decision making. This factor and other negative or dysfunctional attributes will be considered below.

Negative Generic Qualities

Time, Space, and Other Obstacles

Each decision-making model analyzed in this text shares common qualities. One quality, thought to be dysfunctional or negative, is the "fragmentation factor." This factor is most readily observed in the context of the political model where decisions are made in bits and pieces (by increments) and in widely segmented processes or places (committee structures). Fragmentation of time and space occurs in the rational process as well. Indeed, formal coordination becomes a major need in hierarchical business environments with complex, multidepartment organizations processing data in a variety of centers and subunits. In the legal world, as well, there is very little formal integration of the system. Each court, each area of law, each level of the judiciary operates as an independent entity jealously guarding its hard-earned prerogatives.[7]

Such fragmentation is manifest. *Arguendo*, it is even desirable ala the checks and balances notion that it is healthy (1) to have multiple points of access and (2) to have built-in countervailing forces. But despite these very legitimate and very thoughtful justifications, fragmentation is perceived by managers and decision makers to be undesirable. Fragmentation is viewed as a logistical hurdle to integrated, wholistic approaches that will better serve the common good whether the commonwealth be a business organization, a political community, or a legal society.

It is the quest for wholeness, the drive toward integration, that emerges as a major concern of decision making. Thus fragmentation is a negative factor only in the sense that it runs counter to the human impulse for continuity, integration, and completeness. A related impulse today is for immediate, quick, and complete responses to problems, no matter how complex or multivariate the causes. In part this impulse is fostered by electronic technology, which creates at least the illusion of the potential for wholeness and integration of decision-making circuitry. In part the impulse is nurtured by a frustration with crazy quilt, administrative layers, which serve primarily to impede effective decisions. Regardless, with both positive and negative forces operating to push for change, fragmentation emerges as a major negative obstacle to sound decision making. Thus any decisional structures for the future must overcome the organizational, political, and legal barriers to what is viewed as the goal of complete integrated approaches.

Technology, Politics, and Control

An individual's seeming inability to transcend the physical limitations of time and space is potentially altered by new technologies. Generally, the emergence of technology is viewed as a beneficence—that is, professional decision makers and lay people both are generally optimistic about the prospects for enhanced quality of life as a result of new technology. This is because technology is perceived as value neutral or as ethically objective. The argument is that technology is just a machine; the machine has no values or ideology; thus the machine or technology ethically is neutral.

This reasoning is fallacious and dangerous for two reasons. First, as Daniel Bell notes:

> Technology is not simply a "machine," but a systematic disciplined approach to objectives, using a calculus of precision and measurement and a concept of system that are quite at variance with traditional and customary religious, asthetic and intuitive modes.[8]

Bell argues that instead of a machine technology we face an increasingly potent "intellectual technology" whereby powerful theoretical frameworks create new machine/electronic possibilities. Those who control the intellectual technology (math, law, psychology) will control the machine or tool (computer, wiretap, polygraph, etcetera). Thus the machine may be value neutral, but the technology behind the machine is not. Control of this technology emerges as the central ethical and political issue of the 1980s and 1990s.

The second fallacy and danger behind the technology-is-neutral argument is noted by Christopher Lasch, who argues that such an interpretation is "designed to reassure."[9] Lasch means that those who understand the power of technology want to keep close control and thus seek to discourage the public/outsiders from asking critical questions. The vagueness of technology, the definition of *machine*, the illusion of neutrality—all serve to reinforce the capability of an elite few to control this "tool."

Thus technology is not ethically neutral. It is deliberately designed to concentrate control and power in the hands of a few key decision makers. Accordingly, control, and not technology, emerges as the key referent for analysis of decision making. People do not like to talk about control because it is linked to politics, which is considered unseemly or dirty. But it is there. Control is the philosophy or ethic that guides the use and misuse of modern technology, not the reverse. It is the philosophy of control that must be illuminated as a major force in decision making, regardless of field or discipline. Control is an imperialistic impulse; its logic is to expand and to monopolize. Thus control may be an illogical impulse in a society where democratic participatory values are cherished. For example, on a purely conceptual level, it is troubling to some theorists that rational criteria are not considered relevant to power models of decision or to political models of organization.[10] The application of conscious, rational, strategic criteria has its own built-in theoretical limitations.

Nonetheless, it is the presence of control as a philosophy, aided by the illusory impact of technology, that emerges as a central difficulty in reaching legitimate criteria for decision making in the near future. The centrality of control as a decisional criterion is a major limitation on policy development in a pluralistic, democratic, constitutional society.

Language, Culture, and Other Buzzwords

Words carry symbolic meaning. Words have consequences for behavior. Indeed, certain words or phrases have a deadening effect; they convey little meaning, but they numb the brain. For example, buzzwords like *state of the art* or *bottom line* or *viable options* convey very little specific content. Yet these words have a larger meaning; in effect they cause critical analysis to cease. In short they prevent further examination or intelligent analysis.

We have examined this curious and dangerous phenomenon by looking at the meaning and the impact of the phrase *public sector/private sector* as if there actually exist such discrete orbits of interaction.

The latest rage word is *culture*, as in "the culture of the corporation." In classrooms, conferences, board meetings, and cocktail parties, the word sweeps like a prairie fire over intelligent conversation. What does the word mean? In reality most users actually are referring to a business style or to a corporate strategy. Others use the word to refer to an atmosphere (open/closed, autocratic/democratic) of decision making. In either case the word is misused. Twenty-five years ago when poverty studies were the rage, some writers talked about a "culture of poverty." Anthropologists and other serious scholars tried to point out that *culture* is a very precise word with specific meaning. The word *culture*, they noted, can only be used when a community has certain language characteristics, intergenerationally shared customs and values, tangible and distinct artifacts, and tools such as knives or hammers. By this meaning there is no "corporate culture." Why then is the word used? Probably to embellish or to enhance the concept of "strategy," which otherwise might carry negative connotations. And so, what is wrong with a little puffing? Nothing except that academics, practitioners, and others actually begin to believe that a culture, with all its sophisticated implications, exists. And what is the problem with this? It is deceptive. It creates illusion. It masks reality. It points people in wrong directions. Students study the wrong stuff. Professors create artificial worlds. Managers evade reality and responsibility. Lawyers get tangled up in meaningless jargon. The public is put off.

Sometimes the buzzword or jargon has severe consequences. For example, the words *interdict the harbor at Haiphong* or *terminate with prejudice* mask the hideous implications of death and mass destruction. This is precisely the intent. Likewise, words like *program parameters* and *micromanagement of conflict* hide the actual implications of such terms. So what?

The point is that such jargon is inherent in contemporary decisional models. These buzzwords serve not so much to convey meaning as to short-circuit analysis. As such, they are dangerous in a world of complex, adversarial relationships. Buzzwords do little to improve decision making. Thus language emerges as a critical aspect of decisional theory.

PROGRESS, INTEGRATION, AND THE FUTURE

The notion that current decision is ineffective prompts the thought that decision making could be, or should be, *more* effective. This is to suggest that a concept of progress is inherent in the critical analysis. In short, things can be better, and so they should be better. This would be an accurate reading of this text despite contemporary thinking, which suggests a minimalist approach to social intervention.

The idea and the ideal of *progress* is inherent in man's impulse to act. Why act unless one believes the act will be efficacious? To decide is to act. Thus progress, or some positive intellectual equivalent, is inherent in decision models. Yet progress as a concept has been debunked in the face of the shortcomings of modernization (urban blight, environmental destruction, increasing militarization) and in the context of technocratic lust (the horrors of the holocaust, the degradation of work, and growing gaps between rich and poor).

Upon closer analysis, however, it appears that progress is not discredited but that the intellectual ingredients essential to progress have fallen away. This is the persuasive argument of Leo Marx, who sees the absence of moral perception, the ideology of engineering, and a fixation on material benefits as the false gods of progress. Against these lesser ideals progress will fail. Yet earlier generations in America believed in progress and they succeeded. Why? Henry Steele Commager has a thought.

> The generation of the founding fathers solved the problems that confronted them not so much by the application of mechanical or scientific expertise as by the application of philosophy—a broad term which covers the humanities. . . .
> Scientific and technological expertise can solve any number of particular problems, but has great difficulty with general problems. . . . It is not certain that philosophy can solve these problems, but it is certain that without philosophy they will not be solved. . . . What is called for are new philosophical and moral approaches. . . . I return once again to the central theme of this argument: that what we lack on a global scale is not the technical or scientific expertise; it is political responsibility. This cannot be achieved by edifying admonitions. It cannot even be achieved by formal education—what we are officially addicted to—for formal education is but a part of the larger education of society.[11]

The technocratic goal of material progress as the basis for general progress misses the point of the enlightenment ideal, which shaped this society: the ideal of progress in the service of society.

Aside from the traditional (and sometimes sentimental) exhortations for "better education" or for "more humanities in the curriculum,"[12] what can be done? There are several possibilities.

Social Needs versus Material Needs

The beauty of each of the above models is that they concern people. People, human beings, are the only element in the universe of decisional factors who care about what is decided. Buildings do not care; paper does not care; dollar bills do not care. It is each model's inability absolutely to reject the human element that transfigures the rational, political, and legal approaches. Likewise, it is this common element that provides the substantive basis for decision making. This fact needs to be highlighted simply because it is commonly ignored, particularly in the rational model. Nonetheless, the basic social ingredient is present. It needs only to be operationalized.

Penetrating Symbols

How to operationalize (or implement) lofty principles is always the question. Nonspecific prodding, or moralizing, is of little or even negative value. What specifically can be done to reemphasize the objective of social good versus material good? The answer depends on what the problem is. If the problem is that symbols with their overpowering force cause critical thinking to decrease, then the issue is how to penetrate the symbol and therby enhance social perception.

Journalists are increasingly aware of this problem—especially electronic media journalists who find it difficult to penetrate the rhetoric, dramaturgy, and ritual of political and governmental activities. For example, in the presidential election of 1984 the press thoroughly covered graphically visible and technically concrete matters such as the federal budget and the "Star Wars" proposal. What the press fumbled "were issues that are subjective, abstract, and morally ambiguous" such as "religious freedom," the "new patriotism," and "good feelings about America." Constrained by traditions that emphasize "coverage of the palpable and the factual, the press finds itself losing ground in covering contemporary politics, with its stress on image and abstraction."[13]

Some journalists, recognizing the trap of manipulation by symbol (and worrying that the press itself is becoming a tool in the hands of political drama managers), suggest penetrating those areas heretofore off-limits, namely personality, character, and values. While these are risky areas, very often they are the issues that matter most.

What is the lesson for decision making in general? Precisely the same. The focus must be on the decision maker and on his/her personality character and values and not on the process that deflects hard questions and that causes the critical public to acquiesce in omnipotent ritual, rhetoric and routine.

Elitism and Separation of Power

In the modern organization, whether it be a business corporation, a governmental institution, or a judicial body, one would not tolerate the use of a sledgehammer to fix a computer or a guru to solve a personnel problem. Such tools are inappropriate to problem solving in the context of subjective decisions. Likewise, a dull, insensitive or untrained mind is an inappropriate resource for decisions that are complex and for solutions that require a broad base of social, historical, and linguistic skill. This is to say that decision making is not a field open to anyone. It is open only to those who qualify by possession of certain intellectual resources—intellectual property by another name.

The generation of the Founders possessed such property; they were beneficiaries of education in linguistics, philosophy, math, history, science, architecture, and other diverse fields. They applied this background to the fields of law, engineering, and military and business life. They were philosophers first; lawyers, businessmen, and politicians second. Their backgrounds were generic; later they specialized. Today it is the reverse; and this fact, partly, produces the lack of an integrating framework for decision makers.

To argue such an elitist training is to argue "elitism." This is true. At the same time, the procedural checks and balances and the constitutional separation of powers as envisioned by the Founders can be preserved. We should, however, discard the fiction that a Ph.D. is prepared to make decisions of a nontechnical nature; or that a J.D. is prepared to understand broad social questions; or that an M.B.A. can discuss social costs and benefits. A broader intellectual framework is the prerequisite to decision making. Specialization via a profession or a discipline does not provide the necessary credentials for membership in the decision maker's elite club.

A Working Vision of the Future

The future is not tomorrow or even the next 10 to 20 years. The future is what we *presently* imagine it to be and what we carefully plan for. In this context it will be at least two generations (20 to 50 years) before integrated models of decision making will emerge—models that are based on transcendent philosophical principles as opposed to narrow personal/professional specializations. A generation must be nurtured to rediscover the value of intellectual property based on philosophical precept; a second generation must be educated to apply such resources to actual problems.

What are the confines or the contours of this integrated framework? For starters, the conceptual framework and the intellectual skill requisite to integration will be an ability to transcend *process* criteria. The limitations of time and space are largely evaporating. For example, a political decision in Washington, D.C., can be transmitted to a bank in Chicago in a second. A disaster in Bhopal hits the stock market in minutes.

Thus it is possible to imagine decisional modes that eliminate physical limitations. Indeed, this may be the most provocative point in the most recent work of James March concerning his "garbage can model" of decision making, a model that envisions a situation in which both access and decision structures are completely open.[14] Although there are linkages among actors and choices, and although there are time constraints, these factors are not controlled or structured as rationalist, political, or legal processes would presume them to be. If the garbage can model is only partially accurate as an instructive device, the implications are enormous. Depending on one's point of view, decision making can be viewed as a stream of creativeness or as a runaway train.

Thus as we are close, intellectually, to a break-through; close to the historical moment when the only theoretical limitations are momentum (the force created once a policy is set into motion) and imagination. The possibilities are exciting. Nonetheless, these are important limitations. For example, the physical laws of future decision making (momentum and mass) unimpeded by friction or process (space and time) will punish false steps in an unforgiving manner. The old cushions of check and balance, specialization and departmentalization, and levels of appeal will no longer be operative. Thus the features of the decisional framework will incorporate a decisional command post, which necessarily implies central command or strict hierarchical elitism. This much is certain. Will the elitist command post, with interlocking directorates, be accompanied by the necessary humanistic training that is requisite to integrated social body? This is by no means certain. Accordingly, the following concluding thoughts are offered.

NOTES

1. The importance of *theory* (a set of generalizations that guide actual operations) cannot be overstated. For example, without a mathematical theory there would be no computer technology; without economic theory there would be little organized commerce; without a legal theory there would be few cases to promulgate law. Thus theory is seen as the intellectual prerequisite to any operational activity.

2. One obvious *generic* quality is the fact that each method has both positive and negative aspects or elements.

3. For example, poor communication may be a symptom (manifestation) of deeper underlying cleavages (the causal factors); but often communication is thought to be the problem, or the cause.

4. For example, the now-outmoded (medical) "germ" theory of decisions argues that there is a single cause or single germ behind a breakdown or problem.

5. Murray Edelman, *The Symbolic Uses of Power* (Urbana:University of Illinois Press, 1964), pp. 4–7.

6. Jeffrey Pfeffer, *Organizations and Organization Theory* (Boston: Pitman, 1982), p. 62.

7. Thus bankruptcy "judges" are forbidden the perquisites of other federal-level judiciary.

8. Daniel Bell, "The Year 2000—The Trajectory of an Idea," in *Toward the Year 2000*, ed. Daniel Bell (Boston: Houghton, Mifflin, 1968). p. 1.

9. Christopher Lasch, Address titled "Technology and the Degradation of Work," presented at the Conference on "The Human Side of High Tech" sponsored by DePaul University, Chicago, Illinois, November 29, 1984). Christopher Lasch is Professor of History, University of Rochester.

10. James G. March, "Bounded Rationality, Ambiguity, and the Engineering of Choice," *Bell Journal of Economics*, Vol. 9, pp. 587–608, 1978.

11. Henry Steele Commager, *Illinois Humanities*, 1, no. 1(1974):1.

12. Please note that this writer thinks that humanistic education is precisely the essential prerequisite to improvement or progress.

13. Carl Sessions Stepp, "Weakness in Coverage," *New York Times*, November 17, 1984, p. 19.

14. James G. March and Roger Weissinger-Baylon, *Ambiguity and Command: Organizational Perspectives on Military Decision Making* (unpublished manuscript, Boston: Pitman Publishing, Inc., May, 1985) pp. 6–7.

I am sometimes reproached for not reaching any definite conclusion. But this is less a legitimate desire which people express than a trap which is set for me. Everyone understands that the modern world is a kind of upside-down world, but does that matter? People always hope to get used to living standing on their heads. They allow you to show them that their position is not normal, but if you talk to them about standing properly they think you aren't observing the rules of the game.

Georges Bernanos
"Why Freedom?"

Conclusion

CRITERIA FOR ACTION

STANDING PROPERLY AND FIRST STEPS

Beyond Neoclassicism: The Death of Jazz and Other Tragedies

It is no accident that this work quotes from, and relies heavily upon, dated classical studies and traditional writers such as Simon, Easton, Edelman, Bell, Frank, Wilson, and Buber. The work will be criticized for this noncontemporary emphasis. But the idea is that useful insights will be found only by studying the "original score" and not in the "variation of the theme." The situation is similar to the neoclassic phase in jazz, an era in which current musicians concentrate on producing, in the words of critic Sam Friedman, "personally stamped recombinations of existing knowledge."[1]

This is not unlike the situation with current organizational research: In law, in business, and in behavioral sciences the incentives and pressures lead to a "sharpening of the pin," an emulation and colonization of the classical work. The result is merely a replay on the theme. As with modern jazz, no one would deny that current decisional research has produced some exciting sounds; but the results are erratic, discordant, and unrelated. The personal impulse muffles the integrating theme.

So, too, in academic research. Young scholars and junior professors are forced to develop "new" and "different" material—else it is not salable and publishable. The pressure is to polish the pin. But the tip of the pin eventually will become so brittle it will break.

Thus, as a first step, university administrators should reemphasize the classics and reward faculty accordingly. A "deprioritization"[2] of costly semi-pro, "slam-dunk" athletics might provide the operational base for implementing such a decision. The intellectual base will be found in resources like the "Great Books." If universities and centers of learning cannot take even this meager step, it surely will not be taken at IBM or at the Office of Management and Budget or at the Supreme Court.

Generic Structures, Integrated Disciplines, and the New Generation

Integrated models require integrated structures. There is some evidence that such generic systems are already emerging. For example, in various parts of the nation, several traditional business schools (Yale, Northwestern, Arizona) have, with mixed degrees of success, attempted to integrate public administration with business administration. Likewise, professors of law and political science are being invited to join Colleges of Commerce, as the AACSB (American Assembly of Collegiate Schools of Business [the Business School accrediting association]) requires more courses in "business and law" and "government regulation." On the theory that "Mohammed must go to the mountain" public sector faculty often find a ready and receptive audience in such "nonpublic" settings. The dean of a preeminent law school is arguing a strong case for a legal education based on an interdisciplinary approach embracing economics, history, government, and other areas heretofore ignored in traditional curricula.[3]

Interdisciplinary studies enjoyed a brief but never vigorous life twenty years ago. The difference today is that a range of federal and state agencies, as well as private foundations and distinguished scholars, is calling for a change in curricula to place more emphasis on inquiry (abstract thinking), literacy (reading, writing, speaking), historical consciousness, science, values, art and multicultural experiences.[4] Regardless of ideological orientation, the emergence to power of a new generation of classically trained conservatives is bringing to Washington and to other regional centers of decision making a sense of historical purpose and social value. Such a trend can only restore and reinvigorate the public debate regarding academic fundamentals and thereby expand thinking regarding outmoded, process-oriented, specialized, and remote curricula. Hard-core, liberal academics should pay attention to the fact that much is to be learned from conservative educators with their insistence on the basics. Academics must take the lead in the "re-conversion" to the classical models. If we do not, we are false to our own values and we deserve to lose even more credibility.

Business Leadership, Rugged Individualism, and Cultural Aphasia

The rhetoric and the incentives of the corporate world are the language of individualism. The language of individualism comes in several varieties:[5] the utilitarian individualism of Benjamin Franklin and the contemporary individualism of textile cost-benefit analysts; the expressive individualism of Walt Whitman, and the self-centered individualism of Werner Erhard. In the business community the tension will be between the self-made man (the materialistic nouveau riche) and the self-actualized man (the renaissance entrepreneur). Is it not time for the business community to join with powerless academics in the search for integrated, cultural wholeness and for a deemphasis on material goals and short-run profits? This is not an idle question. There are practical incentives: the business community desperately needs personnel who can communicate—that is, speak, read, write, and listen. And there are moral imperatives: business leaders are in a unique position themselves to become truly self-actualized by exerting influence on integrated systems and on classical education. Has financial abundance brought social or personal happiness? Has technical prowess resulted in more joyful family life? Has material acquisition resulted in spiritual completeness? Businesspeople must be concerned with these cultural questions. At any rate there will be no more "soft" toilet paper if the landscape is "deforested." We had better pay attention to these matters, and cost-benefit analysis is not the only way to do it.

The Acropolis, the Snake Dance, and Policy Externships

Professor Vincent Scully gives a marvelous one hour slide show/lecture on the ancient Greeks and the modern Hopi.[6] The Greeks, he states, were determined to be apart from nature. Thus they built their Acropolis as a separate structure high on a hill remote and distinct against the landscape. The Hopi Indians of the American Southwest live more in touch with nature and with their natural surroundings: the mountains, the fauna, the wildlife. To remember and to celebrate the integration of human life with nonhuman life, the Hopi, each year, perform the awe-inspiring Snake Dance, which forces the dancers and the community (the people) to relive the integration and connection between humans (the highest form of life) and snakes (the lowest form of life). The contrast (and its implication) is clear: one society seeks to remove and be separate from nature; the other culture forces a constant reminder of closeness with even the most repulsive, fearsome, and meanest elements of the life cycle.

Political scientists and policy analysts should be trained to do a snake dance; to crawl into mines and caverns, to confront snakes. This training should occur early in their academic preparation and should be an annual part of a required continuing education program so that upon graduation to a "center" for governmental studies or to a "job" in government as a bureaucrat, public affairs officials do not lose touch. The Acropolis as a symbol of remote fragmented, incrementalist, specialization is not the appropriate vision for a democracy or its practitioners. It is not healthy to enshrine the dissociated, disintegrated practice of public administration in such a theoretical framework. Political scientists and their counterparts in public administration must break away from the isolating remote "buildings" of Government and reunite with society through required externships and through training in the fields of art, history, science, and language.

Making Sausage and Selling It: The Law and Administrative Reform

If they involve important matters, decisions in business or in government are controversial decisions. Ultimately and inevitably, they become legal decisions. They wind up in the lap of the law. Therefore, the way lawyers think, and particularly the way judges reason, becomes a central concern.

Perhaps this study offers a naive view of justice; after all, entire areas of law (contract law, criminal law) were avoided. On the other hand, administration is generic to all areas of the law, and the administrative state has emerged as the primary concern of practitioners and theorists alike. Administrative issues (procedural due process, for example) are threshold issues. It is in this context that the cases are drawn from administrative law: they illustrate the problems. They reveal how the legal process works and how judges reason.

Is there a rule of reason operating? Arguably not. Would anyone (even minimally conversant with the facts) believe that Justice Frankfurter would have/could have written the *Merrill* opinion if he had spent three days on a wheat farm in Idaho? Is it reasonable to expect or to ask farmers to start their daily chores and morning coffee with the *Federal Register*? What accounts for this gross gap between reality and the rule; this palpable "absurdity" to quote Chancellor Kent.

Part of the problem is that lawyers and judges have become removed (set apart) from society. Interdisciplinary curricula in law schools will help in broadening one's vision. But nothing will replace experience. To judge someone's life we must understand that life. Is it naive to suggest that judges, as a prerequisite to judicial appointment, should have practiced law, preferably not in a large law firm where the first several years involve document handling? Is there not something humbling about actually making sausage on the factory floor as opposed to merely selling it or watching it being made? And is not this humbling experience healthy for those who ultimately will judge or process the problems of the wheat farmers of the land?

If we seek administrative reform, and if the law is the fulcrum for such reform, the focus should be on the key participants and particularly on judges and their life experiences. The rest will follow.

* * * * *

Is this flight of fancy? Wishful vague thinking? Hopelessly immature? Arguably. But arguably not. Three hundred years ago would it have been realistic for Louis Joliet, paddling along the shore of Lake Michigan, to imagine a corporate structure (Sears Tower) rising more than 100 stories high, on the banks of the Chicago River? Two hundred years ago, in drafting the *Federalist Papers* would it have been practical for James Madison and John Jay to envision the demise of a quill-pen Congress and the emergence of computerized policy making programs? Little more than 100 years ago sitting at his President's desk at Washington College,[17] would it have been possible for General Robert E. Lee, "the King of Spades", to imagine armies using intercontinental ballistic missiles and Star Wars satellite systems? Fifty years ago would it have been reasonable for a state court in Utah to forsee as a critical legal issue the implantation of a baboon's heart in a child's body? Since these past fantasies are now present realities is it not possible to imagine a time when comprehensive, integrated approaches will be the norm? And against this possibility are not these so-called fanciful ideas actually rather mundane and practical?

The magic of the mind is that nothing is unimaginable. Given the breakdowns in our present fragmented and disintegrated decisional methodologies, we search for approaches that are complete and integrated. The integrating mechanism is the mind, not a machine, although the machine (technology) eliminates certain procedural constraints. The intellectual criteria for integration include broad humanistic training in areas that transcend specialization.

In taking these steps it may be well to remember the admonition of Georges Bernanos:[8] *A thought which does not result in an action is nothing much, and an action which does not proceed from a thought is nothing at all.*

NOTES

1. Larry Kart "The Death of Jazz," *Chicago Tribune*, February 24, 1985, p. 5.
2. This obviously is not a word; but the meaning is widely understood.
3. James Warren, "Dean of Law Enters Plea for New Tradition," *Chicago Tribune*, 4(1978):1587−608.
4. See the recent "Reports" on curriculum revisions of the Association of American Colleges (1985) and the National Institute of Education (1985) as prime examples.
5. Peter Steinfels, "Up From Individualism" *New York Times: Book Review*, p. 1. April 14, 1985.
6. Vincent J. Scully, Jr. is art historian at Yale, and this paragraph is truly a "synopsis" of his presentation.
7. It is now called Washington and Lee College.
8. George Bernanos as quoted in "Reason and Society: John Dewey" by Albert William Levi, *Philosophy and the Modern World* (Bloomington: Indiana University Press, 1959) p. 283.

GLOSSARY: SOME IMPORTANT DEFINITIONS

administration. (p. 106) The process of effecting and achieving the optimal level of organizational goals; also, the management process in the "public sector"; the application of values set by authoritative policy-makers.

administrative model. (p. 129) A process of decision making based on a profile of feasibility whereby choices are adapted (in a screening process) to the various social, financial, racial, historical, psychological, and other "administrative" interests on which these choices impinge.

avoidance theory. (p. 153) A model of decision making, conceptualizing a two step process whereby controversial risky issues are submerged and safe neutral issues are surfaced in order to give the impression that the decision-maker is doing his job.

cognitive dissonance. (p. 25) Any perceived incompatibility between an individual's beliefs or between an individual's behavior and his beliefs.

common law. (p. 46) Case law (or judge made-law) as opposed to constitutional, statutory, or administrative law.

decision making. (p. 10) The process by which courses of action are chosen (from among alternatives) in pursuit of organizational goals.

discretion. (p. 193) Intuitive responses to influences: an intellectual approach to problems based on nonobjective, nonscientific processes.

discretionary models. (p. 37) A process of decision making (characterized by vague, arbitrary, often nonaccountable factors) based on sophisticated/deliberate choice criteria leading to the resolution of controversial, complex matters through an admixture of law, fact, and influence.

dysfunctional. (pp. 29n, 44) Negative consequences or conditions resultant from the action of a *structure* over time.

eufunctional. (pp. 29n, 44) Positive consequences or conditions resultant from the action of a *structure* over time.

functions. (pp. 1n, 43) Consequences or conditions resultant from the action (operation or persistence) of a structure over time. There are *eufunctions* and *dysfunctions* (defined).

garbage can model. (pp. 31−32) A process of decision making whereby solutions (decisions) are not determined a priori but are the products of solutions and problems joined together by "simultaneous availability" and by simultaneous demands on the decision maker's time.

groupthink. (p. 176) The process of making decisions whereby group members seek to achieve a consensus (above all) and consequently seek to suppress dissent or disagreement.

generic. (p. 195) The state of sharing common qualities; the opposite of *discrete*.

history. (p. 131) The continuing process of interaction between the historian and his facts; an unending dialogue between the present and the past.

ideology. (p. 132) The preferential choice (the right or wrong choice) that the administrator makes on an individual level.

irrationality. (pp. 15, 81) The opposite of *rationality*: the rational process that is inconsistent with rational (self-interest) ends.

irrational models. (p. 56) A process of decision making whereby intentional behavior results in choices that; (1) are inconsistent with some

Glossary

organizational (or individual) goal or (2) are misdirected because of process factors (structure, and the like).

legal model. (p. 36) A process of decision making based on the "rule of law," whereby solutions derive from the sum total of principles and procedures that a legal society has adopted.

law. (p. 37) The sum total of principles and procedures that a legal society has adopted and that it relies on and enforces in order to function properly; (1) the aggregate of legal precepts (judicial and administrative rules and regulations); (2) the judicial process (the ritualized, formal institutional system).

macro-organizational behavior. (p. 30) The study of organizations based on analysis of structural and functional elements (the big picture).

management. (p. 104) The *process* of achieving the optimum attainment of organizational goals; also, the *status* of belonging to a corporate hierarchy.

micro-organizational behavior. (p. 30) The study of organizations based on analysis of individual and group behavior (the small picture).

model. (p. 12) An abstraction of reality or a simplified representation of some real-world phenomenon.

mores. (p. 156) The ways of doing things that are current in a society to satisfy human needs and desires, together with the faiths, notions, codes, and standards of well living that inhere in those ways.

"muddling through" models. (pp. 30–31) *Ad hoc*, incremental, fragmented, and nonscientific processes of decision making; based on suboptimizing, noneconomic (read *political*) criteria.

organization. (p. 8) A *structure* (defined) made up of two or more persons who accept coordinated direction to achieve certain goals and that has certain *functions* (defined) or consequences.

organic. (p. 86) Units that respond to change or to stimuli.

policy. (p. 45) Authoritative values that emanate from a formal or informal body or source.

political model. (p. 29) A process of decision making that seeks to maximize the authoritative allocation of values for a society (see **politics**) through incrementally achieved preferences. The four-part process whereby the authoritative institutions of society identify problems; select preferred problem-solving approaches (choices); formulate a problem definition to rationalize these programs; and finally administer resources accordingly.

political system. (pp. 29–30) A concept that presumes that the study of political phenomena can reach the level of other social sciences, and that politics constitutes as separate and distinctive a theoretical field as economics or sociology. Political system refers to the complex of processes and institutions that allocate the authoritative values for a society.

politics. (pp. 29–30) The authoritative allocation of values for a society.

power. (p. 26) A relational concept (as opposed to a physical property to be possessed) that describes one person's ability to influence the behavior of another or others.

public. (p. 77) That group or element in society that is indirectly affected by the decisions of policymakers.

rational model. (pp. 13–18) A process of decision making based on systematic analysis of means and ends (see **rational**); the process whereby programs (read choices) are derived from an analysis of causation and change.

rational. (p. 52) Deliberative evaluation and choice based on objectively calculated data; ideally a value-free systematic matching of means and ends; opposed to intuitive (hunch) thinking.

rationality. (p. 54) The process of rational thought—and one that is based on systematically calculated data and choices: deliberate selection of means to reach ends.

rationalism. (p. 52) The goal of rational thought—and one that is based on objectively calculated goals and objectives: maximization of ends.

social system. (p. 43) A patterned collection of elements in action (operation or persistence) that involves a plurality of interacting individuals, and that is capable of lasting longer than its members' life span.

Glossary

socialization. (p. 175) The process whereby one learns to adopt those values and norms that are essential to full-fledged membership in an organization.

stare decisis. (p. 37) Stand by the decision; the rule of precedent.

static. (p. 86) Units that are fixed (in time and place) and not responsive to change or stimuli.

structures. (pp. 1n, 43) Patterns (observable uniformities) of action (operation or persistence) of a time.

symbol. (p. 219) Visual or verbal representations of some real-world phenomenon that assume a meaning that transcends itself, thereby causing observers of the symbol to acquiesce (hold one's critical factors in abeyance) under the potent spell of the symbol.

system. (pp. 8–51) A bounded region in space and time, with component parts that interact with each other causing stresses and strains, inputs and outputs, and feedback over time.

systems theory. (pp. 9–10) The "black box" approach, which sees inputs filtered through an abstract system of interacting parts and ultimately converted into outputs, which in turn are transformed via a feedback loop into other inputs.

third sector. (p. 45) A sector or organizational activity that is neither public nor private but that possesses characteristics (voluntarism, collegiality) unique to its institutional setting (unions, colleges, zoos, museums, and the like).

technology. (p. 222) Not (simply) a machine but a systematic disciplined approach to objectives using a calculus of precision and measurement and a concept of system that are quite at variance with traditional and customary religious, aesthetic and intuitive modes.

values. (pp. 12, 43) Basic convictions that specific modes of conduct or end states of existence are personally or socially preferable to opposite or converse modes of conduct or end states.

ANNOTATED RECOMMENDED READINGS

These recommended references and readings are not necessarily cited in the text. They are offered for those who want to read further. Also, materials cited in the text are not all relisted here. (See the Author Index for a complete list of referenced material.) Required readings are noted by an asterisk(*).

Alston, William P. *Philosophy of Language*. Englewood Cliffs, N.J.: Prentice-Hall, 1964.

> A philosophical discourse on the many uses and misuses of words. Fundamental philosophy.

Bell, Daniel. *The End of Ideology*. New York: Free Press, 1962.

> The inspirational source of the neoconservative movement. The ideological content is self evident.

Bell, Daniel, *Toward the Year 2000*. Boston: Houghton Mifflin, 1968.

> Insightful look at the future. An update is eagerly awaited.

Berkeley, George, *The Craft of Public Administration*. Boston: Allyn & Bacon, 1972.

Great cases, sound organization. Tells us why public administration is important.

Buber, Martin. *Drei Reden über das Judentums*. Frankfurt am Main: Rutten & Loening, 1916.

The roots of "I and Thou." Buber explored man's relationship to his universe before he explained man's relationship to man (*Ich und Du*). The relationship always is an ethical one.

Buchholz, Rogene. *Business Environment and Public Policy*. Englewood Cliffs, N.J.:Prentice-Hall, 1982.

Finally, a comprehensive, albeit superficial collection of all one needs to know about this interdisciplinary field. Good teaching instrument.

Carr, Edward Hallett. *What Is History?* New York: Alfred A. Knopf, 1963.

Old-school stuff. Carr answers the question. Readable discussion of the meaning of history.

Davis, Kenneth Culp. *Discretionary Justice: A Preliminary Inquiry*. 3rd ed. Urbana:University of Illinois Press, 1976.

This third edition, published during the Bicentennial, forces the question: In a society of laws, why did it take lawyers so long to penetrate the widespread phenomenon of discretion?

Dewey, John. *The Public and Its Problems*. New York: Holt, 1927.

The Roaring twenties were great for film, music, sports . . . and social philosophy. Dewey is the Babe Ruth of Modern Social Thought.

Drucker, Peter. *The Practice of Management*. New York: Harper Brothers, 1954.

The Bible. Answers all the questions—but still we have the problems.

Easton, David. *The Political System*. New York: Alfred A. Knopf, 1953.

The godfather of systems theory in the social sciences. Promotes the credibility of a science of politics, but takes the politics out of poli sci.

*Edelman, Murray. *The Symbolic Uses of Politics*. Urbana: University of Illinois Press, 1964.

A humble presentation with profound thoughts—doesn't get nearly the recognition it deserves. Read and reread. Like fine classical music, it takes awhile to sink in. Disturbingly prophetic. Required.

Elbing, Alvard. *Behavioral Decisions in Organizations.* Glenview, Ill.: Scott Foresman, 1970.

Terrific step-by-step analysis of decision making at the micro (individual) and macro (organizational) levels.

Elster, Jon. *Ulysses and the Sirens: Studies in Rationality and Irrationality.* Cambridge: Cambridge University Press, 1979.

A self-confessed frustrated poet and mathematician explores rational and irrational behavior. Edmund Husserl to Groucho Marx with Pascal and Descartes along the way.

Etzioni, Amitai. *Modern Organizations.* Englewood Cliffs, N.J.: Prentice-Hall, 1964.

Early Etzioni. A mix of sociology, administration, and sophisticated common sense.

Fisher, Bruce D., and Phillips, Michael J. *The Legal Environment of Business.* St. Paul: West, 1983.

Between two covers, this work covers the waterfront. Complete and up-to-date; discussion questions included. It's all here.

Gross, Bertram. *Friendly Facism: The New Face of Power in America.* New York: M. Evans, 1980.

A solid citizen and academic of high stature puts himself on the line and identifies the lack of humanistic education as a central moral problem of our times.

Hardin, Russel. *Collective Action.* Baltimore: Johns Hopkins University Press, 1982.

How a mob can be just as rational as a calculating mathematician.

Harrison E. Frank. *The Managerial Decision Making Process.* Boston: Houghton Mifflin, 1975.

Good overview of terms, concepts, theories, and materials presented in sound management jargon. Helpful and inclusive; not real deep.

Annotated Recommended Readings 245

Hollis, Martin and Lukes, Steven. *Rationality and Relativism.* Cambridge: MIT Press, 1982.

Cutting but not always clear philosophical argument on why rationality is not "value free." Collection of good readings.

*Hoos, Ida R. *Systems Analysis in Public Policy.* Berkeley: University of California Press, 1972.

Powerful language and cogent thoughts. Scathing indictment of "systems" thinking. Required.

Levitt, Theodore. *The Third Sector.* New York: AMACOM, 1973.

Early exploration into the twilight zone of "neither public nor private."

Levy, Marion J. *The Structure of Society.* Princeton: Princeton University Press, 1952

Essential interpretation of "Parsonian" terminology and concepts. Basic grounding in structural-functional analysis. Hard-core sociology in usable terms. Great for definitions.

Lindblom, Charles. "The Science of Muddling Through," *Public Administration Review* 19, no. 2 (1959): pp. 79–88.

Interesting, serious, revealing, and significant thoughts on how administration really works. Dated, but so is Hitchcock. The later article "Still Muddling, Not Yet Through," *Public Administration Review*, Nov-Dec 1979, pp. 517–26, brings us up-to-date.

Long, Norton E. "Public Policy and Administration: The Goals of Rationality and Responsibility." *Public Administration Review*, 14, no. 1 (Winter 1954) pp. 22–31.

Anything he writes is worth reading, at least once.

Lowi, Theodore J. *The End of Liberalism.* New York: W. W. Norton, 1969.

Elegantly crafted thesis on why some ex-liberals find Senator Gary Hart's packaging more relevant then Hubert Humphrey's revivalism.

*March, James G., and Olsen, Johan P. *Ambiguity and Choice in Organizations.* Bergen, Norway: Universitetsforlaget, 1976. See also Cohen,

Michael D.; March, James G.; and Olsen, Johan P. "A Garbage Can Model of Organizational Choice." *Administrative Science Quarterly* 17, no. 1 (March 1972).

Very few academics come up with original thoughts. March and coworkers are in a select group. Eclectic thoughts break new ground. Exciting stuff. Required.

McClennan, Edward F. *Social Theory and Practice* 9, nos. 2–3 (1983).

Overview article on the rational model in the public arena, where it works amazingly well.

Miles, Robert H. *Macro Organizational Behavior*. Santa Monica: Goodyear, 1980.

Surveys the field. A rich resource for graduate students seeking an overview of the literature and the theories. Uses relevant cases.

Nagel, Ernest. *The Structure of Science*. New York: Harcourt Brace, 1961.

Presumes to say that anyone who has not mastered science is not educated. True, but it leaves a lot of us out.

Nisbet, Robert. *History of the Idea of Progress*. New York: Basic Books, 1980.

Heavy going but serious history. Loses some steam in the middle.

Pears, David. *Motivated Irrationality*. Oxford: Clarendon Press, 1984.

Easy to read philosophical treatise on the rewards of altruism and other so-called "irrational" behaviors.

Perry, James L., and Kramer, Kenneth L. *Public Management: Public and Private Perspectives*. Palo Alto, Calif. Mayfield, 1983.

Collection of readable past and present essays on a "generic" topic. Woodrow Wilson to Michael Murray. What a drop.

Pfeffer, Jeffrey. *Organizations and Organization Theory*. Boston: Pitman, 1982.

Clear, forceful, complete. One of the best studies on organizations in the last decade.

Pfeffer, Jeffrey. *Power in Organizations*. Boston: Pitman, 1981.

Finally, someone took the central but "dirty" topic and made the "purist" think about it. Important.

Plato. *The Republic*. New York: Bollingen Foundation, 1969.

The modern organization is the "republic." Read it in this context.

*Rawls, John. *A Theory of Justice*. Cambridge: Harvard University Press, Belknap Press, 1971.

Comprehensive and serious. Morally intelligent thoughts on the most elusive of topics. Required.

Robbins, Stephen P. *Organizational Behavior*. Englewood Cliffs, N.J.: Prentice-Hall, 1984.

The only text around that will keep a night class of overworked graduate students alert and informed for three and one-half hours. The dedication alone assures us that the rest will not be that bad.

Rokeach, Milton, *The Nature of Human Values*. New York: Free Press, 1973.

Adequate warmup for thinking about a disturbingly complex area.

Rousseau, Jean Jacques, *The Social Contract*. New York: E. P. Sutton, 1954.

The basis for legal, moral, political, and organizational relations.

Sharkansky, Ira. *Public Administration: Policy Making in Government Agencies*. Chicago: Markham, 1972.

Among several public administration readers available, Sharkansky's is the most durable, even though the cases and articles are dated.

Simon, Herbert A. *Administrative Behavior*. New York: Free Press, 1965.

Simon says and says—and still it is refreshingly relevant.

Skinner, B. F. *Beyond Freedom and Dignity*. New York: Knopf, 1971.

The ultimate rat psychologist here preaches what he practices.

Stigler, George J. *Essays in the History of Economics.* Chicago: University of Chicago Press, 1965.

One of the first and best explanations of how Economic man can also be Political Man (with less emphasis on the vice versa).

Stigler, George. *The Citizen and the State.* Chicago:University of Chicago Press, 1982.

Nobel Prize winner's update on how Rational man is Political man. Essential reading.

Uniform Commercial Code (UCC). (Various editions. See *Ill. Rev. Stat.* 1977, ch. 26, and various other state codes.)

Why not? The annotated cases are great for detail and insight. A reference for *any* business school class. At least make students aware of the UCC.

Wildavsky, Aaron. *The Politics of the Budgetary Process.* Boston: Little, Brown, 1964).

There are updated versions of this "classic" piece; and condensed presentations in texts such as Richard Stillman's *Public Administration.* Like Wagnerian music, Wildavsky's work is not as good as it sounds.

*Wilson, Woodrow. "The Study of Administration." *Political Science Quarterly*, Vol. II, No. 2, June 1887, pp. 197–222.

Public administration's star student gets the ball rolling. Required.

NAME INDEX

Alston, William, 8−9
Argyris, Chris, 96
Augustine, St., 97
Austin, John, 106, 163

Balfe, Ruth, 22
Bell, Daniel, 132, 222
Bentham, Jeremy, 52
Bernanos, Georges, 230
Blake, Robert, 98
Buber, Martin, 50

Cardozo, Benjamin N., 37
Carr, Edward Hallett, 132
Commager, Henry Steele, 225
Cummings, E. E., 162
Curley, Michael, 26

Davis, Kenneth Culp, 37−38, 194
Dewey, John, 50, 105, 216
Douglas, Justice, 182−183

Easton, David, 164
Edelman, Murray, 39−41, 102, 220

Eliot, T. S., 128
Erhard, Werner, 233
Etzioni, Amitai, 17−18

Fiedler, Fred, 14, 98
Frank, Jerome, 37, 179
Frankfurter, Justice, 204, 206, 234
Franklin, Benjamin, 233

Gluckman, Max, 197
Goethe, Johann Wolfgang, 48
Gordon, Lawrence, 13
Gross, Bertram, 94

Hardin, Russell, 16
Holmes, Oliver Wendell, 37
Hoos, Ida, 84−86
House, Robert, 14

Kent, Chancellor, 192, 234

Lasch, Christopher, 222
Lawler, Edward, 53
Lindblom, Charles, 14, 30−32, 107

Long, Norton, 106

Machiavelli, 179–180
March, James, 31–32, 223, 228
Martin, John Bartlow, 134
McClennon, Edward, 50
Miles, Robert H., 23, 88
Mill, John Stuart, 52
Miller, Danny, 13
Mintzberg, Henry, 13
Mouton, Jane, 98
Murray, Michael, 59

O'Rourke, Gene, 18

Parmenides, 6
Pears, David, 81–82
Penner, Rudolph G., 33
Pfeffer, Jeffrey, 117, 122
Plato, 166

Rauh, Morton, 67
Rhode, John, 53
Rousseau, Jean-Jacques, 211–212

Sartre, Jean Paul, xiv, 1
Schelling, Thomas, 115
Scully, Vincent, 233
Simon, Herbert, 21–22, 54
Smith, Adam, 52
Speer, Albert, 80, 94
Steinbruner, John, 11, 13
Stigler, George, 16
Sumner, William, 156

Theresa, Mother, 82

Vroom, V. H., 14–15

Wamsley, Gary, 117
Whitman, Walt, 233
Wiesel, Elie, 2
Wildavsky, Aaron, 107–108, 115, 118, 120–121
Williamson, Oliver, 21–22
Wilson, Woodrow, 106

Yetton, P. W., 15

Zald, Mayer, 117

SUBJECT INDEX

ABC, Inc. case, 18-20
Academic decisions, 61-62. *See also*
    Modern management applied to
    academic decisions case
Accountability, 152-153
Acropolis, 233-234
Administration
    business, 157
    in discretionary model, 204-205
    process of, 157-158
    public, 157
    versus management, 103-104
    versus policy, 106-107
Administrative models. *See also* Centralia
    Blast case
    definitions and concepts
        administrative factors, 130-131
        class, 133
        history, 131-132

ideology, 132-133
race, 133
screening model, 129-130
Administrative technique, 38
Ambiguity
    and garbage can model, 31-32
    and justice, 166-168
American Textile case
    conclusion of, 184-185
    description of, 169-175
    review of
        application of principles, 183
        balancing test, 181-182
        case law, logic of, 183-184
        case method, 179-180, 184-185
        consensus, 176
        deduction, 177-179
        deference, 179
        definitions, 180-181, 183

251

deflection, 180–181
distinction versus difference, 176–177
groupthink, 176
induction, 177–179
judicial strategies, 182–183
organizational behavior, 175–176
power, 183–185
problems, 183
rational relationships, 182
ricorsi, 179–180
selectivity, 183
values approach, basic, 177
American Textile Manufacturers Institute Inc., et al. v. Donovan, Secretary of Labor, et al, See American Textile case
Analytic phase, 10
Arbitrary, 195
Automation, 97
Avoidance, 153
Avoidance theory, 153

Balance test, 166, 169–170
Balancing test, 181–182
Bargaining, 121
Bartose people, 197
"Bay of Pigs" decision, 176
Behavior
  covert, 122
  human, 93–94
  organizational, 175–176
Behavioral acceptability, 94–95
Biases, 153–154, 208–209
"Black box" approach, 10
Board of trustees, 67–68
Boards of governors, 68
Body politic, 211
Bounded rationality, 50
Brown lung. See American Textile case
Brown v. *Board of Education of Topeca et al.*, 176–177
Budgeting as political process case
  calculation of budget in
    description of, 109–110
    expectations of participants, 110–111

incremental method, 110
    simplification, 110
  conclusion of, 124
  coordination in, 111–112
  description of, 107–109
  goals of budget in, 112–113
  review of
    actual goals, 118–119
    bargaining, 121–122
    careerism, 119
    complexity, 115
    comprehensiveness, 116, 119–120
    congruence of goals, 124
    coordination, 120–121
    covert behavior, 122
    demerits, 121
    fair share, 116–117
    fragmentation, 120–121
    incrementalism, 116
    legitimacy, 122
    legitimation, 123–124
    merits, 121
    organizationalism, 119
    political perspective, 117
    public goals, 118–119
    secrecy, 121–122
    selectivity, 122–123
    simplicity, 115
    subunit differentiation, 119–120
    truth, 117
  strategies of budget in, 113–115
  supervision in, 111–112
Bureaucracy, 210–211
Bureau of budget, 68–69
Business. See Rational models; specific cases in
Business leadership, 233. See also Management
Buzzwords, 223–224

Careerism, 119
Case method, 179–180, 184–185
Centralia Blast case
  blame for, 150–151
  cleanup in, partial, 140–141

Index

complaint in, 138–139
conclusion of, 158
crisis in, 140–141
description of, 133–135
and federal control of mines, 145–146
history behind, 135–138
inspection in, 139–140
and Krug-Lewis agreement, 147–148
letter to governor in, 143–145
political aspects of, 148–150
report to federal government in, 146–147
review of
  accountability, 152–153
  administration, 156–157
  administration process, 157–158
  avoidance, 152–153
  bias, 153–154
  business admnistration, 157
  change, 157
  deliberate or accidental, 154–155
  ethic, 155–156
  fact versus value, 152
  mores and morals, 156
  public administration, 157
  status, 154
  tangibles and intangibles, 155
  triage and mitigating disasters, 155
CFR, 199
"Chadi" justice, 197, 211
Choice phase, 10
City of Burbank et al. v. Lockheed Air Terminal, Inc., et al., 182–183
Class, 133, 154
Code of Federal Regulations (CFR), 199
Codified justice, 197
Cognitive dissonance, 25
Collective rationality, 16
Collegiate Common Market. *See* Modern management applied to academic decisions case
Competition, 96–97
Complexity, 85, 115, 205
"Complex situations," 11
Comprehensiveness, 116, 119–120

Conflict, 60–61, 76–77. *See also* Political models
Conflict resolution models. *See* Political models
Congressional budget process case, 33–35
Consensus, 176
Controllable quantitative processes, 71
Coordination, 120–121
Cost-benefit analysis, 169–170
Covert behavior, 122
Culture, 223–224

Decisional blindness, 95
Decision making. *See also* specific approaches and models of
approaches to, intellectual, 1–4, 7
beyond neoclassicism, 231–232
in business, 11
business leadership in, 233
and conservative generation, 232–233
cultural aphasia in, 233
definition of, 10
depoliticization of, 73
externships in, 233–234
generic structures in, 232
in government, 11
in higher education, 62–65
illustrations of, 2–3
individualism in, 233
integrated disciplines in, 232–233
in law, 12
law and administrative reform in, 234–235
and mind, 235–236
in organizations, 7–8
phases of, 10–11
process of, 11–12
"Decision tree," 14–15
Deduction, 177–179
Deductive model, 184
DEF Corporation case, 22–24
Deference, 179
Deflection, 180–181
Delegalization, 210–211
Deliberative factor, 54

Demerits, 121
Design phase, 10
Discretion
  as abstraction, 194–195
  and arbitrariness, 196
  and delegalization, 210–211
  as game playing, 39
  and generic approach, 195
  and justice, 195–197
  and law, 37–38, 193–194
  in operation, 197–198
Discretionary Justice (Davis), 194
Discretionary models. *See also Merrill* case
  definitions and concepts
    abstraction of discretion, 194–195
    distinction of discretion, 193–194
    generic approach, 195
    justice and discretion, 195–197
    methodological elements, 198–199
    operation of discretion, 197–198
    operative elements, 199
Disincentives, 95
Disintegrated approaches. *See also* Legal models; Political models; Rational models
  definitions and assumptions
    decision making, 10–12
    models, 12–13
    organizations, 7–10
    systems, 7–10
Disorganization, 85
Due process, 209–210
Dysfunctions, 9

"Easy" case, 87–88
Education, higher. *See* Modern management applied to academic decisions case
Elitism, 226–227
Environmental Protection Agency (EPA), 11
Eufunction, 8, 124

Fair share, 116–117
Federal Crop Insurance Corporation v. *Merrill et al.* See *Merrill* case

Federal Register, 199
Federal Register Act of 1935, 199
Foreign Corrupt Practices Act of 1977, 18–21
Formalism, 198
Fragmentation, 120–121, 221–222
Frankfurt-Brandeis "political connection," 183
Furman v. *Georgia*, 196
Functional explanation, 184
Functions, 8

Game playing, 39
Garbage can model, 31–32, 228
General Motors. *See* Lordstown Fiasco case
General Motors Assembly Division (GMAD). *See* Lordstown Fiasco case
Generic approach, 195
GMAD. *See* Lordstown Fiasco case
Goss, et al. v. *Lopez et al.*, 209
Government. *See* Political models; *specific cases in*
Government Manual, 199
Groupthink, 176

"Hard" case, 58–59
Harvard Decision Tree of means-end analysis, 3
History, 131–132, 153
Hopi Indians, 233–234

Ideology, 132–133, 154, 211
Illinois case. *See* Modern management applied to academic decisions case
Imperialist impulse, 70–71
Implementation phase, 10
Incentives, 95
Incrementalism, 30–32, 116
Individualism, 233
Induction, 177–179
Inductive model, 184
Informal mechanisms, 210
Informational factor, 54
Inside Warren Court (Schwartz and Lesher), 183

Index

Integrated approaches,
  commonalities of models, 217–218
  future, working version of, 227–228
  and integration
    of elitism and separation of power, 226–227
    of social needs versus material needs, 225–226
    of symbols, 226
  negative generic qualities of
    buzzwords, 223–224
    control, 222–223
    culture, 223–224
    language, 223–224
    obstacles, other, 221–222
    politics, 222–223
    space, 221–222
    technology, 222–223
    time, 221–222
  positive generic qualities of
    behavioral or human problems, 219
    causation, 218–219
    decisions, 218–219
    symbols, 219–221
    truth, 218–219
  progress, 224–225
Intellectual approaches. *See* Legal models; Political models; Rational models
Interest group liberalism, 36
Internal Revenue Service (IRS) case, 26–29
Intuition, 177–179
Irrationality, 15–16, 56–57
Irrational models. *See also* Lordstown Fiasco case
  definitions and concepts
    definition of rationality, 81–82
    irrationality, 82–83
    limits of rationality, 84–86
    scientific methods, 83
    systems, 83–84
IRS case, 26–29

Jargon, elitist, 70
Justice

  as abstraction, 164–165
  and ambiguity, 166–168
  balance test of, 166
  ethic, 165–166

Language, 223–224
Law. *See also* Legal models; specific cases
  in and decision making, 234–235
  definition of, 37
  meaning of, 37, 163–164
  positive, 163, 167
Law of probability, 184
Legal authority, 164
Legalism, 163–164
Legalism case, 39–41
Legal models. *See also American Textile* case; Legalism case
  criticism of, 37–41
  definitions and concepts
    characteristics of, 165–169
    justice, 164–165
    legalism, 163–164
    positivism, 163–164
  and legal process, 35–36
  and rule of law, 36
Legal process. *See* Law
Legal reasoning. *See* Law
Legal sector, 3
Legal superiors, 164
Legal technique, 38
Legislature, 69
Legitimacy, 122–123
Legitimation, 123–124
Lordstown Fiasco case
  assessment of, 92–93
  "beating the line" tactics in, 91–92
  conclusion of, 99–100
  description of, 88–89
  efficiency experts in, 89–90
  management in, 91
  review of
    automation of line, 97
    behavior, 93–94
    behavioral acceptability, 94–95
    competition, 96–97

decisional blinders, 95
disincentives, 95
effects of, 99
goals, 98
incentives, 95
management styles, new, 98–99
participative versus authoritarian approaches, 98
rational analysis, 97–98
rationalism, implications of, 99
risk calculation, 96
segregated decisional structures, 96
sunk-costs syndrome, 97
technical threshold, 94–95
technocratic monopolism, 94
strike in, 91
worker reaction in, 90–91

Management. *See also* Modern management applied to academic decisions case
authoritarian, 98
definition of, 61
forms of, new, 74–75
limits of, 72–73
participative, 98
styles of, new, 98–99
versus administration, 103–104
Management by objectives (MBO), 16
Management information system (MIS), 67
Marbury v. *Madison*, 179
MBO, 16
Means-end analysis, 14, 54–56
Merits, 121
Merrill case
conclusion of, 211–212
description of, 199–204
review of
administration, 204–205
biases of discretionary process, 208–209
body politic, death of, 211
bureaucracy, 210–211
complexity, 205
conditions of discretionary process, 207
delegalization, 210–211
due process, 209–210
issues of discretionary process, 208
limitation rhetoric, 206
participation ideology, 211
rule of law, 210–211
square corners notion, 206
technicality, 206–207
MIS, 67
Models 12. *See also* Legal models; Political models; Rational models
Modern management applied to academic decisions case
conclusion of, 75–77
conflict in, inherent, 60–61
definitions of terms in, 61–62
description of, 59–60
illustration of
board of trustees, 67–68
boards of governors, 68
bureau of budget, 68–69
classification of, 65–66
legislature, 69
university management, 66–67
policy issues in
budget, 62–63
curriculum, 63
faculty, 63–64
physical plant, 65
recruiting, 64–65
students, 64–65
review of
academic leaders, 73
alternatives of management, 72
budget issues, 71
changes of management, 74–75
controllable quantitative processes, 71
depoliticization of decision making, 73
effects of, 75
elitist jargon, 70
future, 75
imperialist impulse, 70–71
limits of management, 72–73
nonacademics, 74

Index

professionalization, 73—74
stereotypes, 74
summary of, 70
Monopoly, technocratic, 94
Morals, 156
Mores, 156
Motivated Irrationality (Pears), 81—82
"Muddling through" models, 30—31, 107

Narrow rationality, 16
Negative injunctions, 179
Nonarbitrary, 195
Non optimizing strategy, 168—169
Nonpublic, 50. *See also* Private
Nonrationalism, 82
Nonrationality, 56—58

Occupational Safety and Health Act, 170. See also *American Textile* case
Occupational Safety and Health Administration (OSHA), 11, 170
Organism, 86
Organization
  complex, 1—2
  definition of, 7—8
  goals of, 13—14
  versus disorganization, 85
Organizational behavior, 175—176
OSHA, 11, 170

Participant goals, 18
Plessy v. *Ferguson*, 176—177
Policy, 106—107
Political analysis, 30
Political models. *See also* Budgeting as political process case; Congressional budget process case
  and ambiguity, 31—32
  criticism of, 32—35
  decision maker in, 30
  definitions and concepts
    management versus administration, 103—104
    muddling process, 107
    policy versus administration, 106—107

public versus private, 104—105
and incrementalism, 30—32
and political system, 29—30
preference of, 32
and rational models, 130
Political system, 29—30
Politics
  definition of, 29—30
  in discretionary models, 196
  in integrated approaches, 222—223
  in political model, 117
Positive injunctions, 179
Positive law, 163, 167
Positivism, 163—164
Power, 163, 183—184
PPBS, 16, 66
Preanalysis, 10
Private, 104—105. *See also* Nonpublic
Private sector, 1—4
Procedural matters, 198
Professionalization, 73—74
Program planning and budgeting system (PPBS), 16, 66
Public
  Dewey's definition of, 50, 105
  versus private, 104—105
Public sector, 1—4

Queen v. *Dudley and Stephens*, 12

Race, 133, 154
RAMs, 67
Rational analysis, 97—98
Rationalism. *See* Rationality
Rationality
  and behavior, 53—54
  bounded, 50
  collective, 16
  and competition, 96—97
  in contemporary context, 49—50
  data deficiencies of
    domination of tools and machines, 87
    measures of success and cycles of defeat, 87
    misuses of data, 86—87

as goal, 52–53
  implication of, 99
  and means-end analysis, 54–56
  narrow, 16
  and nonrationality, 56
  in Occidental man, 50–51
  in Oriental man, 50–51
  as process, 53–54
  in rational models, 15–16, 49
  and systems analysis, 51–52
  theory deficiencies
    organization versus disorganization, 85
    simplicity versus complexity, 85
    statism versus organism, 86
  value of, 58
Rational models. See also ABC Inc. case; Modern management applied to academic decisions case
  criticism of
    individual context, 24–29
    societal context, 17–21
    subunit context, 21–24
  decision maker in, 13
  definitions and concepts of
    goal-process elements, 49–52
    irrationality, 56–58
    means-end analysis, 54–56
    nonrationality, 56–58
    rationalism, 52–53
    rationality, 53–54
  and elitist jargon, 70
  goals of, 13–14
  and political models, 130
  process of, 14
  theories of, 14–16
Resource allocation models (RAMs), 67
Resource sharing. See Modern management applied to academic decisions case
Ricorsi, 179–180
Risks, 96
Rule of law, 36, 210–211

Sanctions, 164

Screening process, 129–130
Selectivity, 122–123, 183–184
Self-interest
  and rational models, 15–16
  and social interest, 121
  and truth, 118
Simplicity, 85
Simplification, 115
Social goals, 18
Societal goals, 18
South Carolina State Highway Department et al. v. Barnwell Brothers, Inc. et al., 182
Southern Pacific Co. v. Arizona ex nel Sullivan, Attorney General, 166, 181–182
Specialization, 96, 227
Square corners notion, 206
Stare decisis, 176
Statism, 86
Status, 154
Stereotypes, 74
Structures, 96
Substantive matters, 198
Subunit differentiation, 119–120
Sunk-costs syndrome, 97
Symbols, 219–221, 226
System, 7–8
System goals, 18
Systems analysis, 7–8, 51–52
Systems theory, 9–10, 83–84

Technicality, 198, 206–207
Technical quality, 94–95
Technology, 222–223
Teleological explanation, 184
Third sector, 1
Threshold phase, 10

University adminsitration, 66–67

Values, 15, 177

QUOTE SOURCES

Preface: Albert Einstein: From "Albert Einstein" in *Living Philosophies* (New York: Simon and Schuster, 1931) p. 1.

Introduction: Jean-Paul Sartre: From "The Imaginary Life" in Jean-Paul Sartre, *The Psychology of Imagination* (New York: Washington Square Press, 1966) p. 169.

Chapter One: Plato on the One: "The Hypothesis in Parmenides" in H. N. Fowler, *Plato in Twelve Volumes* (Cambridge: Harvard University Press, 1926) Vol. IV, p. 253.

Chapter Two: Mephistopheles: From Goethe's "Faust" in *The Permanent Goethe* ed. by Thomas Mann (New York: Dial, 1948) p. 77.

Chapter Three: Albert Speer: In "Conclusions" to Albert Speer, *Inside the Third Reich* (New York: Macmillan, 1970) p. 521.

Chapter Four: Murray Edelman: In "Introduction" to Murray Edelman, *The Symbolic Uses of Politics* (Urbana: University of Illinois Press, 1964) p. 2.

Chapter Five: T. S. Eliot: From "The Wasteland—A Game of Chess" in *The Complete Poems and Plays of T. S. Eliot* (London: Faber and Faber, 1969) p. 65.

Chapter Six: e. e. cummings: From "Voices to Voices, Lip to Lip" in E. E. Cummings, *Complete Poems, 1913–1962* (New York: Harcourt, Brace, Jovanovich, 1972) p. 264.

Chapter Seven: Chancellor Kent: From James Kent, *Commentaries on American Law* ed. by O. W. Holmes, Jr. (Boston: Little, Brown, 1896) Vol. I, 12th ed., p. 462.

Chapter Eight: John Dewey: From "John Dewey" in *Living Philosophies* (New York: Simon and Schuster, 1931) p. 33.

Conclusion: Georges Bernanos: From "Why Freedom?" in Georges Bernanos, *The Last Essays of Georges Bernanos* (Chicago: Regnery, 1955) p. 95.